The Europeanization of National Political Parties

This book offers a detailed exploration of how national political parties have responded to the increasing relevance of European governance.

This is the first empirical study to examine the effects of the European Union on the internal organizational dynamics of national political parties. It draws on the results of a major, cross-national project and is based on documentary analysis and some 150 interviews with senior party actors in six EU member states (Austria, Britain, France, Germany, Spain and Sweden).

Situated in the context of the debate on Europeanization, this book illustrates that national political parties have been surprisingly well equipped to handle the challenges of the increasing importance of multi-level governance in Europe. Following a rigorous analytical framework set out in the introductory chapter, the country studies examine all relevant national political parties (a total of 30) and systematically address a clearly defined set of empirical questions. The volume ends with two comparative chapters that analyse the findings from a cross-national perspective and offer theoretical insights into the problems of party government amid increasing European integration.

This text will appeal to all those researching in the fields of European Studies, Political Science and Comparative Politics.

Thomas Poguntke is Professor of Political Science at the University of Bochum and Fellow at the Mannheim Centre for European Social Research, Germany.

Nicholas Aylott is Senior Lecturer (docent) in Political Science at Södertörn University College, Sweden.

Elisabeth Carter is Lecturer in Political Science at Keele University, UK.

Robert Ladrech is Senior Lecturer in Politics at Keele University, UK.

Kurt Richard Luther is Senior Lecturer in Politics at Keele University, UK.

The Europeanization of National Political Parties

Power and organizational adaptation

Edited by Thomas Poguntke, Nicholas Aylott, Elisabeth Carter, Robert Ladrech and Kurt Richard Luther

Routledge
Taylor & Francis Group

LONDON AND NEW YORK

First published 2007
by Routledge
2 Park Square, Milton Park, Abingdon, Oxon, OX14 4RN

Simultaneously published in the USA and Canada
by Routledge
270 Madison Avenue, New York, NY 10016

*Routledge is an imprint of the Taylor & Francis Group,
an informa business*

Transferred to Digital Printing 2008

Typeset in Times New Roman by
Prepress Projects Ltd, Perth, UK

British Library Cataloguing in Publication Data
A catalogue record for this book is available from the British Library

Library of Congress Cataloging in Publication Data
The Europeanization of national political parties: power and organizational
adaptation/edited by Thomas Poguntke ... [*et al.*].
p.cm.–(Routledge advances in European politics; 45)
ISBN-13: 978-0-415-40191-3 (hardback: alk. paper) 1. Political Parties–
Europe. 2. Europe–Politics and government–1989–I. Poguntke, Thomas.
JN50.E87 2007
324.2094–dc22
2006024258

ISBN10: 0-415-40191-7 (hbk)
ISBN10: 0-415-47978-9 (pbk)
ISBN10: 0-203-08734-8 (ebk)

ISBN13: 978-0-415-40191-3 (hbk)
ISBN13: 978-0-415-47978-3 (pbk)
ISBN13: 978-0-203-08734-3 (ebk)

Contents

Tables

List of contributors

Nicholas Aylott is Senior Lecturer (*docent*) in political science at Södertörn University College, Sweden. He previously worked at Umeå University, Sweden, and at Keele University, UK. His main fields in teaching and research are comparative politics and political institutions, especially political parties. He has published a book and several chapters and journal articles on, among other topics, the impact of European integration on party politics in the Scandinavian countries.

Elisabeth Carter is Lecturer in Political Science at Keele University, UK. Her main research interests include political parties and party systems, electoral institutions and electoral behaviour, and right-wing extremism. She has written a number of articles and chapters on electoral institutions (in particular on their impact on small parties) and is author of *The Extreme Right in Western Europe: Success or Failure?* (Manchester University Press 2005).

Robert Ladrech is Senior Lecturer in Politics at Keele University, UK. He specializes in social democratic parties, French politics and Europeanization of party politics. Recent articles, book chapters and books include 'Europeanization and Party Politics', *Party Politics* (2002), 'The Europeanization of Interest Groups and Political Parties', in Simon Bulmer and Christian Lequesne (eds), *The Member States of the European Union* (Oxford University Press 2005) and *Social Democracy and the Challenge of European Union* (Lynne Rienner 2000).

Kurt Richard Luther is Senior Lecturer in Politics at Keele University, UK. He is Convenor of the Keele European Parties Research Unit (KEPRU) and of the Parties Standing Group of the European Consortium for Political Research. His research interests embrace party organization, right-wing radical parties, consociational democracy, Austrian political parties and party system, as well as federalism. His publications include *Political Parties in the New Europe: Political and Analytical Challenges* (co-editor, Oxford University Press 2002 and 2005) and *Political Elites in Divided Societies: Political Parties in Consociational Democracy* (co-editor, Routledge 1999).

Laura Morales is assistant professor of Political Science at the Universidad de Murcia, Spain. Her interests lie especially in the areas of political parties, electoral behaviour and political participation. She is currently coordinating the project LOCALMULTIDEM (funded by the 6th Framework Programme). Her book *Nations of Political Joiners?* (a revised version of her Ph.D. thesis, which was awarded the ECPR and the Spanish Political Science Association prizes for the best Ph.D. thesis in 2004) will be published by ECPR Press in 2007.

Thomas Poguntke is Professor of Political Science at the University of Bochum and Fellow at the Mannheim Centre for European Social Research. He has taught previously at the universities of Stuttgart, Mannheim, Bielefeld, Keele and Birmingham. He is series editor of the *Routledge/ECPR Studies in European Political Science* and is author and editor of numerous publications including *Parteiorganisation im Wandel: Gesellschaftliche Verankerung und organisatorische Anpassung im Europäischen Vergleich* (Westdeutscher Verlag 2000), and *The Presidentialization of Politics: A Comparative Study of Modern Democracies* (Oxford University Press 2005; with Paul Webb). His main research interests focus on New Politics, party system change, political parties and the comparative analysis of democratic regimes.

Luis Ramiro is associate professor in Political Science at the Universidad de Murcia, Spain. His interests lie especially in the areas of political parties and Spanish politics. Among his most recent publications are 'Programmatic Adaptation and Organizational Centralization: The Case of the AP-PP', *South European Society and Politics* (2005) and *The Crisis of Communism and Party Change: The Evolution of Communists and Post-Communists Parties in Western Europe* (ICPS 2003).

Preface and acknowledgments

Political science has witnessed several 'growth industries' over the years. Research on postmaterialism and neo-corporatism comes to mind, as does the literature on new social movements, and, more recently, on social capital, to name but a few. What sets European integration research apart from these is the fact that there can be very little doubt about the existence and relevance of the phenomenon. Furthermore, the phenomenon itself, i.e. the European Union, has been rather proactive in stimulating research through a series of funding initiatives. Hence, when we began to investigate how increasing European integration might have influenced the internal dynamics of national political parties, we were surprised to find that very little had been written on this aspect. While almost every conceivable feature of Europeanization had been covered in the literature, virtually no attention had been given to how the central political actors in nation states, that is, national political parties, had adapted organizationally to the challenges of multi-level governance. Therefore, when we set out to investigate how the growing importance of the EU might have changed the internal balance of power in national political parties, we were largely exploring new territory.

The original research proposal was formulated by Nicholas Aylott, Robert Ladrech, Kurt Richard Luther and Thomas Poguntke (principal investigator), who were all based at Keele University at the time. We were joined by Elisabeth Carter at Keele, and Laura Morales and Luis Ramiro, who took care of the Spanish case study. Over the years, several members of the group have changed institutional affiliations and even countries of residence: Nicholas Aylott first moved to Umeå University in Sweden and will now soon take up a post at Södertörn University College, Huddinge/Stockholm; Laura Morales and Luis Ramiro moved from Madrid to the University of Murcia; and Thomas Poguntke moved down the road from Keele to Birmingham.

Despite geographical distance, we succeeded in collaborating very closely, and the coherence of this book testifies to this. Supported by a grant from the British Economic and Social Research Council (Grant No. R000 23 9793) and additional funding from the Keele University Research Investment Scheme, we were able to coordinate systematic research on all relevant parties in six EU member states following a common framework of analysis. Key to our success was the possibility of meeting twice a year since early 2003 in order to discuss and refine our theoretical perspective and make sure that our interviews were conducted according to a unified set of guidelines. In the end, we completed about 150 interviews with leading party politicians in 30 parties in Austria, Britain, France, Germany, Spain and Sweden and, most importantly, we are confident that our results are comparable across countries and parties.

Along the way, we have received generous help from a large number of colleagues. Many of them assisted us with a mail survey of all relevant parties in the 15 pre-2004 enlargement EU member states, the results of which will be reported elsewhere. The meeting to discuss the questionnaire was held in Murcia in May 2004 and was generously supported by the Spanish Ministry of Education and Science (Acción Especial SEC2002–11872-E). Clearly, the present volume has benefited tremendously from the stimulating discussions in Murcia. Others joined us at subsequent presentations of initial results, like at the ECPR general conferences in Marburg and Budapest, while many attended our end of project meeting in Brussels in May 2006. The European Policy Centre hosted an event in which we were able to discuss our results with practitioners, and the Fondation Universitaire provided us with a wonderful environment for a concluding panel and a round table. Not only did we benefit tremendously from the insights of many colleagues, but we were also reassured by our friends that our endeavours were indeed worth the effort. We are deeply grateful to Luciano Bardi, Stefano Bartolini, Marina Costa Lobo, Kris Deschouwer, Patrick Dumont, David Farrell, Karl Magnus Johansson, Ruud Koole, Sylvia Kritzinger, Christopher Lord, Gail McElroy, Alessia Mosca, Gerassimos Moschonas, Karina Pedersen, Philippe Poirier, Tapio Raunio, Martine van Assche, Edwin van Rooyen and Alberto Vannucci for their inspiration, help and support along the way.

Elisabeth Carter, Keele
Thomas Poguntke, Birmingham
July 2006

1 European integration and internal party dynamics

Elisabeth Carter, Kurt Richard Luther and Thomas Poguntke

Academic research on 'Europeanization' has become a veritable growth industry over the last decade. The number of works that have addressed this theme in one form or another has soared (see Featherstone 2003; Mair 2004) and the numerous doctoral studies on the subject suggest that this trend will continue for some time to come. And little wonder: on the one hand, over this time period, European integration has grown both in terms of the number of policy areas now affected by the European Union (EU) and in terms of the number of member states which are now part of the Union. On the other hand, the concept of Europeanization is sometimes understood so broadly that this research agenda is incredibly wide, allowing for a whole range of subfields of political science and international relations to be potentially examined through the lens of Europeanization.

Within this body of work, scores of studies have investigated the Europeanization of domestic institutions, including central government and national administrations, local government and territorial institutions, national parliaments, national courts, and trade unions. Others have examined the influence of the European Union on policy-making in the member states (including monetary policy, transport policy, telecommunications policy and environmental policy), while still others have explored the impact of European integration on national interest intermediation, political contention, business–government relations, domestic news coverage, and public understandings of citizenship and of nation state identities.[1]

In spite of such activity, there has been relatively little research into the effects of European integration on national political parties, party systems, elections and voters. Gabel (2000) has analysed whether issues of European integration influence national electoral behaviour, and Mair (2000) has examined the impact of Europe on national party systems. Similarly, in regard to political parties, Ladrech (2002) has put forward a useful framework for analysis that identifies five possible areas of investigation for evidence of Europeanization, some of which have since been examined. Indeed, Raunio (2002) has considered the impact of European integration on the autonomy of party leaderships, and Pennings (2006) and Dorussen and Nanou (2006) have investigated the influence of integration on national party manifestos. A number of works have also examined the European policy of individual parties (for example Gaffney 1996; Daniels 1998; Raunio 1999; Sloam

2004; Smith 2005). But this list remains relatively short, and it is still the case that this area of research is underdeveloped.

Indeed, in a review of two influential volumes on Europeanization, Mair bemoaned this very fact, arguing that 'the politics of Europeanization . . . continues to be neglected' (2004: 345), a point he later repeated when he claimed that 'far too little systematic attention has been paid to analyzing the indirect impact of Europeanization on parties and party systems, especially at the domestic level where it is likely to be more important' (2006).

The lack of attention paid to the domestic level is particularly striking when one considers how much research has been devoted to electoral and party developments at the supranational level. After all, numerous studies have concerned themselves with elections to the European Parliament (EP), while many others have explored the dynamics of party competition and the composition and behaviour of party groups within the EP, and a further body of work has focused on the development of extra-parliamentary parties at the European level, i.e. Europarties.[2]

The fact that so little work has examined the impact of European integration on national political parties is all the more remarkable given that, after all, political parties provide the essential link between government and electorates in modern parliamentary (and to a lesser extent semi-presidential) democracies (Lawson 1988; Poguntke 2002). Furthermore, it is somewhat surprising that, of the few studies that have investigated the relationship between political parties and European integration, with the exception of the conceptual framework put forward by Poguntke *et al.* (2007 forthcoming), none has explored the possible effects of increasing European integration on how parties organize. This is a notable omission because parties are organizations that, to varying degrees, pursue the classic goals of office, votes and policy, and at the heart of party organization lies the formal and informal distribution of power that shapes how these goals are prioritized and pursued. And these goals are (in theory) affected by European integration since decisions made at the EU level increasingly shape national policies, and hence directly mould the environment within which national parties operate. Growing European integration should therefore influence the ability of parties to achieve their desired goals and, in turn, it is reasonable to expect party organizations to adapt to such thorough changes in their environment so as to minimize potentially disruptive effects of European integration and exploit new opportunities that such environmental changes might offer.

In light of this, this volume focuses its attention on the impact of European integration on the internal organizational dynamics of national political parties. It investigates both formal and informal changes in national party organizations that arise from European integration and, in so doing, it examines the extent to which European integration has altered the distribution of power within national political parties. As well as filling an important gap in the research on parties and European integration, through its theoretical foundations and its research design it seeks to answer Mair's call for more studies that provide 'robust comparative evidence concerning the impact of Europe at the national level' (2006).

Given that this study is located within the wider literature on Europeanization, the next section of this chapter turns its attention to how this multi-faceted concept has, to date, been defined and understood. The chapter then moves to examine why and how European integration might have induced change in national political parties, and it then considers factors that may explain variation in this change. It concludes with an overview of the research design of the study.

The meaning of 'Europeanization'

Europeanization has become a fashionable term in contemporary political debate and in political science research. However, the concept to which the term refers is a contested one, with scholars using it to point to a number of different processes and phenomena. As a result, many maintain that there is no 'theory of Europeanization' (Olsen 2002: 944; Featherstone and Radaelli 2003: 333; Bulmer and Lequesne 2005: 11), while others have even questioned the usefulness of the term as an organizing concept (Kassim 2000: 238).

In reviewing the literature on Europeanization, authors have highlighted different definitions of the term. Particularly useful is Olsen's list, which identifies five possible uses of the term: (1) changes in external boundaries; (2) developing institutions at the European level; (3) central penetration of national systems of governance; (4) exporting forms of political organization; and (5) a political unification project (2002: 923–4). Of these five uses, the third, which points to a 'top-down' process whereby domestic political actors or institutions have adapted to the pressures of European integration, has been particularly widespread and influential, especially in the field of comparative politics. One of the first definitions of Europeanization seen from such a perspective, and one which has since been widely cited, is that offered by Ladrech, who characterizes Europeanization as 'an incremental process re-orienting the direction and shape of politics to the degree that EC political and economic dynamics become part of the organizational logic of national politics and policy-making' (1994: 69). In a similar fashion, Héritier *et al.* define Europeanization as 'the process of influence deriving from European decisions and impacting member states' policies and political and administrative structures' (2001: 3).

With the reservation that these two definitions obscure the role of individuals and policy entrepreneurs, Radaelli offers a more detailed definition of Europeanization as 'processes of a) construction b) diffusion and c) institutionalization of formal and informal rules, procedures, policy paradigms, styles, "ways of doing things" and shared beliefs and norms which are first defined and consolidated in the EU policy process and then incorporated in the logic of domestic (national and subnational) discourse, political structures and public policies' (2000: 4). By putting forward this definition Radaelli first broadens the definitions offered by Ladrech and Héritier *et al.*

In addition, however, by arguing that these processes are first defined and consolidated at the EU level, Radaelli touches on the second use of the term in Olsen's list, namely the 'developing [of] institutions at the European level'. This notion is even more explicit in the work of Risse *et al.*, who define Europeanization as 'the emergence and the development at the European level of distinct structures of governance, that is, of political, legal, and social institutions associated with political problem-solving that formalizes interactions among the actors, and of policy networks specializing in the creation of authoritative European rules' (2001: 2).

Thus, unlike Ladrech, Héritier *et al.*, Radaelli and others, Risse *et al.* do not understand Europeanization as encompassing domestic change brought about by the impact of the influence of 'Europe'. Instead, they view Europeanization as an institutionalization of the European political system, and they then proceed to examine the impact of this institutionalization on the domestic structures of member states (see Mair 2004: 339–40). Risse *et al.* have come in for some criticism for their usage of the term. In particular, questions have been raised over the extent to which their concept of Europeanization differs from, or overlaps with, the concept of European integration (Bomberg and Peterson, 2000: 3–4; Radaelli 2000: 3; Howell 2004: 8; Bulmer and Lequesne 2005: 13). That said, they remain very aware of the differences between European integration and (their concept of) Europeanization, arguing that 'much of the literature on European integration . . . treats the process of integration as the end point of a causal process beginning with domestic and transnational societal interests and ending with European outcomes' (2001: 12), whereas their approach focuses on the post-ontological stage of research, namely explaining processes and outcomes of European integration (see also Caporaso 1996; Radaelli 2000: 6).

Despite differences in definitions, there are similarities in the studies mentioned above, in that all focus on a 'top-down' process of Europeanization, since all are concerned with the impact of European dynamics, decisions, processes, institutions and/or policy networks on domestic politics, policies or polities. That said, however, some studies have also pointed to the existence of so-called 'bottom-up' Europeanization by acknowledging that member states are not only affected by 'Europe', but may also seek to shape institutions, processes and policies. Indeed, Risse *et al.* recognize that their approach 'rests on a circular flow, a system of causal relationships closed by feedback loops' (2001: 12). Similarly, Bomberg and Peterson explicitly point out that 'Europeanization is a two-way process' and go on to define it as 'a shorthand term for a complex process whereby national and sub-national institutions, political actors, and citizens adapt to, and seek to shape, the trajectory of European integration in general, and EU policies in particular' (2000: 7; see also Börzel 2002: 193–4).

Some of the relatively early studies of Europeanization mentioned above implicitly viewed European integration as an independent variable, and identified the change in domestic structures or processes that came about in response to integration (or the Europeanization of these domestic structures or processes) as the dependent variable (Hix and Goetz 2000). However, the interconnectivity of the 'top-down' and 'bottom-up' dimensions of Europeanization has, to some extent, meant that a reconceptualization of the relationship between European integration and Europeanization is required. Indeed, as Howell argues, 'the relationship between European integration and Europeanization is interactive and the distinction between the dependent and independent variable obscured' (2004: 3; see also Bulmer and Burch 2001: 78).

This review of (some of) the different definitions of Europeanization and the discussion of the various 'dimensions' of Europeanization are important, in the first instance, because they provide an overview and an assessment of the literature on the subject. Yet it has also been appropriate to provide a (short) literature review in this introductory chapter to the volume so as to place the present project in the wider 'Europeanization framework'.

Since the aim of the present project is to examine the ways in which and the extent to which national political parties have adapted their organizations in the face of growing European integration, this volume is very much concerned with the 'top-down' dimension of Europeanization. In this sense, it adopts a definition of Europeanization akin to those put forward by Ladrech (1994) and Héritier *et al.* (2001). In short, it conceptualizes Europeanization as intra-organizational change in national political parties that is induced by the ongoing process of European integration. This in turn means that, throughout the volume, European integration is indeed treated as the independent variable, and change or adaptation in the organizations of national parties is treated as the dependent variable. This said, however, the chapters that follow do not lose sight of the fact that Europeanization is a two-way process and that various 'feedback loops' between the domestic and the supranational level exist. Indeed, the country study chapters that follow and the concluding chapters to the volume spend considerable time discussing the finding that party elites, especially when in office, have become further empowered as a result of European integration and thus are able to attempt to upload their preferences onto the supranational level. Thus, while the research underpinning the volume focuses squarely on the 'top-down' dimension of Europeanization, the implications of the findings are very much discussed with both dimensions of the concept in mind.

Before turning to outlining the theory on which the project is based and presenting the hypotheses it advances, two further points should be made about Europeanization. Firstly, it is worth emphasizing that the literature on Europeanization fully acknowledges that the impact of European integration on domestic actors and the extent to which these actors may or may not engage in any adaptation is likely to be non-uniform, within countries, across countries, and over time. Börzel has examined this issue in some depth and suggests that the 'differential impact of Europe is explained by the "goodness of fit" between European and national policies, institutions, and processes, on the one hand, and the existence of "mediating factors" or intervening variables that filter the domestic impact of Europe, on the other hand' (2005: 50; see also Ladrech 1994; Börzel and Risse 2000; Risse *et al.* 2001).

Institutional variables are perhaps the most obvious of these intervening variables, but authors have also drawn attention to the importance of 'systems of policy beliefs' (Radaelli 2000: 24), and of values, discourses and identities (Dyson 2000; Checkel 2001). Furthermore, as Mair (2004) has pointed out, even

though to date much of the academic literature has largely ignored them, the political preferences of actors, the extent to which European integration (and indeed
Europeanization) may create political or partisan contestation, and the extent to
which this may then be mobilized should also be considered as crucial intervening
variables. This question of intervening variables will be picked up later in this
chapter when the intervening variables judged most important to the study will be
discussed. In their quest to explain any variation in the extent to which national
parties have adapted their organizations in response to European integration, the
country chapters will also pay attention to these variables. Similarly, Chapter 8
will explore the effect of intervening variables in some depth, given that it focuses
its attention squarely on the issue of variation.

The second point to be made about Europeanization concerns its measurement
and centres around the question of isolating the effects of European integration on
domestic actors. As Goetz has warned, European integration 'is but one of several
"drivers of change"' (2000: 225), and hence, as Bulmer and Lequesne explain,
'there is the very clear risk that Europeanization studies may attribute all empirical findings of adjustment to EU-effects' (2005: 14). This issue will be returned to
in some detail later in the chapter when the study's research design is explained,
since, as will become clear, if an appropriate and careful research strategy is pursued, it does indeed become possible to isolate the effects of European integration
on domestic actors.

Before the chapter can turn its attention to outlining the types of party organizational changes it expects to have taken place, and before its hypotheses can be
presented, it is necessary to briefly discuss the most relevant institutional changes
of the EU so as to appreciate the environment in which national political parties
exist today.

How European integration has changed the environment of national parties

A series of treaty revisions since the late 1980s has fundamentally altered the fab-
ric of European governance. Essentially, these treaties have expanded the powers
of the European Parliament, and in so doing have strengthened some of the supranational elements of the EU and widened the Union's scope. The EP has gained
power through various waves of institutional reform. The Single European Act,
which came into force in 1987, brought in the cooperation procedure, which gave
the EP the right to a second reading over certain legislation. The Maastricht treaty
then established the co-decision procedure, which makes legislation subject to a
third reading by the EP before it can be adopted by the Council of Ministers, and
which allows the EP to prevent legislation from being adopted should an absolute
majority of its members oppose it. The Amsterdam treaty then extended the use of
co-decision, meaning the EP has increasingly become a veto-player in European
law-making.

In addition to gaining power as a result of changes in the legislative process,
the EP has also become stronger vis-à-vis the Commission. At Maastricht it won

the right to confirm an incoming Commission (en bloc), while at Amsterdam it became able to vet the President of the Commission and subject individual commissioner-candidates to parliamentary hearings (Bache and George 2006: 297). The EP used its newly acquired rights in 2004 when it forced the designated President of the Commission, José Manuel Barroso, to withdraw the controversial Italian candidate Rocco Buttiglione.

The supranational logic of the EU was further strengthened after Amsterdam when qualified majority voting (QMV) in the Council of Ministers was extended to most policy areas in the EC pillar (Nugent 2003: 77), although clearly, if disagreements do exist between states, proposals are not normally pushed to a vote. Furthermore, the treaty of Amsterdam saw visa, asylum and immigration policy move into the EC pillar of the Union, and hence fall under QMV, and also introduced QMV to the Common Foreign and Security Policy pillar for adopting and implementing joint actions and common positions.

At the same time, the scope of EU legislation greatly expanded and an increasing portion of legislation is now shaped in Brussels (Börzel and Risse 2000: 3). The Single European Act widened the scope of European-level jurisdiction to many economic areas, and the Maastricht treaty brought consumer protection policy, public health policy, transport policy and education policy under the jurisdiction of the EU. It also extended the EU's competencies in areas of social policy, the environment, and economic and social cohesion (McCormick 2005: 71–8).

Taken together, these institutional changes have had three effects. First, the substantial extension of the powers of the EP has enhanced the supranational elements of the EU. Second, the widened possibilities for QMV have, albeit gradually, shifted the logic of decision-making in the Council of Ministers towards a supranational logic. And third, the overall scope of EU decision-making has been extended considerably, thereby increasing the immediate relevance of decisions made by the Council of Ministers, the European Council and the EP for national politics.

The strengthening of the EP through both institutional reform and through its increased policy remit raises important questions concerning the goodness of fit between the organization and decision-making routines of national political parties on the one hand, and the need to integrate the increasingly important activities of Members of the European Parliament (MEPs) into the political routines of national political parties on the other (Raunio 2000). After all, even though EP party groups are composed of national delegations, the organizing principle of the EP is ideological families, not national delegations. The EP does mix both logics since it requires that a certain number of nations be represented in party groups, and national representation and ideological affinity will compete with each other when it comes to the internal dynamics of EP groups. But how national parties deal with this question, and how much room for manoeuvre MEPs are accorded, have become increasingly relevant issues for national political parties.

The increased use of QMV in the Council of Ministers raises equally important questions about how national political parties accommodate the fact that party politicians in executive office participate in policy decisions which are binding for the nation state without being able to veto them. Although QMV is only invoked in rare cases, its very existence and the 'threat' of its use may shield politicians from criticisms from their national constituency because they may claim that they had to agree to a compromise in order to avoid QMV being applied (Kassim 2005: 288). Likewise, national parties and national parliaments have little ability to scrutinize decisions made in the European Council (where QMV is not employed), even though it is here that the most important choices about the EU's direction are usually made.

In short, since EU decision-making has become far more important for national politics it is only reasonable to expect that national political parties are likely to have come under pressure to adapt. In the past, parties controlled national legislation and had developed mechanisms which would keep their government ministers in check and ensure a reasonable degree of implementation of their programme goals once in power (Klingemann *et al.* 1994). Furthermore, traditionally, the spheres of domestic politics and foreign relations were clearly distinguishable, even though there were limits to controlling a government when it was engaged in foreign policy. Today, however, the emigration of a considerable portion of policy-making to the European level has muddied the waters and, in theory, national political parties should have developed new mechanisms with which to cope with this challenge.

From the perspective of party theory, European integration constitutes a system-level trend that provides stimuli for political parties to adapt their organizations. At its simplest, this means the state-centric paradigm in which political parties have traditionally operated is gradually being replaced by a system of 'unbounded territories' (Bartolini 1999). Moreover, the supranational level impacts directly upon in particular two of the three key goals that the party literature (e.g. Müller and Strøm 1999) ascribes to political parties, namely votes and policy. Since 1979, parties need to organize to compete for votes in elections to the EP, and issues related to European integration can also shape interaction within and between parties competing for votes in national (and even regional) elections. In addition, European integration impacts on parties' pursuit of policy. Not only has the EU led to the establishment of intergovernmental and supranational arenas in which policy-seeking occurs (including above all the EP, the Council of Ministers, the European Council and intergovernmental conferences (IGCs)), but the extended scope of EU-level decision-making might further stimulate parties to adapt their internal processes of manifesto formulation and intra-party decision-making on policy priorities, not least to incorporate EU-level party actors.

Indeed, European integration has created new categories of party actors and caused changes in the roles that some party actors play. The new categories of party actors it has generated include MEPs, who function predominantly at the supranational level. Other party actors continue to operate for the most part at the national level, but are now charged with maintaining regular links between the national and supranational levels. Over time, both these categories of actor develop expertise in EU-related issues and processes. In 1988, Panebianco identified another category of party expert whose intra-organizational position, he argued, had been privileged by system-level change. These were 'electoral professionals' (Panebianco 1988: 262–7), whose value to their parties derived from their mastery of technologies that became increasingly indispensable for vote-seeking. As party actors with a specialization in EU-related issues and processes are nowhere near as indispensable for the pursuit of political parties' key goals, they are unlikely to acquire the same degree of intra-party influence as electoral professionals. Nonetheless, given the importance which the EU level has assumed, so-called 'EU specialists' may well see some increased influence.

In line with party organizational theory, it is therefore reasonable to expect parties to have engaged in formal or informal organizational adaptation given that European integration has greatly increased the complexity of the environment within which parties operate. Yet, as the literature on party organizational change also makes clear (e.g. Harmel and Janda 1994), parties tend to be averse to organizational change. Hence it cannot be assumed that external stimuli will necessarily lead to organizational change. Furthermore, if change does occur, it may be neither identical nor irreversible. This can be attributed in part to the conservative nature of all organizations, but also highlights the importance of taking a number of potentially intervening factors into account. In the language of Panebianco, 'organizational innovation' – especially of the formal variety – is most likely to occur when exogenous stimuli coincide with internal pressure on a party's 'dominant coalition' (Panebianco 1988: 239–50).

In his recent evaluation of approaches to explaining party organizational change, Harmel points out that the focus on system-level trends is best suited to explaining general processes of cumulative or incremental organizational change that arise from gradual environmental change (2002: 132–3). By contrast, what he labels the 'discrete change approach' focuses mainly on explaining abrupt organizational change, which exponents of this approach (e.g. Janda 1990; Harmel and Janda 1994) often attribute to some sort of internal or external 'shock'. The discrete change approach thus appears *prima facie* ill-suited to explaining organizational change resulting from the slow-moving processes of European integration. However, this assumes that parties are exposed to the external stimulus of European integration over a long period of time, which is an assumption that may be less appropriate for parties in countries that only recently joined the Union. For them, the need for rapid adjustment to the exigencies of European integration might well be considered a form of 'external shock'.

European integration as a cause of party change

Parties are likely to have adapted to European integration in a number of ways. They might have changed their policy preferences and the content of their manifestos, and they might have adapted the way they organize European election campaigns. In turn, the structure of party competition might have also changed. As mentioned above, a number of studies have already addressed these issues.

Significantly, however, the impact of European integration on the organization of national political parties has so far been largely neglected. This is therefore the object of the present empirical investigation.

Essentially, party organization is about the informal and formal distribution of power within a party that will give power-holders the authority to pursue their preferred goals relating to office, votes and policy. Following Max Weber, power is conceptualized here as the ability to achieve a desired outcome, even against resistance (Weber 1980: 28). In other words, those who have power within a party can decisively influence what a party stands for, how it competes in different electoral arenas, and who will be elected to party and public offices. This power can flow from direct control over these aspects, that is, from the autonomy to decide without outside interference, or it can be the result of access to resources that can be used to overcome resistance by others. Party politicians 'who enjoy greater autonomy have a larger sphere of action in which they are protected from outside interference. To this extent they can effectively ignore other actors. Their overall power is, then, the combination of the scope of this protected area and their ability to use all their power resources to overcome potential resistance by others outside this protected area' (Poguntke and Webb 2005a: 7).

Clearly, there is never complete autonomy in a democracy because politicians need to anticipate the mechanisms of democratic accountability, which, at the very least, make themselves felt at the next election. In addition, democracies have developed a set of *ex ante* and *ex post* mechanisms in order to restrict the size of these zones of autonomy or, in other words, facilitate accountability (Bergmann *et al.* 2000; Strøm 2000; Strøm *et al.* 2003). However, politicians need to have freedom to manoeuvre in order to conduct their business of bargaining and achieving compromise. The very nature of EU decision-making with its strong bias towards negotiation and compromise inherently requires large zones of autonomy and restricts the feasibility of keeping those acting in EU institutions on a tight leash (Hix and Goetz 2000: 11).

Consequently, the general expectation is that increasing European integration has induced organizational adaptation within national political parties which has led to a power shift in favour of two partially overlapping groups: (1) party elites and (2) those specializing in EU affairs. These two groups should have gained formal competences and *de facto* freedom of manoeuvre (i.e. autonomy) and access to resources (e.g. access to and control over information, expertise, money, staff). This in turn should have given them stronger leverage in intra-party power games. These power gains are likely to have occurred mainly at the expense of ordinary MPs and middle-level party elites.

Party elites

The growing importance of EU politics has increased the relevance and the frequency of involvement of national party politicians in European-level arenas. Mainly, this relates to the institutions of the EU, but it also includes participation in Europarty politics. Party elites, that is, the inner party leadership and, when in government, cabinet members, are increasingly involved in EU-level decision-making that produces binding outcomes for national parties and national politics.

To a limited degree, this applies to party elites participating in the leadership bodies of Europarties since they partake in decisions that may have some bearing on how their national parties position themselves programmatically and strategically, particularly in European election campaigns (Hix and Lord 1997; Bardi 2002; Poguntke and Pütz 2006). Normally, membership in Europarty leadership bodies depends on a prior senior position within the national party and will not add much to an incumbent's national political weight because Europarties still play a limited role in European party politics. That said, a leading position in a Europarty may well strengthen party elites from smaller parties and smaller countries where easy access to international networks might otherwise be less readily available.

First and foremost, however, the above-mentioned involvement in binding decision-making for national politics applies to the Council of Ministers and the European Council (and IGCs). Essentially, it is the logic of intergovernmental negotiations which prevails here: those present in negotiations need to have sufficient autonomy in order to be able to achieve compromise, and this restricts the scope for effective *ex ante* controls by relevant party or parliamentary actors considerably. Those engaged in these negotiations also enjoy greater resources since they have access to the expertise provided by governmental bureaucracies, at both the national and the European level (Hix and Goetz 2000: 13).

When it comes to *ex post* control it is usually very difficult, if not inconceivable, for parliamentary parties that support a government to veto decisions in which their ministers, or even heads of government, have participated. In the first instance, this applies to the 'grand' decisions reached by European summit meetings where heads of government often find themselves locked into marathon meetings attempting to break deadlocks, but the intrinsic logic applies also to regular policy-making by the Council of Ministers where national cabinet members are increasingly involved in nationally binding legislation. To be sure, there is some national variation as regards the strength of European affairs committees (Raunio and Hix 2000; Raunio 2005) and there is more scope for detailed scrutiny in the ongoing process of policy-making by the Council of Ministers. Nevertheless, it is undeniable that EU policy-making has a strong 'executive bias', favouring members of the government and giving them more power vis-à-vis national legislatures and national party arenas to determine policies.

This inherent imbalance is augmented by the fact that those involved in negotiations have considerable control over the *ex post* presentation of which options were available, because Council meetings take place behind closed doors (Raunio and Hix 2000: 145). As mentioned above, the extension of QMV may have strengthened the autonomy of individual negotiators vis-à-vis their principals even further. Although this is not a one-way process because the growing relevance of European governance is likely to have induced the creation of countervailing mechanisms designed to limit power gains by party elites, it is nonetheless reasonable to expect a power shift to have occurred in favour of party elites as a result of ongoing European integration. These power gains flow from the changes in EU decision-making and, above all, from the greatly widened scope of EU governance. On this basis, the following hypothesis may be advanced:

Hypothesis I

European integration has resulted in a shift of power within national political parties in favour of national party elites.

EU specialists

EU specialists are a heterogeneous group of actors who are characterized by the fact that a considerable part of their political activity is related to the process or substance of European governance. They share a specific expertise in the functioning of the EU as a multi-level system. This is often reflected in the fact that they will meet more or less regularly across the functional divisions within their party and their national political system. In other words, they represent an identifiable group within parties. EU specialists include MEPs, members of national parliamentary EU affairs committees, EU spokespersons, members of the party head office staff who are involved in EU affairs, EP group staff and so on. It is important to keep in mind that party politicians (and even staff) often combine several functions. This is particularly true for smaller parties in which, for example, a deputy head of the parliamentary party may also be the senior member of the national parliamentary EU affairs committee and the link person to the Europarty. Despite this overlap, it is still quite possible to distinguish analytically between these roles. Elite interviews in the context of this study have shown that politicians are normally acutely aware about which particular hat they wear in a specific political situation.

Three main groups of EU specialists are identified in this study: MEPs; national politicians with an EU brief (such as members of national parliamentary EU affairs committees and party spokespersons on EU affairs); and party staff who are concerned with the management and organization of EU-related activities. As their roles in the political process differ substantially, they might have benefited from ongoing European integration in different ways. Each group is discussed in turn.

MEPs

The institutional changes outlined above have had three interrelated effects on the political role of MEPs. First, as the powers of the EP have grown, MEPs have now collectively attained considerable power in the legislative process of the EU. Second, as these powers have been extended to a larger number of policy areas, the frequency with which MEPs can exert power has grown. And, third, as EU decision-making has become so much more relevant for national politics, there is likely to have been a growing demand for the expertise of MEPs in national politics. While expertise on European matters should be an important resource which MEPs might be able to use in intra-party discussions and power games, the increasing power of the EP has also considerably enhanced their autonomy as legislators. As a result, national parties are likely to have created new mechanisms to integrate MEPs more closely into party decision-making routines so as to improve their accountability. While this may, to a certain degree, reduce the autonomy of MEPs as EP legislators, it is likely to augment their weight in internal party politics because it increases their involvement in national debates and allows them to use their expertise and their enhanced legislative powers in the EP as a resource in national intra-party power games.

National politicians with an EU brief

This group of EU specialists includes all those national party politicians without senior executive office who specialize in European affairs, such as members of national parliaments' European affairs committees, party spokespersons on EU affairs inside and outside parliament and, where applicable, the minister for European affairs.[3] In territorially decentralized states, many of these positions also exist at the sub-national level, which considerably increases the size of this group. As a result of the growing relevance of the EU, this group should have experienced a growing demand for its expertise. Furthermore, as the scope of the EU has grown, so the involvement of these actors should have been extended to a larger number of policy areas. In other words, the expertise of these people should have become a more valuable resource and, in those cases where EU specialists have decision-making powers, the number and the scope of their zones of autonomy will have increased. This should, in turn, have given them a stronger role in shaping their party's programmatic documents and, in the case of those who are also parliamentarians, their party's legislative behaviour. The latter is particularly relevant for senior members of European affairs committees in national (and sub-national) parliaments, which, in some cases, play an important role in influencing their country's European politics. Finally, national EU specialists are also expected to have better access to material resources such as staff or travel allowances as parties and parliaments have to accommodate their increased role.

Staff with an EU brief

The last main sub-group of EU specialists consists of those people employed by parties and parliamentary parties at sub-national, national and EU levels who are concerned with the management and organization of EU-related activities. As they are not elected, strictly speaking, unlike elected politicians, they have no decision-making powers. Instead, they are a resource to the other two groups of EU specialists. At the same time, however, these staff may often be quite influential in drafting policy or programmatic documents, for example, as elected politicians will, in most cases, lack the time to actually draft such documents and are likely to only become involved in the editing stages. This gives staffers the power to shape decisions even if they do not take those decisions themselves. Hence, their expertise is an important resource that they should be able to use in order to influence their party's position. Furthermore, as the EU has become more relevant for national parties, the demand for their expertise, and hence their power, should have grown.

In short, all three categories are likely to have gained intra-party power because their expertise in EU affairs has become an increasingly useful resource in internal party politics. At the same time, the growing relevance of European integration should have improved their access to material resources such as staff and money. In addition, MEPs and national politicians with an EU brief (categories 1 and 2 above) should have gained power because their zones of autonomous decision-making have become larger and/or are invoked more frequently: MEPs benefit from the fact that the EP is more powerful *and* is now involved in a greater number of policy areas. Likewise, members of national European affairs committees may have benefited from a strengthening of their committee's formal powers, and all national and sub-national EU specialists are likely to have experienced an increasing demand for their specific role as a result of the progressing 'intrusion' of European into national (and sub-national) politics. In light of this, a second hypothesis is formulated as follows:

Hypothesis II

European integration has resulted in a shift of power within national political parties in favour of EU specialists.

Countervailing forces

No doubt, the influence of growing European integration on the internal distribution of power within national political parties will be moderated by a range of factors specific to individual parties and countries. The most important of these potential intervening variables will be discussed below. In addition, it cannot be emphasized enough that the likely changes outlined above will, in many cases, be alleviated by countervailing forces. An obvious example has already been mentioned in passing: as legislative authority migrates to the institutions of the EU, national and indeed sub-national parliaments will begin to create structures and implement routines designed to recapture some of the lost control or, at the very minimum, reduce the erosion of national legislative powers (Auel 2005: 305–7). One such example are mechanisms that attempt to reduce the autonomy of cabinet members in Council of Ministers meetings (Raunio and Hix 2000; Holzhacker 2005). In addition to these mechanisms, the EU itself has brought in some (limited) measures to alleviate some of the adaptive pressures it has created, for example deciding in June 2006 to open some of the proceedings of the Council of Ministers to the public.

The hypothesized changes outlined above are also likely to be affected by perception, which, after all, is a very important factor in politics. National politicians may not have fully realized how much is now determined by 'Brussels'; as a result, it could be that EU specialists may not have seen their influence in national party politics grow as much as it might. Similarly, national and sub-national parliaments may have been slow in reacting to the erosion of their legislative authority. Consequently, European and national (including sub-national) party politics may have remained more detached from each other than the *de facto* integration of national and European policy-making would suggest. The very fact that EP elections have remained second order elections is a clear indication that parties and mass publics are lagging behind the institutional changes (Reif and Schmitt 1980; van der Eijk and Franklin 1996). That said, to some degree, this detachment makes sense, given that the vast majority of offices (and relevant votes for achieving them) are still won within the confines of the nation state, although when it comes to the third essential party goal, namely policy, continuing detachment is clearly less rational.

Sources of potential variation

As noted earlier in this chapter, research has shown that parties tend not to respond to environmental change in a uniform manner. Numerous factors could mediate the impact of European integration on the internal lives of parties and many of them will be discussed in the six country studies contained in this volume. Although the relatively small number of countries means that these potential sources of variation cannot be subjected to rigorous testing, some will be examined comparatively in Chapter 8. For now, it will suffice to note two broad types of factor that have the potential to explain variation in the impact of European integration on party organization.

The first relates to differences at the level of the member states, and prominent amongst these are aspects of the countries' institutional framework. In the first instance, the way in which European integration affects party organization is likely to be affected by whether a country has a parliamentary or a semi-presidential executive. Similarly, differences are likely between unitary systems on the one hand, and federal systems and those characterized by marked territorial autonomy on the other, since the latter provide significant sub-state sites of party encounters. This could, in turn, militate against the hypothesized strengthening of national party elites, but it could also mean that EU specialists are incorporated more into regional subdivisions of the party, rather than into its national organization.

The effectiveness of the structures set up to scrutinize EU affairs is also likely to cause cross-national variation in the impact of European integration on party organization. Other things being equal, a comparatively strong EU affairs committee is likely to mitigate the executive bias of EU decision-making and is likely to strengthen the parliamentary wing of the party in public office vis-à-vis its governmental wing. Finally, the way in which countries organize their elections to the EP is also likely to account for cross-national variation. The hypothesized intra-party strengthening of party elites is likely to be greater where EP elections are fought in a single constituency, or where the list is closed.

The length of a country's membership of the EU might also help explain variation in the degree to which parties have adapted their organizations. That said, two equally plausible and yet contrasting arguments can be made about the likely effects of the length of a country's membership. On the one hand, it can be argued that membership longevity gives parties more time to adapt their organizations to the exigencies of supranational governance and makes them accustomed to the sight of their elites exercising considerable autonomy when engaging in EU-level decision-making. From this it would follow that the longer a country has been a member of the EU, the more likely it is that EU specialists and party elites will have been empowered. On the other hand, however, it is equally reasonable to argue that joining the EU, particularly in the post-Maastricht era, might have constituted an 'external shock' for parties in countries that have only recently become members, in which case rapid and significant organizational adaptation would be expected. Moreover, since EU-specialization will be less widespread within those parties, persons with such expertise are likely to be in greater demand and thus to enjoy more intra-party influence.

The final country-specific factor concerns public opinion on the EU and the nature of national discourse on EU-related matters. Where a 'permissive consensus' on EU affairs exists and anti-EU sentiment is not mobilized, party elites are likely to have greater autonomy when acting at the EU level and thus more potential to increase their intra-party power. Conversely, where European integration is controversial, or specific EU-related issues are politically divisive, elite autonomy is likely to be constrained.

A second type of intervening factor relates to the nature of the individual parties themselves. Firstly, the level of internal party consensus or division over EU-related issues is likely to be important. Clearly, the more divided a party is over EU-related issues, then the more constrained its leadership is likely to be in making decisions about these issues (Aylott 2002). This, in turn, should militate against the intra-party empowerment of both party elites active in EU-level executive organs and EU specialists. The organizational responses of parties to European integration are also likely to be related to their organizational type and the party family to which they belong. Given the significance that notions of grassroots democracy assume in the organizational ethos of 'new politics' parties (Poguntke 1987), this type of party is expected to offer considerable resistance to the pressures for elite empowerment. By contrast, the ethos of parties that approximate to the 'catch-all' (Kirchheimer 1966) or 'cartel' (Katz and Mair 1995) models, in which the extra-parliamentary party is comparatively weaker, is likely to be more receptive to a further strengthening of elite autonomy. Party organizational size is also a potentially important intervening variable. Small parties are likely to be limited in their capacity to engage in extensive functional differentiation and are therefore unlikely to be able to establish a significant cadre of EU specialists.

Finally, incumbency is likely to be an important party-specific intervening variable. As elite empowerment will primarily flow from the involvement of government members in EU decision-making organs, European integration is expected to result in greater elite empowerment within incumbent than opposition parties. The very fact that elite empowerment is so directly related to incumbency also suggests that this is likely to be at least partially reversed once a party loses office. The emphasis is on 'partially', however: although the decision-making powers are directly linked to incumbency, the power resources flowing from enhanced expertise in EU politics and personal networks remain.

Research design

The research design employed to investigate this project's hypotheses is predicated upon a series of in-depth and predominantly qualitative country studies. The countries were selected according to the logic of a 'most different systems' design (Przeworski and Teune 1970). In line with the discussion in the preceding section of this chapter, this meant seeking to maximize variance in country-level factors such as date of entry, form of government, degree of territorial concentration, overall level of EU scepticism and the existence of a significant Eurosceptic party. With these considerations in mind, the following countries were chosen: Austria, Britain, France, Germany, Spain and Sweden. The ten most recent EU member states were not included in the analysis on the grounds that parties in these countries were not in a position to adapt their organizations over a significant time period in which European integration gradually increased. The pressures for adaptation have therefore been very different for parties in the newest member states as, from the very start of their country's membership, they had to contend with a Union characterized by a high degree of integration, and they have had only a short period of time to respond to this new environment.

This study includes all parties that can be considered 'relevant' according to the criteria of coalition and blackmail potential suggested by Sartori (1976: 122–5). There are between three (Britain) and seven (Sweden) such parties per country, bringing the total number of parties studied by this project to 30.[4]

When examining these parties' organizations, the focus was on both formal and informal change. *Formal* change was taken to mean alterations to party structures, broadly conceived. Party structures can be regarded as the binding framework for internal party politics and thus as significant determinants of the power resources available to actors competing in internal power games. Accordingly, formal organizational change is likely to reflect shifts in the balance of intra-party power (Katz and Mair 1992: 7–8). The empirical investigation examined whether parties had changed their statutes to grant EU specialists *ex officio* seats on their executive bodies, or had over time permitted EU specialists to increase their regularised access to power resources such as money and staff. It also explored whether parties had changed their rules on EP candidate selection and whether they created structures designed to integrate EU specialists more closely into the internal decision-making processes.

However, formal change sometimes captures merely the 'official story' of party organizational adaptation (Katz and Mair 1992). To understand the 'real story' of intra-organizational power relations, it is also necessary to investigate *informal* organizational change, which can be viewed as change in the behaviour of actors within the constraints of party structures. When examining informal organizational change, it was important to establish, for example, whether EU specialists' involvement in intra-party processes such as manifesto formulation had grown, and whether EU-specialization was perceived to be an asset in intra-party power relations. It was also important to investigate the level of autonomy accorded by national parties to their EU specialists and to their elites active in EU-level arenas and, conversely, the degree of accountability to which these actors were subjected. To this end, the investigation focused on matters such as the nature and effectiveness of intra-party mechanisms designed to exercise *ex ante* or *ex post* controls over this type activity. The study also sought to ascertain whether European integration had led to informal organizational change that might have strengthened party elites' influence over the selection of EU specialists, as well as how (the absence of) intra-party divisions over EU-related issues might have impacted upon party elites' intra-party power.

Two main types of data were used to investigate formal and informal organizational change. Firstly, party documents were analysed. These included party statutes and other internal party documents that provided information on topics such as *ex officio* seats for MEPs in national party executives, the rules for candidate selection for EP elections, and possible changes in the number of party staff specializing in EU affairs. Secondly, extensive semi-structured elite interviews were conducted with EU specialists and party elites, and these interviews provided the project with its most important data. Seven categories of key informants were identified: the parties' current or recent leaders; their general secretaries; their parliamentary party chairpersons; their chief representatives on their national parliament's European affairs committee; the leaders of their EP delegations; their international secretaries; and EU specialist staff. Where the target interviewees were unavailable, it was usually possible to interview either a former holder of the relevant office or the office-holder's key assistant. Inevitably, there was variation between parties and countries as regards the availability of interviewees. Furthermore, not all the targeted positions exist in all parties (e.g. a parliamentary party chairperson or an international secretary). Notwithstanding this, some 150 interviews were conducted in the course of this study.

While it was often possible to trace back formal changes to the date of the first direct elections to the EP in 1979 (or later in Austria, Spain and Sweden), it was not realistically feasible to consider informal changes over the same time period. Therefore, in the elite interviews interviewees were asked to evaluate changes over the past decade or so. As the interviews were conducted between 2003 and 2005, this allowed the impact of the post-Maastricht EU-institutional changes on internal party politics to be assessed.

As acknowledged in an earlier section of this chapter, shifts in the internal dynamics of political parties cannot be attributed solely to ongoing European integration. There is much to be said for the proposition that any systematic increase in the intra-party significance of EU specialists would necessarily be directly linked to European integration. However, the situation is very different when it comes to accounting for a strengthening of the intra-party power of party elites. After all, a major theme of the party literature has for some years been that party elites are growing stronger, a trend which has been variously attributed to factors such as the greater significance of personality voting and the 'presidentialization' of politics, to name but two (Bean and Mughan 1989; Kaase 1994; King 2002; Poguntke and Webb 2005b).

As Bulmer and Burch argue, therefore, 'the methodological challenge of Europeanization is to ensure that the research strategy adopted can derive sound results and reasonable inferences about causality' (2005: 864). In this vein, the semi-structured interviews on which this project is based were designed in such a manner as to enable the study to establish, with a fair degree of confidence, the specific effect of increasing European integration on the balance of power within national political parties. In the first instance, party informants were questioned in a manner consistent with the logic of 'process-tracing' (Brady and Collier 2004; George and Bennett 2005). The detailed questioning was designed to reveal causality by asking interviewees directly about their evaluation of exactly how the EU-related role of party elites had impacted upon their position and the position of others within their party organization. In addition, interviews with actors from the same party did not in practice give rise to contradictory evaluations, something that added to the strength of the conclusions reached.

The majority of the project's detailed findings are presented in the six country case study chapters, which are followed by a comparative analysis of similarities and differences across countries and groups of parties (Chapter 8) and a concluding chapter. The country chapters are structured in the following way: first, they discuss potentially relevant country-specific and party-specific background factors. Thereafter, each chapter has a section on 'structural adaptation', in which the 'official story' of organizational adaptation is presented. As party elites are by definition at the centre of party decision-making, the analyses of structural adaptation focus on formal change in respect of the intra-party position of EU specialists. Then the chapters move to the 'real story', dealing first with informal change in the national party arena. Here too, the focus is primarily upon EU specialists. Amongst other things, the authors examine the general intra-party influence of the different categories of EU specialists and the nature and extent of their role in manifesto formulation. The final substantive section of each chapter deals with the 'real story' with respect to the activities of EU specialists and party elites operating at the supranational level. This section is organized by reference to three main arenas: the European Parliament, Europarties and EU decision-making bodies where party elites interact as members of national governments (i.e. Council of Ministers, European Council and IGCs).

Conclusion

This study contributes to answering a number of important questions related to the ongoing process of European integration. Essentially, it investigates the extent to which the model of party government prevalent in the old 15 EU member states has been hollowed out by European integration through a gradual and substantial shift of power towards those party elites who are in government and a relatively small cadre of EU specialists. If the hypotheses are borne out, this would mean that national political parties have lost a considerable portion of their control over national policies. Given that parties are the essential democratic link between the institutions of government and the electorate (Lawson 1988; Poguntke 2002), this would raise important questions concerning the democratic legitimacy of the European multi-level system of governance. Although it is true that members of national government are democratically legitimized, they nevertheless operate one step further away from their principals in parliament when they are part of EU decision-making bodies.

In addition, QMV has made it more likely that those active in European institutions of governance 'lend' their legitimacy to decisions that they may be able to influence but not veto. In conjunction with the increased powers of the EP this means that the interests of individual EU members states can, in some cases, be overruled by majority voting. Given that EP elections are national second order elections, both MEPs and members of national governments derive their legitimacy from their national electorates, and yet they are part of bodies that may overrule the interest of other countries. To be sure, this may be unavoidable, and even desirable, on the path towards a more integrated Europe. However, if elements of national sovereignty are given up in exchange for increasing European integration, it is essential that those active in the institutions of European governance are linked to national constituencies, and national parties are a crucial linkage in this process.

It is precisely this linkage that, according to this project's hypotheses, might have become weaker. To the extent that elites are empowered by European integration, a substantial disaggregation of the party in public office might be expected. Those in government might become more independent from their parliamentary parties, and the parliamentary parties might find it increasingly difficult to hold their ministers to account. Equally, those in government might gain further dominance over the party central office (Katz 2002). By and large, the party on the ground may have suffered least in that it has, in most cases, become less powerful over the past decades anyway (Harmel 2002: 122–5). To be sure, the ultimate democratic sanction, that is, the loss of power at the ballot box, remains unaffected, but the nature of party democracy might have changed considerably as a result of growing European integration given that there is ever less democratic control over the substance of politics.

Notes

1   On the Europeanization of central government and national administrations see for example Page and Wouters (1995); Bulmer and Burch (1998, 2001, 2005); Harmsen (1999); Dyson (2000); Goetz (2000). On local government and territorial institutions see Goldsmith (1993); Ladrech (1994); Goetz (1995); Börzel (1999). On national parliaments see Raunio and Hix (2000); Hansen and Scholl (2002); Auel and Benz (2005); Saalfeld (2005); Wessels (2005). On national courts see Levitsky (1994); Chalmers (2000); Conant (2001); and on trade unions see Turner (1996). On the Europeanization of public policy see Radaelli (2003); Dyson and Featherstone (1999) on monetary

policy; Héritier (2001) on transport policy; Schneider (2001) on telecommunications liberalization; and Börzel (2002) on environmental policy. On the Europeanization of national interest intermediation see Falkner (2000); on political contention see Imig and Tarrow (2000); on business–government relations see Green Cowles (2001); on domestic news coverage see Semetko *et al.* (2000); and on public understandings of citizenship and of nation state identities see Checkel (2001) and Risse (2001).

2 On elections to the EP see for example van der Eijk and Franklin (1996); Blondel *et al.* (1998). On party competition in European elections see among others Aspinwall (2002); Gabel and Hix (2002); Pennings (2002); Marks and Steenbergen (2004). On party competition in the EP and on EP party groups see Hix and Lord (1997); Raunio (1997); Kreppel and Tsebelis (1999); Hix (2001); Bardi (2002). On Europarties see Dietz (2000); Bardi (2002); Johansson and Zervakis (2002); Ladrech (2002); Poguntke and Pütz (2006).

3 Ministers for European affairs are typically not involved in EU decision-making arenas (there is no Council of Ministers for them for example), but instead coordinate EU policies nationally. As such, they qualify as EU-specialists and are not regarded as party elites.

4 The parties included in this project are as follows: Austria: *Die Grünen – Die Grüne Alternative* (Greens), *Sozialdemokratische Partei Österreichs*, SPÖ (Social Democratic Party of Austria), *Österreichische Volkspartei*, ÖVP (Austrian People's Party), *Freiheitliche Partei Österreichs*, FPÖ (Freedom Party of Austria); Britain: Conservative Party, Liberal Democrats, Labour Party; France: *Parti Communiste Français*, PCF (French Communist Party), *Les Verts* (Greens), *Parti Socialiste*, PS (Socialist Party), *Union pour la Démocratie Française*, UDF (Union for French Democracy), *Union pour un Mouvement Populaire*, UMP (Union for a Popular Movement), which incorporates the former *Rassemblement pour la République*, RPR (Rally for the Republic); Germany: *Linkspartei* (Left Party), which incorporates the former *Partei des Demokratischen Sozialismus*, PDS (Party of Democratic Socialism), *Die Grünen* (Greens), *Sozialdemokratische Partei Deutschlands*, SPD (Social Democrats), *Freie Demokratische Partei*, FDP (Free Democrats), *Christlich Demokratische Union*, CDU (Christian Democratic Union), *Christlich Soziale Union*, CSU (Christian Social Union); Spain: *Izquierda Unida*, IU (United Left), *Partido Socialista Obrero Español*, PSOE (Spanish Socialist Workers' Party), *Convergència Democràtica de Catalunya*, CDC (Democratic Convergence of Catalonia), *Partido Nacionalista Vasco*, PNV (Basque Nationalist Party), *Partido Popular*, PP (Popular Party); Sweden: *vänsterpartiet*, v (Left Party), *Sveriges socialdemokratiska arbetarepartiet*, s (Social Democrats), *miljöpartiet de gröna*, mp (Greens), *centerpartiet*, c (Centre Party), *folkpartiet liberalerna*, fp (Liberals), *kristdemokraterna*, kd (Christian Democrats), *moderata samlingspartiet*, m (Moderates).

References

Aspinwall, Mark (2002) 'Preferring Europe: Ideology and National Preferences on European Integration', *European Union Politics*, 3(1): 81–112.

Auel, Katrin (2005) 'Introduction: The Europeanisation of Parliamentary Democracy', *The Journal of Legislative Studies*, 11(3/4): 303–18.

Auel, Katrin and Arthur Benz (2005) 'The Politics of Adaptation: The Europeanisation of National Parliamentary Systems', *Journal of Legislative Studies*, 11(3/4): 372–93.

Aylott, Nicholas (2002) 'Let's Discuss This Later: Party Responses to Euro-Division in Scandinavia', *Party Politics*, 8(4): 441–62.

Bache, Ian and Stephen George (2006) *Politics in the European Union*, second edition, Oxford: Oxford University Press.

Bardi, Luciano (2002) 'Parties and Party Systems in the European Union: National and Supranational Dimensions', in Kurt Richard Luther and Ferdinand Müller-Rommel (eds), *Political Parties in the New Europe: Political and Analytical Challenges*, Oxford: Oxford University Press, pp. 293–321.

Bartolini, Stefano (1999) *Political Representation in Loosely Bounded Territories*, RSC Forum Discussion Paper, Florence: European University Institute.

Bean, Clive and Anthony Mughan (1989) 'Leadership Effects in Parliamentary Elections in Australia and Britain' *American Political Science Review,* 83(4): 1165–79.

Bergmann, Torbjörn, Wolfgang C. Müller and Kaare Strøm (2000) 'Introduction: Parliamentary Democracy and the Chain of Delegation', *European Journal of Political Research,* 37(3): 255–60.

Blondel, Jean, Richard Sinnott and Palle Svensson (1998) *People and Parliament in the European Union: Participation, Democracy and Legitimacy*, Oxford: Clarendon Press.

Bomberg, Elizabeth and John Peterson (2000) 'Policy Transfer and Europeanization: Passing the Heineken Test?', *Queen's Papers on Europeanization*, 2 <http://ideas.repec.org/s/erp/queens.html>.

Börzel, Tanja A. (1999) 'Towards Convergence in Europe? Institutional Adaptation to Europeanization in Germany and Spain', *Journal of Common Market Studies*, 37(4): 573–96.

Börzel, Tanja A. (2002) 'Pace-Setting, Foot-Dragging and Fence-Sitting: Member State Responses to Europeanization', *Journal of Common Market Studies*, 40(2): 193–214.

Börzel, Tanja A. (2005) 'Europeanization: How the European Union Interacts with its Member States', in Simon Bulmer and Christian Lequesne (eds), *The Member States of the European Union*, Oxford: Oxford University Press, pp. 45–69.

Börzel, Tanja A. and Thomas Risse (2000), 'When Europe Hits Home: Europeanization and Domestic Change', *European Integration online Papers (EIoP)*, 4(15) <http://eiop.or.at/eiop/texte/2000-015a.htm>.

Brady, Henry E. and David Collier (eds) (2004) *Rethinking Social Enquiry*, Lanham, MD: Rowman and Littlefield.

Bulmer, Simon and Martin Burch (1998) 'Organizing for Europe: Whitehall, The British State and European Union', *Public Administration*, 76(4): 601–28.

Bulmer, Simon and Martin Burch (2001) 'The "Europeanisation" of Central Government: The UK and Germany in Historical Institutionalist Perspective', in Gerald Schneider and Mark Aspinwall (eds), *The Rules of Integration: Institutionalist Approaches to the Study of Europe*, Manchester: Manchester University Press, pp. 73–100.

Bulmer, Simon and Martin Burch (2005) 'The Europeanization of UK Government: From Quiet Revolution to Explicit Step-Change?', *Public Administration*, 83(4): 861–90.

Bulmer, Simon and Christian Lequesne (2005) 'The European Union and its Member States: An Overview', in Simon Bulmer and Christian Lequesne (eds), *The Member States of the European Union*, Oxford: Oxford University Press, pp. 1–20.

Caporaso, James A. (1996) 'The European Union and Forms of State: Westphalian, Regulatory or Post-Modern?', *Journal of Common Market Studies*, 34(1): 29–52.

Chalmers, Damian (2000) 'The Positioning of EU Judicial Politics within the United Kingdom', *West European Politics*, 23(4): 169–210.

Checkel, Jeffrey T. (2001) 'The Europeanization of Citizenship?', in Maria Green Cowles, James Caporaso and Thomas Risse (eds), *Transforming Europe: Europeanization and Domestic Change*, Ithaca NY: Cornell University Press, pp. 180–97.

Conant, Lisa (2001) 'Europeanization and the Courts: Variable Patterns of Adaptation among National Judiciaries', in Maria Green Cowles, James A. Caporaso and Thomas Risse (eds), *Transforming Europe: Europeanization and Domestic Change*, Ithaca NY: Cornell University Press, pp. 97–115.

Daniels, Philip (1998) 'From Hostility to "Constructive Engagement": The Europeanisation of the Labour Party', *West European Politics*, 21(1): 72–96.

Dietz, Thomas (2000) 'Similar but Different? The European Greens Compared to Other Transnational Federations in Europe', *Party Politics*, 6(2): 199–210.

Dorussen, Han and Kyriaki Nanou (2006) 'European Integration, Intergovernmental Bargaining, and Convergence of Party Programmes', *European Union Politics*, 7(2): 235–56.

Dyson, Kenneth (2000) 'Europeanization, Whitehall Culture and the Treasury as Institutional Veto Player: A Constructivist Approach to Economic and Monetary Union', *Public Administration*, 78(4): 897–914.

Dyson, Kenneth and Kevin Featherstone (1999) *The Road to Maastricht*, Oxford: Oxford University Press.

van der Eijk, Cees, and Mark N. Franklin (eds) (1996) *Choosing Europe? The European Electorate and National Politics in the Face of Union*, Ann Arbor, MI: University of Michigan Press.

Falkner, Gerda (2000) 'Policy Networks in a Multi-level System: Convergence Towards Moderate Diversity?', *West European Politics*, 23(4): 94–120.

Featherstone, Kevin (2003) 'Introduction: In the Name of "Europe"', in Kevin Featherstone and Claudio Radaelli (eds), *The Politics of Europeanization*, Oxford: Oxford University Press, pp. 3–26,.

Featherstone, Kevin and Claudio Radaelli (2003) 'A Conversant Research Agenda', in Kevin Featherstone and Claudio Radaelli (eds), *The Politics of Europeanization*, Oxford: Oxford University Press, pp. 331–41.

Gabel, Matthew (2000) 'European Integration, Voters and National Politics', *West European Politics*, 23(4): 52–74.

Gabel, Matthew and Simon Hix (2002) 'Defining the EU Political Space: An Empirical Study of the European Elections Manifestos, 1979–1999', *Comparative Political Studies*, 35(8): 934–64.

Gaffney, John (ed.) (1996) *Political Parties and the European Union*, London: Routledge.

George, Alexander L. and Andrew Bennett (2005) *Case Studies and Theory Development in the Social Sciences*, Cambridge, MA: MIT Press.

Goetz, Klaus H. (1995) 'National Governance and European Integration: Intergovernmental Relations in Germany', *Journal of Common Market Studies*, 33(1): 91–116.

Goetz, Klaus H. (2000) 'European Integration and National Executives: A Cause in Search of an Effect?', *West European Politics*, 23(4): 211–31.

Goldsmith, Mike (1993) 'The Europeanisation of Local Government', *Urban Studies*, 30(4–5): 683–99.

Green Cowles, Maria (2001) 'The Transatlantic Business Dialogue and Domestic Business-Government Relations', in Maria Green Cowles, James Caporaso and Thomas Risse (eds), *Transforming Europe: Europeanization and Domestic Change*, Ithaca NY: Cornell University Press, pp. 159–79.

Hansen, Troels B. and Bruno Scholl (2002) 'Europeanization and Domestic Parliamentary Adaptation – A Comparative Analysis of the Bundestag and the House of Commons', *European Integration online Papers (EIoP)*, 6(15) <http://eiop.or.at/eiop/texte/2002-015a.htm>.

Harmel, Robert (2002) 'Party Organizational Change: Competing Explanations?', in Kurt Richard Luther and Ferdinand Müller-Rommel (eds), *Political Parties in the New Europe: Political and Analytical Challenges*, Oxford: Oxford University Press, pp. 119–42.

Harmel, Robert and Janda, Kenneth (1994) 'An Integrated Theory of Party Goals and Party Change', *Journal of Theoretical Politics*, 6(4): 259–87.

Harmsen, Robert (1999) 'The Europeanization of National Administrations: A Comparative Study of France and the Netherlands', *Governance*, 12(1): 81–113.

Héritier, Adrienne (2001) 'Differential Europe: National Administrative Responses to Community Policy', in Maria Green Cowles, James A. Caporaso and Thomas Risse (eds), *Transforming Europe: Europeanization and Domestic Change*, Ithaca NY: Cornell University Press, pp. 44–59.

Héritier, Adrienne, Dieter Kerwer, Christoph Lehmkuhl, Michael Teutsch and Anne-Cécile Douillet (2001) *Differential Europe. The European Union Impact on National Policy-making*, Lanham, MD: Rowman and Littlefield.

Hix, Simon (2001) 'Legislative Behaviour and Party Competition in the European Parliament: An Application of Nominate to the EU', *Journal of Common Market Studies*, 39(4): 663–88.

Hix, Simon and Klaus H. Goetz (2000) 'Introduction: European Integration and National Political Systems', *West European Politics*, 23(4): 1–26.

Hix, Simon and Christopher Lord (1997) *Political Parties in the European Union*, Basingstoke: Macmillan.

Holzhacker, Ronald (2005) 'The Power of Opposition Parliamentary Party Groups in European Scrutiny', *Journal of Legislative Studies*, 11(3/4): 428–45

Howell, Kerry E. (2004) 'Developing Conceptualisations of Europeanization: Synthesising Methodological Approaches', *Queen's Papers on Europeanization*, 3 <http://ideas.repec.org/s/erp/queens.html>.

Imig, Doug and Sidney Tarrow (2000) 'Political Contestation in a Europeanising Polity', *West European Politics*, 23(4): 73–93.

Janda, Kenneth (1990) 'Towards a Performance Theory of Change in Political Parties', paper presented at the World Congress of the International Sociological Association, Madrid, 9–13 July.

Johansson, Karl Magnus and Peter A. Zervakis (2002) *European Political Parties between Cooperation and Integration*, Baden-Baden: Nomos.

Kaase, Max (1994) 'Is there Personalization in Politics? Candidates and Voting Behavior in Germany', *International Political Science Review*, 15(3): 211–30.

Kassim, Hussein (2000) 'Conclusion', in Hussein Kassim, B. Guy Peters and Vincent Wright (eds), *The National Co-ordination of EU Policy*, Oxford: Oxford University Press, pp. 235–64.

Kassim, Hussein (2005) 'The Europeanization of Member State Institutions', in Simon Bulmer and Christian Lequesne (eds), *The Member States of the European Union*, Oxford: Oxford University Press, pp. 285–316.

Katz, Richard S. (2002) 'The Internal Life of Parties', in Kurt Richard Luther and Ferdinand Müller-Rommel (eds), *Political Parties in the New Europe: Political and Analytical Challenges*, Oxford: Oxford University Press, pp. 87–118.

Katz, Richard S. and Peter Mair (1992) 'Introduction: The Cross-National Study of Party Organizations', in Richard S. Katz and Peter Mair (eds), *Party Organizations. A Data Handbook on Party Organizations in Western Democracies, 1960–90*, London: Sage, pp. 1–20.

Katz, Richard S. and Peter Mair (1995) 'Changing Models of Party Organization and Party Democracy: The Emergence of the Cartel Party', *Party Politics*, 1(1): 5–28.

King, Anthony (2002) *Leaders' Personalities and the Outcome of Democratic Elections*, Oxford: Oxford University Press.

Kirchheimer, Otto (1966) 'The Transformation of the Western European Party System', in Joseph LaPalombara and Myron Weiner (eds), *Political Parties and Political Development*, Princeton, NJ: Princeton University Press, pp. 177–200.

Klingemann, Hans-Dieter, Richard I. Hofferbert and Ian Budge (1994) *Parties, Policies, and Democracy*, Boulder: Westview.

Kreppel, Amie and George Tsebelis (1999) 'Coalition Formation in the European Parliament', *Comparative Political Studies*, 32(8): 933–66.

Ladrech, R. (1994) 'Europeanization of Domestic Politics and Institutions: The Case of France', *Journal of Common Market Studies*, 32(1): 69–88.

Ladrech, Robert (2000) *Social Democracy and the Challenge of European Union*, Boulder, CO: Lynne Rienner.

Ladrech, Robert (2002) 'Europeanization and Political Parties: Towards a Framework for Analysis', *Party Politics*, 8(4): 389–403.

Lawson, Kay (1988) 'When Linkage Fails', in Kay Lawson and Peter H. Merkl (eds), *When Parties Fail. Emerging Alternative Organizations*, Princeton, NJ: Princeton University Press, pp. 13–38.

Levitsky, Jonathan E. (1994) 'The Europeanization of the British Legal Style', *American Journal of Comparative Law*, 42(2): 347–80.

McCormick, John (2005) *Understanding the European Union: A Concise Introduction*, third edition, Houndmills/New York: Palgrave Macmillan.

Mair, Peter (2000) 'The Limited Impact of Europe on National Party Systems', *West European Politics*, 23(4): 27–51.

Mair, Peter (2004) 'The Europeanization Dimension', *Journal of European Public Policy*, 11(2): 337–48.

Mair, Peter (2006) 'Political Parties and Party Systems', in Paolo Graziano and Maarten P. Vink (eds), *Europeanization: New Research Agendas*, Basingstoke: Palgrave Macmillan.

Marks, Gary and Marco R. Steenbergen (eds) (2004) *European Integration and Political Conflict*, Cambridge: Cambridge University Press.

Müller, Wolfgang C. and Kaare Strøm (eds) (1999) *Policy, Office, or Votes? How Political Parties in Western Europe Make Hard Choices*, Cambridge: Cambridge University Press.

Nugent, Neill (2003) *The Government and Politics of the European Union*, fifth edition, Basingstoke: Palgrave Macmillan.

Olsen, Johan P. (2002) 'The Many Faces of Europeanization', *Journal of Common Market Studies*, 5(5): 921–52.

Page, Edward and Linda Wouters (1995) 'The Europeanization of National Bureaucracies?', in Jon Pierre (ed.), *Bureaucracy in the Modern State: An Introduction to Comparative Public Administration*, Aldershot: Edward Elgar, pp. 185–204.

Panebianco, Angelo (1988) *Political Parties: Organization and Power*, Cambridge: Cambridge University Press.

Pennings, Paul (2002) 'The Dimensionality of the EU Policy Space', *European Union Politics*, 3(1): 59–80.

Pennings, Paul (2006) 'An Empirical Analysis of the Europeanization of National Party Manifestos, 1960–2003', *European Union Politics*, 7(2): 257–70.

Poguntke, Thomas (1987) 'New Politics and Party Systems: The Emergence of a New Type of Party?', *West European Politics*, 10(1): 76–88.

Poguntke, Thomas (2002) 'Parties without Firm Social Roots? Party Organisational Linkage', in Kurt Richard Luther and Ferdinand Müller-Rommel (eds), *Political Parties in the New Europe: Political and Analytical Challenges*, Oxford: Oxford University Press, pp. 43–62.

Poguntke, Thomas and Christine Pütz (2006) 'Parteien in der Europäischen Union: Zu den Entwicklungschancen der Europarteien', *Zeitschrift für Parlamentsfragen*, 37(2): 334–53.

Poguntke, Thomas and Paul Webb (2005a) 'The Presidentialization of Politics in Democratic Societies? A Framework for Analysis', in Thomas Poguntke and Paul Webb (eds), *The Presidentialization of Politics: A Comparative Study of Modern Democracies*, Oxford: Oxford University Press, pp. 1–25.

Poguntke, Thomas and Paul Webb (eds) (2005b) *The Presidentialization of Politics: A Comparative Study of Modern Democracies*, Oxford: Oxford University Press.

Poguntke, Thomas, Nicholas Aylott, Robert Ladrech and Kurt Richard Luther (2007 forthcoming) 'The Europeanization of National Party Organizations: A Conceptual Analysis', *European Journal of Political Research*.

Przeworski, Adam and Henry Teune (1970) *The Logic of Comparative Social Inquiry*, New York: Wiley.

Radaelli, Claudio (2000) 'Whither Europeanization? Concept Stretching and Substantive Change', *European Integration online Papers (EIoP)*, 4(8) <http://eiop.or.at/eiop/texte/2000-008a.htm>.

Radaelli, Claudio M. (2003) 'The Europeanization of Public Policy', in Kevin Featherstone and Claudio Radaelli (eds), *The Politics of Europeanization*, Oxford: Oxford University Press, pp. 27–56.

Raunio, Tapio (1997) *The European Perspective: Transnational Party Groups in the 1989–1994 European Parliament*, Aldershot: Ashgate.

Raunio, Tapio (1999) 'Facing the European Challenge: Finnish Parties Adjust to the Integration Process', *West European Politics*, 22(1): 138–59.

Raunio, Tapio (2000) 'Losing Independence or Finally Gaining Recognition? Contacts Between MEPs and National Parties', *Party Politics*, 6(2): 211–23.

Raunio, Tapio (2002) 'Why European Integration Increases Leadership Autonomy within Political Parties', *Party Politics*, 8(4): 405–22.

Raunio, Tapio (2005) 'Holding Governments Accountable in European Affairs: Explaining Cross-National Variation', *Journal of Legislative Studies*, 11(3/4): 319–42.

Raunio, Tapio and Simon Hix (2000) 'Backbenchers Learn to Fight Back: European Integration and Parliamentary Government', *West European Politics*, 23(4): 142–68.

Reif, Karlheinz and Hermann Schmitt (1980) 'Nine Second-Order National Elections: A Conceptual Framework for the Analysis of European Election Results', *European Journal of Political Research,* 8(1): 3–45.

Risse, Thomas (2001) 'A European Identity? Europeanization and the Evolution of Nation-State Identities', in Maria Green Cowles, James A. Caporaso and Thomas Risse (eds), *Transforming Europe: Europeanization and Domestic Change*, Ithaca, NY: Cornell University Press, pp. 198–216.

Risse, Thomas, Maria Green Cowles and James A. Caporaso (2001) 'Europeanization and Domestic Change: Introduction', in Maria Green Cowles, James A. Caporaso and Thomas Risse (eds), *Transforming Europe: Europeanization and Domestic Change*, Ithaca NY: Cornell University Press, pp. 1–20.

Saalfeld, Thomas (2005) 'Deliberate Delegation or Abdication? Government Backbenchers, Ministers and European Union Legislation', *Journal of Legislative Studies*, 11(3/4): 343–71.

Sartori, Giovanni (1976) *Parties and Party Systems. A Framework for Analysis*, Cambridge: Cambridge University Press.

Schneider, Volker (2001) 'Institutional Reform in Telecommunications: The European Union in Transnational Policy Diffusion', in Maria Green Cowles, James A. Caporaso and Thomas Risse (eds), *Transforming Europe: Europeanization and Domestic Change*, Ithaca NY: Cornell University Press, pp. 60–78.

Semetko, Holli A., Claes H. De Vreese and Jochen Peter (2000) 'Europeanised Politics – Europeanised Media? European Integration and Political Communication', *West European Politics*, 23(4): 121–41.

Sloam, James (2004) *The European Policy of the German Social Democrats: Interpreting a Changing World*, Basingstoke: Palgrave Macmillan.

Smith, Julie (2005) 'A Missed Opportunity? New Labour's European Policy 1997–2005', *International Affairs*, 81(4): 703–21.

Strøm, Kaare (2000) 'Delegation and Accountability in Parliamentary Democracies', *European Journal of Political Research*, 37(3): 261–89.

Strøm, Kaare, Wolfgang C. Müller and Torbjörn Bergman (eds) (2003) *Delegation and Accountability in Parliamentary Democracies*, Oxford: Oxford University Press.

Turner, Lowell (1996) 'The Europeanization of Labour: Structure before Action', *European Journal of Industrial Relations*, 2(3): 325–44.

Weber, Max (1980) *Wirtschaft und Gesellschaft: Grundriß der verstehenden Soziologie*, Tübingen: Mohr.

Wessels, Bernhard (2005) 'Poses and Orientations of Members of Parliament in the EU Context: Congruence or Difference? Europeanisation or Not?', *Journal of Legislative Studies*, 11(3/4): 446–65.

2 Structural adjustment and incumbent elite empowerment

Austrian parties' adaptation to European integration

Kurt Richard Luther

This chapter reports the findings of an investigation into the extent to which the internal life of Austria's four main political parties has changed in response to the country's 1995 accession to the European Union (EU).[1] Although the impact of membership upon domestic politics figures prominently in recent research by Austria specialists (Tálos and Falkner 1996; Müller and Jenny 2000; Dolezal and Müller 2001; Fallend *et al.* 2002; Müller 2002; Neisser and Puntscher Riekmann 2002; Gehler *et al.* 2003; Höll *et al.* 2003), surprisingly little research exists on how integration might have impacted upon the country's political parties (Puntscher Riekmann *et al.* 2001; Pollak and Slominski 2002). For reasons discussed in this volume's opening chapter, we hypothesize that European integration is likely to have enhanced the intra-party power of two partially overlapping categories of party actors: 'EU specialists' and party elites. To investigate these hypotheses, we will initially seek to establish whether Austrian parties have undertaken any structural adaptation to European integration that advantages these actors. We will then consider whether EU integration has privileged EU specialists in processes of intra-party decision-making such as manifesto formulation and if so, which sub-categories of EU specialists have benefited most. The last substantive section reports our findings regarding the degree of autonomy from their parties which EU specialists and party elites enjoy when acting at the EU level. It also considers the nature and extent of their accountability to their parties for those actions. Before commencing our detailed analysis of these issues, we shall briefly discuss the historical background to and conflicts over Austria's EU membership, domestic institutional reform pursuant to Austria's EU membership, and key organizational features of Austria's political parties.

Austria, European integration and political parties

Historical background

Austria's late accession to the EU has much to do with foreign policy constraints related to the 1955 State Treaty. These included the prohibition of 'political or economic union with Germany in any form whatsoever' and Austria's declaration of permanent neutrality. Austria instead played a leading role in the European Free Trade Area and in the early 1970s negotiated with the Economic Community (EC) a series of free trade agreements containing opt-out clauses in the event of conflicts that might compromise its treaty obligations (Lantis and Queen 1998). The EC's move towards the Single European Act caused Austria to reconsider its position and in 1989 the SPÖ–ÖVP government applied for full membership. Negotiations were successfully concluded in April 1994 and in June an obligatory referendum was held (Pelinka 1995). The SPÖ, ÖVP and opposition Liberal Forum (*Liberales Forum* – LiF) campaigned for membership, which was supported by an unexpectedly large majority (66.6 per cent) of the 81.3 per cent who voted. The highest proportions of 'yes' voters were amongst LiF and SPÖ supporters (75 and 73 per cent respectively). Of those expressing a preference for the FPÖ or Greens – who had both campaigned against membership – only 41 and 38 per cent respectively voted for accession (Ogris 1995; Plasser and Ulram 1995). Austria joined the EU on 1 January 1995 and its parties' subsequent strengths in the European Parliament (EP) are detailed in Table 2.1.

Party conflicts over European integration

The ÖVP had been the first of the governing parties to advocate membership, arguing full access to EC markets for export-oriented firms was essential for future prosperity. Its big business interests thought single market deregulation offered the prospect of reducing organized labour's power over economic policy-making. Later, ÖVP farming and small business groups raised concerns regarding subsidies and competitiveness. Within the socialist camp, support for membership was initially confined to elements of the SPÖ leadership and Austrian Trade Union Federation (*Österreichischer Gewerkschaftsbund* – ÖGB). Here too, economic arguments figured prominently: greater price competition would increase

Table 2.1 Elections to the European Parliament in Austria: votes, seats and turnout, 1995–2004

	1995[a]		1996		1999		2004	
	%	Seats	%	Seats	%	Seats	%	Seats
Greens	–	1	6.8	1	9.3	2	12.9	2
SPÖ	–	7	29.2	6	31.7	7	33.3	7
ÖVP	–	6	29.7	7	30.7	7	32.7	6
FPÖ	–	5	27.5	6	23.4	5	6.3	1
LiF	–	1	4.3	1	2.7	0	–	0
Hans-Peter Martin List							14.0	2
Others	–		2.5	–	2.2	0	0.8	0
Turnout/total seats	n/a	20	66.7	21	49.4	21	42.4	18

Source: Austrian Federal Ministry of the Interior

Note
a Appointed by the Nationalrat in proportion to caucus strengths.

economic activity and raise workers' purchasing power and residual income, whilst the growth essential for maintaining social policy benefits would be secured. More left-wing circles remained extremely sceptical about the EC 'capitalist club', favouring at most participation in the single market. Similar sentiments were to be found in the Greens, the party most consistently opposed to accession, which it was argued would result in the pursuit of growth at any cost and undermine existing environmental protection legislation. The Greens also feared the environmental implications of the expected increase in transit traffic, especially by heavy goods vehicles. Finally, they had concerns about the EC's centralism and 'democratic deficit', and these grew as the contours of the Maastricht treaty emerged.

Once accession had been approved in the referendum, the Greens undertook a remarkable volte-face and accepted membership. The FPÖ moved in the reverse direction. Historically, it had been the most steadfast advocate of European integration, a position critics ascribed to lingering pan-Germanic sentiment. The reality was less clear-cut: the party had long felt EC membership would promote Austria's Western integration and counter features of Austrian consensualism it rejected, including neo-corporatism. From the early 1980s, the FPÖ also advanced economic arguments, but in May 1993 effectively reversed its traditional position. Its rejection of membership (at least on the terms negotiated) was ascribed by most observers to the by then markedly populist party's desire to mobilize the public's anxieties and thus maximize its vote potential.

Since 1995, the main integration-related conflicts between and within Austria's parties have been fourfold. The earlier dispute over neutrality lingered for a few years, in particular in relation to Austria's future security policy. The ÖVP (and especially the FPÖ) initially advocated NATO membership, whilst the SPÖ and in particular the Greens defended neutrality. However, this conflict has since subsided, largely because there is no pressure to make a decision and little prospect of the abandonment of neutrality obtaining the necessary two-thirds parliamentary support and a referendum endorsement. The second conflict resulted from the 'sanctions' imposed on Austria in 2000 by the other EU members in response to the FPÖ's entry into government (Karlhofer *et al.* 2001). They weakened the opposition parties, which the government accused of national disloyalty, but probably increased support for the EU in hitherto more sceptical left-wing circles. A third conflict has concerned EU enlargement. Given its historic links with eastern Europe, Austria's elite was largely in favour of eastern enlargement and well placed to promote it. Yet Austria's location adjacent to the EU's permeable economic 'border' with the accession states made it vulnerable to potentially adverse economic consequences, not least for its labour market. The FPÖ milked this issue, which was also highlighted by the SPÖ's trades union wing and the ÖVP's Workers' and Employees' League. More recently, the enlargement issue has concerned Turkey's proposed membership, something only the Greens did not oppose. Finally, there is considerable unease across the political spectrum regarding the EU's allegedly excessively neo-liberal orientation. Such sentiments are strongest amongst Green and SPÖ supporters, but have also been articulated quite strongly by elements within the FPÖ (though the latter has itself been internally divided over this). They also cause some internal dissent within the ÖVP, especially between its (big) business wing and Workers' and Employees League.

The institutional framework and EU integration

Austria is a centralized federation with a weak territorial chamber (Bundesrat) and a parliamentary executive traditionally able to rely upon highly disciplined party behaviour within the lower house (Nationalrat) (Müller *et al.* 2001). Lacking the two-thirds parliamentary majority required to pass the constitutional amendment for EU accession, the SPÖ–ÖVP government was reliant upon the votes of the Greens and LiF, whose price was a set of reforms that together established one of the strongest sets of formal rights of parliamentary control in EU affairs of any EU member state.[2] The reforms require the government to provide full information on EU affairs to the Nationalrat, Bundesrat and Länder (Articles 23e(1) and 23d(1) of the constitution). Of the three new structures they created, that in which the politically most significant encounters regarding integration policy take place is the Main Committee on EU Affairs (Neisser 1998; Fischer 2002),[3] parliament's pre-eminent existing committee convening exclusively for the discussion of EU matters. Parties are represented in proportion to their overall parliamentary strength. In addition, any MEP may attend (§31c Abs. 7 and GOG-NR), and the relevant federal ministers must. The EU Main Committee always convenes prior to European Council meetings. From 1999 to 2004, it met four to eight times per annum. Its most significant power (Article 23e(2) of the constitution) is to issue ministers acting at the EU level with binding opinions, from which they may only deviate 'for urgent foreign and integration policy reasons'. If they do, they must subsequently justify themselves before the Committee. Its tightly worded first binding opinion is widely agreed to have prevented the relevant minister from negotiating a better deal for Austria and the Main Committee has since issued fewer[4] and much more loosely worded opinions.

The second institution is the Main Committee's Standing Sub-Committee on EU Affairs, on which the parties are again represented according to their overall parliamentary strength. It is to this committee – which deals with more technical matters than the Main Committee – that the parliamentary parties tend to delegate their EU specialists. According to the Parliamentary Standing Orders, the Sub-Committee's chairmanship in the 1995–99 legislature should have been held by the FPÖ, but in light of the latter's Euroscepticism, the committee's first meeting was delayed until the subsequent legislature, when the FPÖ no longer had that claim. Like its parent committee, but unlike almost all others, the Sub-Committee normally operates in public and a record of its proceedings is published. It too can require the attendance of relevant government ministers and is entitled to issue binding opinions.[5] The third key institution is the so-called Fire Brigade Committee (§ 31e Abs. 3 GOG-NR), comprising the Chair of the Standing Sub-Committee, plus one representative chosen *ad hoc* by each parliamentary party. Its role is that of an out-of-hours link between parliament and government ministers acting at the EU level, especially in respect of European Council matters on which parliament has issued binding opinions, or where issues are being debated that might have constitutional implications.

The structural profile of Austrian parties

The four parties examined in this chapter[6] exhibit some formal structural similarities. They all attribute sovereign authority to a *party congress*[7] comprising a few hundred delegates. That of the Greens must meet annually, those of the SPÖ and FPÖ biennially and that of the ÖVP only once every four years. Each party also has a *national executive*[8] of between about 30 members (FPÖ, ÖVP and Greens) and 70 (SPÖ). That of the Greens meets quarterly, whilst those of the others meet every four or six weeks. Day-to-day decisions are made by a *national executive committee*[9] that convenes at least fortnightly and has as few as half a dozen members (ÖVP), or over two dozen (FPÖ and SPÖ). Finally, three parties have a *party council*.[10] That of the FPÖ should meet quarterly and is politically marginal, whilst the statutes of the SPÖ and Greens allow for an analogous body to be convened (typically by their national executives) to debate strategic questions and – in the case of the SPÖ – to confirm candidate lists for national parliamentary elections.

In practice, the parties' organizations differ significantly. The SPÖ and ÖVP are traditional mass parties. Their exceptionally high membership densities have more than halved since their late 1970s peak (Katz *et al.* 1992; Müller 1994; Luther 1999), but remain much greater than those of the FPÖ and Greens (Dachs 2006; Luther 2006a), whose basic structure are those of a cadre and new politics party respectively. Moreover, the SPÖ and ÖVP retain links to collateral associations ranging from interest groups operating within Austria's extensive system of neo-corporatism to cultural and sporting associations, whereas the societal rootedness of the FPÖ and Greens is much more modest. The basic organizational units of the parties also differ. Those of the SPÖ, FPÖ and Greens are territorial, whereas the ÖVP is an indirect membership party comprising not only nine Land party groups, but also three main functional 'Leagues' (of Farmers, of Business and of Workers and Employees), through which the internal workings of the party are mediated. The geographical spread of the parties varies. The SPÖ and ÖVP have local units throughout Austria, yet the overwhelming majority of SPÖ members is located in Vienna and Lower Austria, whereas the ÖVP has traditionally dominated western Austria. The Greens and FPÖ are more unevenly organized, being strongest respectively in urban areas and in Upper Austria, Carinthia and Styria.

The preceding aspects help explain considerable variation in the degree of internal party coherence. The most disciplined party has been the SPÖ, whilst the ÖVP's complex dual structure has militated in favour of greater internal dissent and thus lower leadership autonomy, especially during the party's lengthy period in opposition (1970–87). The FPÖ had traditionally been highly decentralized and riven by personal and regional rivalries. Haider's leadership (1986–2000) witnessed a personalization and centralization of power but, even at the height of the party's electoral success, Haider often struggled to keep a grip on the party organization. Once the FPÖ entered government and started to lose elections, internal tensions led to an orgy of political self-destruction, the resignation of the party leadership in 2002 and the establishment by Haider in April 2005 of the rival BZÖ, to which the FPÖ's ministerial team and most of its MPs signed up (Luther 2003, 2006a,b). The Greens retain a strong commitment to the principles of grassroots party democracy, as well as to the at times contradictory principle of holders of public office exercising an independent mandate. Yet after two decades in parliament, the party has abandoned rotation and the strict separation of public and party office, started to move away from the principle of collective leadership and considerably professionalized its organization. Tensions of an ideological or strategic nature also remain, especially between the generally pragmatic national leadership and the more fundamentalist Vienna party.

Structural adaptation to European integration

Formal management and funding of European-related activities

EU membership resulted in two new categories of party EU specialists: MEPs and members of the national parliamentary committees on EU affairs. It also triggered at least two significant changes to parties' formal structures. Statutes have been amended to guarantee the presence of MEPs on national party organs. In all four parties, MEPs are entitled to participate in their respective party congresses in the same way as MPs. In the FPÖ, this derives from MEPs' *ex officio* membership of the party council, whereas in the SPÖ (non-voting) party congress membership is guaranteed for all MEPs not elected as ordinary delegates. The ÖVP and Greens have also granted the leaders of their EP delegation *ex officio* membership of their national executives.[11] Upon entering government, the FPÖ intended to do likewise, but unrelated internal conflict caused the statutory reform package of which this was to have been a part to be abandoned until April 2005. The leader of the SPÖ's EP delegation is not an *ex officio* member of the party's national executive or executive committee, but informal arrangements effectively guarantee his or her presence on both bodies. All four parties have also changed their parliamentary party rules to grant MEPs parliamentary party membership. The SPÖ statutes go further: they specify not only that MEPs should be 'appropriately represented' on the parliamentary party executive (*Klubvorstand*), but also that one of the deputy leaders of the parliamentary party must be the MEP responsible for the delegation's finances.[12] Two of the ten other members of the party's *Klubvorstand* are also EU specialists: the SPÖ's EU spokesperson and its international secretary. By contrast, FPÖ MEPs are merely non-voting caucus members.[13]

EU specialists have acquired greater visibility in most parties' day-to-day life. Predictably, EP delegation leaders have often acted as their parties' EU spokespersons. This has always been the case for the Greens, where this role has since 1991 been exercised by a former party leader. In the FPÖ, this role was usually exercised by the delegation leader, though both before and after the party entered government it would often be exercised simultaneously by a general secretary or – after 1999 – by its key member of the parliamentary EU Sub-Committee. The larger parties' delegation leaders have always held the role of their respective party's EU spokesperson. However, as the ÖVP has held the foreign minister portfolio throughout Austria's EU membership, the foreign minister has *de facto* shared that role. By contrast, though the SPÖ's delegation leader was the party's sole EU spokesperson until 2000, once the party left government, its vice-chair of the *Nationalrat's* EU Sub-Committee became its EU spokesperson in the domestic arena. In sum, the main factors determining the allocation of the EU spokesperson role have been party size and incumbency.

Although EU specialists such as MEPs and the parties' key actors on the parliamentary EU Sub-Committee ultimately owe their positions to public election, the parties typically have (access to) party functionaries or other paid staff with EU expertise. Such persons can be regarded as part of the resources available to 'office-holding' EU specialists. One key functionary position is that of international secretary, a category of party employee that exists in all parties bar the FPÖ. Appointment to this position is formally undertaken by the parties' national executives, though in the SPÖ and ÖVP the decision is *de facto* made by the party leader. In the Greens, the practice has been for this role – which predominantly involves EU-related activities and was only established after Austria's EU accession – to be the subject of a vote and exercised alongside that of party manager,[14] who in the latter capacity is an *ex officio* member of the national executive committee. The SPÖ's international secretariat pre-dates Austria's EU accession and its head is a member of the party's national executive. Though its funding has been roughly halved since 2000, this is a consequence of the party's dire financial position and not of declining intra-party significance of EU agendas. The latter are estimated to have risen to about 80 per cent of the total workload of the secretariat, which still comprises three persons. EU membership caused the ÖVP national headquarters to establish a 'Europe Office' staffed by two persons who work closely with the party's international secretary. The latter is not a member of the party's national executive and, although 80–90 per cent of the work associated with this role is also EU-related, the party's incumbent status means the international secretary constitutes just one of many – often more privileged – sources of EU expertise. However, it is expected that the role will become more important once the party leaves national office.

The parties vary considerably in the number of EU specialist staff available to them. Neither of the smaller parties' central offices has ever employed a staff member charged primarily with providing specialist EU-related support. Though all four party academies occasionally organize EU-related events – inter alia to train their functionaries – only that of the ÖVP employs (three) EU specialist staff. Most of the EU specialist staff upon whose assistance the parties can call are externally financed. Each party caucus employs one or two, primarily to help process EU-related legislation and service their EU committee members, though they also have an important liaison role between their respective party's 'office-holding' EU specialists and elements of the party organization. Most EU specialist staff are attached to the parties' MEPs, however. The EP budget finances at least one per MEP. In addition, major economic interests groups[15] operate 'training' schemes providing graduate assistants to Austrian MEPs in return for the latter paying half their salaries. The majority of these graduate assistants work in Brussels, though some are located in the offices each delegation has in Vienna, where the more senior staff typically help coordinate EU-related business between their EP delegation, national party caucus, party organization and – where relevant – their party's government team. Not least since Austrian MEPs are members of their respective national caucuses, there has at times been pressure – allegedly not always resisted – for EP-funded staff to be utilized by national party organizations in ways that 'stretch' the EP's formal financial regulations.

As they have generally had larger EP delegations and national caucuses, the ÖVP and SPÖ have clearly had access to more parliamentary EU specialist staff than the FPÖ and especially the Greens. This imbalance has been exacerbated by the larger parties' privileged access to EU experts located in their auxiliary associations and the partially overlapping interest groups of Austria's pervasive system of social partnership. Finally, the Greens have been further disadvantaged by their lack of government experience, since incumbent parties not only are able to access civil service expertise, but also employ EU specialists in their ministerial cabinets. In sum, as hypothesized in Chapter 1, the number of EU specialist office holders and staff has generally increased. However, rather than allocating their own resources to fund EU specialist staff, Austria's parties seek where possible to utilize externally funded staff, a strategy that militates strongly against small parties and those with limited experience of incumbency.

MEP candidate selection

A further interesting research question concerns how the parties' candidates for EP elections are selected (see Table 2.2) and, in particular, whether the procedure used enhances the internal power of party elites. Three aspects of the rules governing Austria's EP elections have helped strengthen the intra-party power of party elites. For one, in the two years prior to the first EP elections, the parties delegated serving MPs and Bundesrat members to the EP in proportion to their strengths at the preceding national election. Not only was the candidate pool very small, but decisions about which individuals were delegated to the EP were both highly centralized and lacking in transparency. Moreover, unlike at national elections, for the purposes of EP elections Austria is organized into a single constituency, which militates against the involvement of the 'party on the ground' in the candidate selection process. Finally, as the total number of Austrian MEPs is so small (and was reduced from 21 to 18 in 2004 – see Table 2.1), party elites have an even greater incentive than is normally the case at national elections to determine the top list positions.

According to their respective statutes and the information of numerous interviewees, the FPÖ has the most and the Greens the least elite-dominated system of candidate selection (for both the EP and national elections). Delegates to the

Table 2.2 Candidate selection for European Parliament elections in Austria

	Greens	SPÖ	ÖVP	FPÖ
Statute grants rights of proposal to	National executive	Executive committee and national executive	Executive committee	Not specified
Which interests does the statue require to be reflected?	None	Länder; trades unions; women's group	9 Länder; 6 functional leagues	None
Gender balance required?	Yes	Yes	No	No
Statute grants final decision on list to	Party congress	Party council	National executive	Party leader
Delegation leader *de facto* chosen by	Delegation	Delegation	Party leader	Party leader
Overall influence of leader	Very low	Medium/high	High	Very high

Greens' party congress not only have the final say on the national executive's proposed ordering of the party's electoral list, but can and do also propose any additional names they wish. Successful candidates are thus not beholden to the party leadership, which in turn is unable to discipline them by threatening their de-selection. In the FPÖ, by contrast, MEP candidate selection has been wholly determined by the party leader's personal estimation of candidates' potential to increase the vote (both at the relevant EP election and – indirectly – at national elections). This frequently resulted in the selection of candidates whose party background was minimal or non-existent,[16] which in turn ensured the dependence upon the leader of MEPs wishing to be re-selected. However, the dramatic post-2002 weakening of the FPÖ leadership (Luther 2003) means that its 2004 candidate list was effectively overturned by the party fundamentalists' campaign of preference voting, which resulted in their candidate moving from third place on the list to take the only seat due to the party.

The MEP candidate selection processes of the SPÖ and ÖVP are considerably more bureaucratized, but here too there is evidence that party leaders have greater scope to determine the outcome than is the case in national elections. Both parties have more constituent units from whom a claim for representation in the EP might be expected than there are seats to be distributed. In the SPÖ, the intra-party constituencies that traditionally need to be accommodated at national elections include the nine Land party groups, the trades unions and the women's section. Within the ÖVP, 'claimants' include the nine Land groups and six functional leagues. At EP elections, there are considerably fewer winnable seats to be distributed than at national elections and there are also no local constituencies at which constituent units can press their candidates. Accordingly, although both parties' leaders invite their respective constituent units to submit candidate lists for EP elections, they are better placed to divide and rule at EP than national elections. It is also worth mentioning that, upon assuming the ÖVP leadership in 1995, Schüssel obtained agreement that he personally determine both the first and second positions on the party's EP candidate lists. In sum, with the notable exception of the Greens, Austrian parties' MEP candidate selection procedures enable national party elites to exercise greater influence than they do at domestic elections. Within the SPÖ, the main countervailing influence comes from the regional party organizations, whilst, in the ÖVP, the party's leagues are also important.

Delegation leaders generally exercise a more significant role within both the EP and their respective parties. Though their selection is formally a matter solely for the delegation itself, it is understandable that party leaders might wish to shape that decision. The leader of the Greens has been able to exert virtually no influence on who leads the party's EP delegation. In both 1995 and 1996, the only candidate for the single seat the party expected to win was its former leader and national parliamentary party chairman, Johannes Voggenhuber. In 1999, and again in 2004, he was joined in the EP by a new colleague unable to challenge his pre-eminent role. By contrast, the FPÖ leader had until 2004 always been able to determine the delegation leadership. The ÖVP leader's control over the leadership of his party's delegation derives from his right to determine the top two places on the party's election list. Although in 1996 there was some uncertainly about whether the person heading the list would be perceived by the other ÖVP MEPs to have an entitlement to the delegation leadership, that has since become the accepted wisdom. At the 1996, 1999 and 2004 EP elections, Schüssel chose former TV journalist Ursula Stenzel to head the list. As she had never been an ÖVP member, she lacked a foothold within the party and was thus doubly dependent upon him.

This kind of external candidacy was in vogue in the late 1990s, when it was seen as a potentially useful response to a widespread sense of public dissatisfaction with traditional party politics. Similar considerations underpinned SPÖ leader Viktor Klima's successful attempt to place his own 'outsider' – journalist Hans-Peter Martin – at the top of his party's list for the 1999 EP election. Though he apparently recruited Martin by secretly promising him the delegation leadership, once the election was over, the delegation refused to play ball and elected its own preferred candidate. Martin eventually resigned the party whip and in 2004 stood as an independent anti-corruption candidate, winning 14 per cent of the vote and two seats, in part through attacking members of his erstwhile delegation. These events severely strained relations between the delegation and the national party leadership, but appear ultimately to have enhanced the autonomy of the former. For when the SPÖ's 2004 election list was compiled by the party's new leader, Alfred Gusenbauer, the ordering of highest placed candidates was very much in line with the delegation's wishes.

Change in parties' EU committees and working groups

EU-related change to internal party working groups has been least pronounced in the Eurosceptic FPÖ. Its delegation leader and chief representative on the parliamentary EU Sub-Committee attempted to establish a regular working group to include EU spokespersons in the provincial party organizations and parliaments. However, only half the 15–20 invitees ever showed up and the group had to be abandoned. The Greens have been more successful. Though small, their new EU committee is apparently quite well attended and includes EU specialists located in Brussels and in the national parliamentary party, as well as a couple from provincial party groups. The largest and most vibrant intra-party EU committees are those of the SPÖ and ÖVP. Since the SPÖ has been in opposition, its national executive's EU committee (*die europapolitische Arbeitsgruppe*) has been co-chaired by the party's delegation leader and EU spokesperson. In 2002, it was halved to reduce it to the most active core and now embraces about 30 persons, some of whom are sources and others targets of EU-related information. It meets monthly and in addition to the party's key EU specialists includes for example representatives of the Chamber of Labour and Austrian Trade Union Federation, as well as key foreign policy practitioners. In addition, the 'crème de la crème' of the party's foreign policy experts meet in the *außenpolitische Koordinierung* to discuss broad strategic issues. The ÖVP also has two partially overlapping groups: the EU working group (*EU Fachausschuss*) has usually been chaired by the foreign minister and concerns itself with major policy issues, as well as long-term and strategic questions, whilst the international office (*internationales Büro)* comprises in the main party staffers, is chaired by the party's international secretary and has been oriented predominantly towards the day-to-day coordination of EU-related activities and policies of the party.

Acting nationally

The overall intra-party influence of EU specialists

According to the framework outlined in the introductory chapter of this volume, we expected European integration to strengthen the intra-party significance of those with an EU specialism. A major theme of each interview was thus whether EU specialists have indeed acquired greater influence in intra-party decision-making. Predictably, interviewees' judgements varied. Moreover, given that the Austrian political class is relatively small and the number of EU specialists even smaller, it is at times difficult to disentangle the effect on individuals' intra-party influence of their personal political biographies on the one hand and their EU specialisation on the other. However, at least three interesting patterns were revealed.

For one, the relative intra-party influence of the different types of EU specialist varies. The most significant actors are delegation leaders, in part because they sit on important national party bodies, but also because of their expertise and – with the exception of the Greens – because the party leader has often had a significant role in recruiting them to the party's EP election list. The intra-party influence of ordinary MEPs is much lower. One of the very few ways in which they can acquire significant influence in their national party is by being on an EP committee dealing with a topic of major domestic political significance. In the ÖVP and SPÖ, the influence of ordinary MEPs is usually exercised at the provincial level, or within the parties' auxiliary associations. In the FPÖ since 1996 ordinary MEPs have tended to have no internal party influence whatsoever.

The parties' chief representatives on the parliamentary Sub-Committee on EU Affairs are in general less influential parliamentary actors than initially envisaged. The major reason is because the committee has rarely made full use of its formal powers. Moreover, if an issue acquires major domestic political resonance, members lacking other significant sources of intra-party influence tend to find it is taken over by the caucus leader. Accordingly, the influence of the parties' chief representatives on this committee tends to be limited to the parliamentary party. There are two exceptions, however. The first is where (as in the case of the post-1999 SPÖ incumbent), the individual has a significant prior party career. The second applies to the chair of the Sub-Committee, who by dint of that role, acquires a potentially very significant role in respect to supranational party decision-making (see p. 48 below). International secretaries exist in all parties save the FPÖ. Not least since some are party employees, their intra-party role tends to be limited to service functions such as providing information and maintaining external contacts. This can make them very useful to the party elites, especially in government-oriented parties that find themselves out of office, but they rarely exercise independent political influence. The same applies to the general category of party staffers (albeit with the caveat made below).

Second, the interviews revealed variation by party in EU specialist influence. This reflects the relative value parties attach to EU affairs and has thus been lowest within the Eurosceptic FPÖ, where the roles of MEP and delegation leader in particular were at times so negatively perceived that they actually reduced the incumbents' scope for exercising intra-party influence to 'below zero'. Within the Greens, where Euroscepticism has receded and interest in the EU grown, EU specialization has become more valued, especially where it relates to core party issues such as nuclear energy and transit traffic. Yet it remains of limited intra-party value for two reasons in particular. First, the party has not yet held national office, and so has not been forced to engage with the breadth of the EU's agenda. Second, the small scale of the Greens' national party organization and the limited number of national office holders places a premium on generalists. One interviewee put it thus: 'A Green politician who specialized solely in [the EU] would have no internal party weight whatsoever.'

The larger parties attach much greater value to EU specialization, in part because they have been much more Europhile in recent years, but also because their size and close links to Austria's neo-corporatist 'chambers' permit them this luxury. Within the territorially organized and more centralized SPÖ, EU specialists are active above all at the level of the national party: in its central office, national caucus and – when the party is in government – ministerial cabinets. Within the territorially and functionally differentiated ÖVP, the three main leagues constitute important additional arenas of often very focused EU specialist activity, as well as the vehicles for career progression of EU specialist staff in particular. Finally, the interviews suggest the ÖVP's combination of greater organizational diversity and less prescriptive statutes helps explain why formal structures are perhaps less decisive for the exercise of intra-party influence. ÖVP interviewees were more inclined than their SPÖ counterparts to point to the informal bases of the intra-party influence of EU specialists such as the delegation leader, who is a member of the weekly 'kitchen cabinet' of the current leader.

The interviews also drew attention to two significant types of change over time in the intra-party influence of EU specialists. One relates to when parties move from government to opposition or vice versa. *Ceteris paribus*, when a party moves from opposition to government, the intra-party power of the executive element of the 'party in public office' increases at the expense of the parliamentary element. The relative influence of parliamentary EU spokespersons, EU committee members and delegation leaders is thus reduced in favour of the party's EU-relevant ministers and their EU specialist staffers. This transition was especially pronounced in the FPÖ, whose lack of government experience made for intense competition for EU specialist staff, especially from ministerial cabinets. Conversely, when a governing party moves into opposition it loses a lot of its sources of EU information and regularized contacts, which strengthens the intra-party significance of the parliamentary party and of EU specialists such as delegation leaders, but also of international secretaries. In addition, the interviews highlighted change in the intra-party influence of EU specialists as a consequence of the parties' growing experience of being in the European Union. In other words, as familiarity with EU-related processes and issues spreads, the EU-related expertise upon which EU specialists were able to trade during (and also before) the early years of membership is no longer as scarce a commodity. The consequences of this are visible above all in the two large parties, but perhaps especially so in the ÖVP, where an interviewee likened changes in the intra-party role of EU specialists to a series of 'waves'.[17] In recent years, intra-party EU discourse has become almost exclusively technocratic, but this apparent dissipation of the wave 'masks a much more profound substantive Europeanization than we really make apparent'. If EU expertise has indeed not dissipated, but instead inundated the party, this may explain why another ÖVP interviewee strongly resisted the proposition that one could differentiate between EU specialists and others. Be that as it may, interviewees in both the ÖVP and SPÖ argued EU expertise is still valued within their parties and had indeed been highly beneficial for the careers of a number of relatively young party staffers in particular, since it had brought them into much closer proximity to party elites than would have been the case for many of their peers who are not EU specialists.

EU specialists and manifesto formulation

Our interviews revealed that, in all parties, EU specialist involvement in the formulation of general election manifestos is limited in the main to the sections on the EU. Moreover, the key EU specialist actor is the delegation leader, though on occasion other MEPs also contribute; EU specialist party staffers' role is essentially of a technical or service nature. The two larger parties typically submit an early draft to their internal EU working groups. Of the wider group of EU specialists thereby brought into the process, those most active in formulating the EU chapter appear to be the chief representatives on the parliamentary Sub-Committee for EU Affairs and the parties' international secretaries. In the ÖVP, the foreign minister – and his or her ministerial team – also plays an important role throughout the formulation process.

EU specialists' role in the formulation of manifestos for EP elections is most pronounced in the Greens. In 2004, for example, the manifesto was formulated by the delegation leader 'with virtual full autonomy' from the national party and parliamentary party. Though he consulted with the person placed second on the party's electoral list, he retained 'the absolute final say' on the text. The leader of the FPÖ delegation also assumed a lead role in respect of her party's 1999 and 2004 EP election manifestos, albeit with substantial input from her EP colleagues and under the watchful eye of the party's *de facto* leadership group,[18] whose prime concern was to ensure the manifesto was in tune with the party's domestic political strategy. The party's national parliamentary party – a key actor in the formulation of general election manifestos – was largely irrelevant.

Lower involvement of MPs in EP manifesto formulation is also a feature – albeit less pronounced – in the SPÖ and ÖVP. In both, EU specialists are typically allocated the task of producing an initial manifesto draft and steering it through their parties' respective EU working groups. In 2004, for example, the most significant EU specialist actor in the SPÖ's EP manifesto initiation and formulation process was its international secretary. It was only at a relatively late stage that the party leader and caucus chair got involved. In the ÖVP, the initial manifesto concept was produced by the delegation leader, who discussed it with fellow MEPs and the party's campaign specialists. This process was monitored by the party's pre-eminent informal body, the 'Monday Circle' of which the delegation leader is a member.[19] As in the SPÖ, however, the prime actors in the formulation of the party's EP manifestos are its EU specialists in general and its MEPs and delegation leader in particular.

That MEPs and delegation leaders should play such a prominent role in most parties is a consequence not only of their EU specialization, but also of Austria's electoral system, which militates in favour of campaigns moulded around the leaders of the parties' single national lists. Considerations of electoral advantage also explain the attitude adopted in particular within the SPÖ and ÖVP towards the manifestos produced by their respective Europarties. Interviewees' comments included: 'One has to be very careful that there is nothing in these manifestos produced at the European level that could harm one at home' and 'It is practically impossible that one could be helped by the manifesto, but it is easily possible that it could harm one.'

The interviews also provided three main insights into changes over time in the nature of the manifesto formulation process and the role within it of EU specialists. Though some SPÖ respondents suggested there had been a general increase in the role of the delegation leader, the overall picture both there and in the ÖVP and Greens appears to be one of considerable continuity in the extent and nature of EU specialist involvement in manifesto formulation. In the FPÖ, however, EU specialists such as the delegation leader and MEPs replaced the national caucus members as the key actors in the formulation of EP manifestos, the content of which also became less Eurosceptic. Indeed, this trend had by 2004 so enraged the party's Eurosceptics that it caused them to develop an alternative manifesto. This was distributed amongst party sympathizers, where it is likely to have made a major contribution to their third placed candidate receiving sufficient preference votes to enable him to take the single seat that would have otherwise gone to the leadership's candidate.

The interviews again highlighted the impact upon internal party life of alternation between government and opposition. For example, one SPÖ interviewee explained that whilst the party was in government much of the manifesto formulation process was conducted by the offices of the SPÖ's federal chancellor and ministers, who liaised with the party central office, but thereafter the party caucus has taken on a much more significant role. Finally, interviewees were at pains to stress that their parties attach ever less significance to election manifestos. This trend started and has been most pronounced in the FPÖ, where under Haider 'Written manifestos played no significant role. What counted was the leader's spoken word.' The other parties have also experienced a considerable decline in the significance attached to manifestos in the last ten or so years. Thus the Greens 'no longer attach such value to this', whilst many in the SPÖ 'have become rather tired of manifestos' and one ÖVP interviewee reported that the 2004 EP manifesto was approached as a routine chore (*Pflichtübung*). This seemingly universal trend suggests that any increases in the role of EU specialists in the formulation of party manifestos are perhaps less significant indicators of heightened intra-party influence than they might otherwise have been.

Conveying EU-related policy constraints

When discussing how policy constraints emanating from the EU are conveyed within their national parties, interviewees mentioned debates in their party executive bodies. Indeed, one senior FPÖ interviewee claimed a major aspect of their role to have been 'telling [national executive members] all the things that were not possible'. Interviewees from all parties that had experienced incumbency also identified their caucus chairperson as a key conveyor of EU-related constraints vis-à-vis their parliamentary party.

In the ÖVP, EU-related issues have increasingly become depoliticized and dealt with technocratically. The caucus leader's prime role in these matters has been to guarantee government majorities and to this end, both incumbents to date have ensured the incorporation at the earliest possible stage of the legislative process of the key parliamentary representatives of the party's functional leagues. At times, they have both nonetheless had to insist that such colleagues' demands are incompatible with EU rules or political realities. The impact of incumbency on the EU-related role of the caucus chairperson is most visible in the SPÖ and FPÖ, who have both experienced a change in incumbency status since 1995. Prior to 2000, the SPÖ's (acting) caucus chair's role in EU-related matters was very much akin to that of his ÖVP counterpart. Since then, however, he is less concerned to constrain EU critics within his caucus and has increasingly adopted EU-critical positions, in large measure in order to mobilize (electoral) support in the domestic political arena. Such populist instrumentalization of EU-related issues had until 1999 been expertly demonstrated by the FPÖ's then caucus chair, who saw his role as ensuring that his caucus members (including MEPs) toed the Eurosceptic line. Incumbency meant the FPÖ's new chair had to provide caucus support for a coalition agreement containing a fundamental acceptance of European integration. This brought the him into conflict with his caucus, vis-à-vis which he often had to act as a conveyor of constraints. Though he largely succeeded in forcing through the government's line, growing EU-related conflict within the party as a whole – but also between the party on the ground and the party in public office – contributed to the 2002 intra-party revolt that toppled the FPÖ government team. It was also a motivation for the 2005 founding of the BZÖ. By removing grassroots FPÖ pressure upon the party's MPs and ministers, the BZÖ helped enhance caucus discipline – not least in EU-related matters – and thereby secure the government's survival (Luther 2006b).

Acting supranationally

Parties and their MEPs

Virtually all interviewees rated their MEPs' autonomy in routine EP business as high or very high and as greater overall than that of their MPs. Yet respondents from the SPÖ, ÖVP and FPÖ also stressed that their national parties regularly seek to limit MEP discretion in two partially overlapping circumstances. The first is when the issue in question is highly contested in the domestic party system. This typically includes not only major issues of integration policy with constitutional ramifications, such as enlargement or the EU constitution, but also policy areas of particular salience in Austria, such as traffic, nuclear power and security. The second is when issues pertain to matters of particular sensitivity within individual parties, usually because they relate to core party values, or are internally contested, typically between rival ideological factions or client groups.[20] One might conclude that, although Austrian MEPs' autonomy within the EP is in general very high, it is severely constrained in matters of political import. Yet at least two caveats are in order.

MEPs frequently deal with EU-related issues well before their domestic colleagues are fully aware of them and/or their implications. Accordingly, the 'routine' EP business in respect of which MEPs exercise considerable autonomy can and does contain matters that turn out to be of greater significance for domestic politics than appreciated by national parties at the time. Moreover, parties vary considerably in their capacity to constrain their MEPs' actions, even in 'important' issues. Such constraint has been virtually absent vis-à-vis Green MEPs, who are 'almost completely free' to act as they see fit. Indeed, the delegation leader's position has frequently been diametrically opposed to that of his national party.

Similar conflicts have also occurred with the SPÖ, albeit less often. Some suggest the last five years have witnessed a small increase in the autonomy of SPÖ MEPs and one reported that most in the national party think it has been too high. The latter judgement might reflect the SPÖ tradition that, as one interviewee put it, 'at the provincial . . . and national level, parliamentarians do what they are told'. The ÖVP has expected similar levels of discipline from its domestic parliamentarians. It is thus perhaps not surprising that one ÖVP interlocutor reported that, in respect of virtually all important issues of recent years, the party's EP delegation leader has received voting guidance from the chancellor – either directly, or through his *chef de cabinet*, or foreign policy advisor. Moreover, not only has she sought to ensure compliance, but there were also numerous examples of 'pre-emptive compliance'. Taken as a whole, our interviews suggest that, since 1995, ÖVP MEPs have generally been subjected to somewhat greater national party discipline than other parties' MEPs. The autonomy of FPÖ MEPs has been the most variable over time. A member of the FPÖ's national leadership argued that, for the first two or three years, MEPs' EP actions corresponded closely with the party's policy, but then became ever more 'decoupled' from and eventually completely 'alien' to the party. The national parliamentary party thus, according to one interviewee, 'increasingly had the impression that the MEPs came to tell [it] what the party's EU policy should be'. The implication is that the delegation went 'native', ignoring party instructions. An alternative FPÖ interpretation is that the national party's interest in EU affairs was limited to issues it could utilize for domestic electoral advantage and, in the absence of party guidance on any other issue, the delegation was left to its own devices. Yet, once in government, the FPÖ leadership considerably attenuated its Euroscepticism and was thus clearly more in tune with the *de facto* policy of the delegation, over which it sought to exercise much greater control. Conversely, the EU policy of both the leadership and delegation became increasingly distant from the still predominantly Europhobic views of the party on the ground.

The interviews produced a number of interesting insights into the nature and extent of MEPs' linkage with – and thus potential accountability to – their national parties. For one, no national party has any formal rules requiring MEPs to report back to them, which helps explain why virtually all interviewees considered MEPs' accountability to be lower than that of MPs. Furthermore, in the two larger parties (and to a lesser extent in the FPÖ), 'ordinary' MEPs' linkage is less with the national party than with its constituent units. In the case of the SPÖ, this means above all the provincial party organizations, some of which have in recent years become more interested in EU-related issues and thus in influencing their MEPs. As provincial parties help determine the party's EP election list, it is in MEPs' interest to maintain good relations with them. Ordinary ÖVP MEPs maintain analogous links with their regional parties and their in part very powerful leaders. As a rule, they are also very well embedded within one of the party's three main leagues.

It is in all cases the delegation leader who maintains the most frequent and intense links to the national party. Formal linkage occurs above all in three types of site, the first of which are party bodies. Though delegation leaders routinely speak at party congresses, make occasional appearances in their parties' executive committees and in the case of the two large parties play a significant role in their party's EU committee, the politically most important body they regularly attend is their respective national executive. The EU is routinely a significant agenda item in the national executives of the Greens and ÖVP, and one on which their delegation leaders are expected to speak. Delegation leader reporting has in recent years been more *ad hoc* in the SPÖ's national executive. In the FPÖ, all but the domestically most emotionally charged of EU-related issues tended to be placed at the end of the agenda and nodded through, often whilst people were already packing their bags. A second site of institutionalized linkage is national caucuses. Though caucus linkage is considered important by both MEPs and MPs, delegation leader attendance at caucus plenaries and executive meetings tends to be infrequent; for example, it averages once every two months in the Greens and only two or three times a year in the ÖVP. Though this causes resentment in some caucuses, it is largely an unavoidable consequence of the conflicting schedules of the national and European parliaments. The third potential site of institutionalized linkage is meetings of the party in national executive office. It applied to the SPÖ from 1995 to 2000 and to the FPÖ from 2000 until 2004, but in the case of the ÖVP has been relevant ever since 1995. The most prestigious are the weekly pre-cabinet meetings attended by the respective party's ministerial team, general secretary, caucus chair and other key figures from its constituent units. This and the chancellor's even smaller 'kitchen cabinet' – the so-called 'Monday Circle' (*Montagsrunde*) – that immediately precedes it have been the politically most important site of party linkage for the ÖVP's delegation leader. From 2000 until 2004, the FPÖ delegation leader also maintained regular links to the 'party-in-government' via the vice-chancellor's office.[21]

Most interviewees stressed the frequency and importance of the immensely diverse examples of informal links between MEPs and their national parties. These can include *ad hoc* meetings or simply telephone contact with other EU specialists, or with MPs, the caucus chair, party leader, or members of the party's national bodies. Finally, interviewees were asked about change over time in links. Those from the Greens and SPÖ stated there had been no significant change in recent years, but some reported an intention on the part of their national parties to make linkage more regularized and intense. In the case of the SPÖ, this reflects the fact that, having lost office and the excellent EU connections this entailed, the party places greater value upon the information on current EU affairs its MEPs can provide. Given their small size, the Greens are even more reliant upon their MEPs. On the other hand, numerous FPÖ and ÖVP respondents reported significant increase over recent years in the frequency and intensity of linkage between their MEPs and national parties. However, one ÖVP interviewee was at pains to stress that this should not be interpreted as indicative of greater constraint upon MEP behaviour, since the proportion of *ex post* MEP reporting had not declined. A similar pattern appears to pertain in the FPÖ and SPÖ.[22]

To summarize, MEPs' generally high autonomy within the EP can be constrained on some issues and *ceteris paribus* is more likely to occur when their national party is in government. Though there is linkage between MEPs and national party bodies, this is mainly limited to the delegation leaders. Moreover, some of the most frequent and important linkage takes place elsewhere, namely either through informal contacts with party elites, or – when the party is in government – with the party in national executive office. As a proportion of overall linkage, institutionalized forms that involve the party *qua* party are thus relatively infrequent and often *ex post*.

Parties and their Europarties

The ÖVP, SPÖ and Greens all belong to Europarties.[23] The Greens' international secretary played a significant role within the pan-European European Federation of Green Parties and its executive committee continues to delegate two MPs (currently its party manager and foreign policy spokeswoman) to the council of what in 2004 became the European Green Party (EGP). Although the intra-party significance of this Europarty activity has to date been virtually non-existent, two factors militate in favour of this changing. First, the EGP is becoming more EU-oriented and less of an exclusively discussion forum for mid-level party functionaries, as witnessed by its recent introduction of leaders' meetings. Second, the Greens' leadership has started to consider the potential utility of the EU-level networking the EPG might offer, were the party to enter national government, a prospect regarded as much more likely since 2000. Indicative of this is that the party leader's first-ever EU-level activity was his attendance in late 2004 at an EGP party leaders' meeting.

The ÖVP and SPÖ have long been closely involved in their respective Europarties: the European People's Party (EPP) and the Party of European Socialists (PES). The EPP and PES differ in the organization and labelling of their internal structures – which have also changed over time – but essentially function as transnational sites for party networking and coordination. The following comments will be limited to their secretariats (PES: Coordination Team; EPP: Political Bureau), to which the parties' international secretaries are delegated, and to their leaders' meetings.

Interviewees agreed that, when acting in their Europarties, international secretaries have a very high degree of discretion, and that this reflects the fact that the decisions they make relate almost exclusively to the coordination of the member parties' activities, rather than to matters of political substance. Yet the networking role of international secretaries is highly valued by their parties. The SPÖ had traditionally attached the greater significance to such networking, and had joined the PES even before Austria's accession to the EU. Moreover, its erstwhile Nationalrat president and deputy leader Heinz Fischer took a very active role in the PES, of which he was a vice-president from 1992 until being elected President of Austria in 2004. The SPÖ's move into opposition in 2000 removed at a stroke many of the other channels of international networking to which it had become accustomed, making the party's Europarty links all the more highly prized. 2000 was also a key year for the ÖVP's Europarty links, though the catalyst here was the EU's 'sanctions': 'From one day to the next [the role of international secretary] became very important . . . both within and outside the party. . . . A major legacy was . . . external contacts are no longer taken for granted.' Given the matters they deal with in their Europarties, international secretaries' linkage to their parties occur less through formal party bodies than via their respective EU working groups. In part, they also report directly to other EU specialists and to holders of key national office, such as the general secretary, caucus chair and party leader. The exigencies of incumbency mean that, in the ÖVP, feedback is on balance less extensive, governed more by considerations of the immediate political agenda, and of course includes reports to the party's ministerial team.

Their composition and timing make leaders' meetings the most important type of Europarty activity in which the SPÖ and ÖVP are involved. Amongst the significant differences worthy of note are variations in individual continuity. Whilst the ÖVP has had the same leader since April 1995, the SPÖ has had three. The first (Franz Vranitzky)[24] attached enormous significance to PES leaders' meetings, which in his day were less closely linked to European Council meetings and provided considerably greater scope for brainstorming and strategic thinking. His successor (Viktor Klima) was allegedly much less international in his orientation, which contributed to him being less committed to and effective in leaders' meetings. The SPÖ's present leader, Alfred Gusenbauer, has a marked foreign policy background and again attaches great significance to leaders' meetings.

Incumbency also matters. The ÖVP has been in government since accession; until 2000 it held the vice-chancellorship and thereafter the chancellorship. By contrast, the SPÖ's leader held the chancellorship until 2000, but has since been in opposition. The ÖVP's current leader thus attends EPP leaders' meetings as a head of government who will shortly be engaging in substantive European Council negotiations. By contrast, though PES leaders' meetings are one of the most prestigious networking opportunities available to the current SPÖ leader, for non-incumbent leaders they have little immediate political significance, serving instead as a sort of 'consolation prize'. *Prima facie* somewhat paradoxically, an interviewee from each party argued that, when a party is in government, leaders' meetings (but to some extent Europarty meetings of international secretaries also) are of less party significance, since what is being discussed is above all the foreign policy of the state, rather than of the party. The logical corollary of this argument is that the 'partyness' of Europarty activity is greater when a party is in opposition. An analogous logic is apparent in respect of the processes whereby party leaders' communicate with their parties about their activities in leaders' meetings. In both parties, leaders report back to their executive committees and on the most significant issues also to their national executives. However, at least as much weight is attached to the caucus. In the case of the ÖVP, the most important sites of both *ex ante* and *ex post* discussion are the Monday Circle and pre-cabinet meeting. Numerous interviewees suggested that *ex ante* and *ex post* party constraints are significantly lower in the case of leaders who are simultaneously prime minister.

Parties and their ministers

At least three aspects of Austria's institutional framework have the potential to enhance party elites' autonomy in EU-level executive decision-making. First, it might enable ministers to circumvent some of the constraints of cabinet decision-making. Constitutionally, ministers have full discretion in their national and European-level actions, but convention dictates cabinet decisions require unanimity, which can place considerable political pressure upon ministers to act within overall government policy. At the EU level, they can more easily ignore the wishes of their coalition partner. The best example to date is ÖVP ministers' 2002 approval of the Czech Republic's accession. Though they acted in accordance with the ÖVP's wishes, their effective avoidance of a potential cabinet veto by the FPÖ generated considerable intra-party difficulties for the latter's ministerial team. Ministers' EU-level autonomy can also be affected by the partial lack of 'fit' between their domestic portfolios and the briefs of the Councils of Ministers they attend. This has led to ministers making decisions in policy areas that are domestically the responsibility of other cabinet colleagues, or indeed of ministers from another party,[25] which in turn can undermine ministerial accountability to their parties. Finally, the discretion of party elites in general is enhanced by the *de facto* operation of the 'Fire Brigade Committee', a virtual committee through which ministers liaise with representatives of the parliamentary parties regarding the current state of council negotiations and any changes they believe are necessary to their positions. The conduit for this liaison is the chair of the Standing Sub-Committee on EU Affairs. When eliciting the parties' positions for onward transmission to the minister (or chancellor), he consults not only the committee's formal members, but a range of elites from all parties and from their key auxiliary associations. In really important issues, he – or even the chancellor himself – will communicate directly with the leaders of the other parties. Accordingly, the Fire Brigade Committee not only permits domestic EU specialists to liaise with party elites acting in EU-level executive organs, but also promotes direct consultation on EU decision-making across a wide range of party elites, both within and outside government. In sum, although the Fire Brigade Committee was primarily designed to enable parliament to constrain ministers' EU-level actions, an unintended consequence of its actual operation has arguably been a strengthening of the role in EU issues of party elites in general.

To date, only the SPÖ, ÖVP and FPÖ have had ministers active in EU-level executive bodies. Notwithstanding institutional constraints and the political exigencies of coalition government, interviewees from all three agreed that, when acting at the EU level, ministers have considerably greater discretion vis-à-vis their own parties than they do in the domestic arena. Prominent amongst their explanations for this were the high intra-party status of ministers, the physical distance and relative lack of transparency of EU decision-making, the highly technical nature of issues ministers decide upon, and the paucity of domestic interest in the majority of EU business. As with MEPs, 'the more domestic political relevance an issue has, the greater is the degree of *de facto* constraint [upon ministers]', though it is important to note that 'not everything that is important in the Union has domestic political relevance and vice versa'. The majority of ÖVP and FPÖ respondents maintained their ministers' discretion has increased in recent years. Unsurprisingly, most ÖVP interviewees emphasized that their party leader's discretion has increased most, a development which in their opinion had in turn further strengthened the chancellor's intra-party power. They were also inclined to explain the general increase in ministerial autonomy by reference to arguments amounting to the proposition that the party's growing experience of EU decision-making has resulted in a 'permissive familiarity'.

The overall picture of ministers' party linkage painted by the interviews is one of significant similarities between the parties, as the following statement highlights: 'Ministers in effect receive three sets of instruction: from their party, from cabinet and from parliament. Of these, those they receive from their party are the least important.' There was universal agreement that, whilst ministers seek to maintain linkage to both the legislative and executive wings of their party in public office, the latter is more important and takes place above all in pre-ministerial party meetings. Moreover, it is above all here that ministers engage in not only *ex post* but also significant *ex ante* discussion of their EU-level actions. The second most important arena of ministerial linkage to their parties is the caucus. When the SPÖ was in government, there would regularly be plenary meetings of the SPÖ caucus at which the chancellor and ministers reported on their EU-level activities. These were regarded by at least one minister as a useful form of political insurance for when things got tough. ÖVP ministers have also regularly attended analogous meetings, the frequency of which has increased in recent years. Individual ÖVP ministers also report back to the league subdivisions of the party caucus. Given that the FPÖ repeatedly faced potential rebellion by its MPs, it is not surprising that the caucus was considered by the FPÖ's leadership as by far the most important site of ministerial linkage with the party.

The linkage of ÖVP and FPÖ ministers to their respective party organizations has usually been much less regular and more rudimentary than to their parties in public office. When explaining this, these parties' respondents wished to stress that it is often more difficult for ministers to consult fully with their parties in respect of EU-level than national-level decisions. The arguments they cited included distance, the complex technical nature of many decisions and the infrequency with which formal party bodies meet. Similar considerations applied when the SPÖ was in government, though some interviewees suggested party bodies were perhaps slightly less insignificant than (more recently) in the ÖVP and SPÖ.

In all parties, the most significant party bodies in which linkage occurs are executive committees and national executives, though even here most discussions of ministers' EU-level activities are conducted on an *ex post* basis. As one ÖVP respondent put it: 'The national party is not kept constantly informed other than in respect of tactical, strategic or electoral matters.' Accordingly, EU-related decisions are only very rarely made in the ÖVP national executive. In the Eurosceptic FPÖ, the rare discussions of EU-level activities were undertaken 'only at a relatively simplistic level', something a senior FPÖ interviewee attributed to executive committee members' lack of EU expertise and preoccupation with domestic politics.

Ministers of both large parties seek to maintain linkage to their key auxiliary associations. For example, whilst the SPÖ was in government, its chancellor made occasional appearances at the weekly meetings of the social democratic caucus of trade unionists. ÖVP ministers have much closer and regular links to the three functional leagues. Indeed, ÖVP ministers chair the relevant party policy committee (*Fachausschuss*), upon which they and their ministries exercise considerable influence. Finally, though ministers and at times even (vice-)chancellors report on their EU-level activities to their respective party congresses, the latter meet at best every year or two and, not least for that reason, rarely offer any opportunity for the party on the ground to influence their ministers' EU-level actions.

In sum, the interviews provided a considerable body of evidence in support of the hypothesis that European integration has further strengthened the intra-party influence of party elites. However, they also provided numerous comments that highlighted the in part very different patterns of linkage between parties and their ministers. Thus a leading member of the FPÖ, in which EU policy has been highly contentious between the party in public office and the party on the ground, stated the party's 'ministers of course have greater discretion, but have paid dearly for it'.[26] An SPÖ interviewee who had personal experience of voting at the EU level against the national party's line was more sanguine about the intra-party consequences: 'One would then naturally have conflict at home, but one can deal with that. The matter has by then of course been decided.' Many ÖVP interviewees were dismissive of the significance of linkage between a minister and the party *qua* party, insisting instead that EU-level decision-making by its party elites was governed above all by the decisions of the leader and small groups of elites that meet regularly in informal bodies. Especially in the case of the ÖVP, linkage to the party's key constituent elements (i.e. the provincial parties, but in particular the leagues) is in large measure a product of the fact that individual ministers are themselves frequently recruited through and remain embedded in the latter.

Conclusion

Our analysis of Austrian parties' organizational adaptation to European integration covers only the relatively short period up to the end of 2005, so it is impossible to be sure if the trends we have highlighted will endure. On the other hand, Austria's relatively new status within the Union means its parties' organizational adaptation is more recent and thus to some extent more visible. For one, it is has necessarily been less incremental than in states with longer EU membership. Moreover, both intra-party documentation and interviewees' memories have perhaps been fuller than might otherwise have been the case.

As this chapter has demonstrated, the internal life of all four Austrian parties has changed in response to European integration, albeit not dramatically. There has been a considerable growth in EU specialists, whom all four parties have guaranteed *ex officio* presence on national party bodies via formal statutory change.

The resources allocated to EU-specialist activities have increased, though overwhelmingly from external bodies such as the EP, neo-corporatist interest groups and government ministries. EU-specialist involvement in manifesto formulation has grown, but remains limited above all to (the albeit growing range of) EU-specific topics. Within the two major parties, EU specialists were particularly highly valued in the years immediately prior to accession and in the first few years thereafter. As EU expertise becomes more widespread within these parties, however, so the intra-party status and career benefits of that specialization decline. This may help explain why overall, we did not find consistent evidence in support of the hypothesis that EU specialists would become increasingly significant players in internal power games.

On the other hand, party actors involved in decision-making at the supranational level enjoy in part considerably higher levels of autonomy from – and lower levels of accountability to – their national parties than is the case in analogous national arenas. Though this finding applies to MEPs and those active in Europarties, as well as to those who attend Councils of Ministers or European Councils, few of these actors can convert their supranational-level autonomy into enhanced intra-party power. Europarty activity other than leaders' meetings has the least currency in national-level intra-party power games and that of 'ordinary' MEPs as a rule not much more. By comparison, delegation leadership can have considerably greater value. However, our evidence very much supports this volume's hypothesis that involvement in decision-making within EU-level executive bodies does enhances the intra-party power of party elites and in particular of party leaders.

There are a number of country-specific factors that may well help account for why Austrian parties' organizational adaptation to European integration has proceeded as indicated in this chapter. Certain features of Austria's institutional framework have been important, including its peculiar system of parliamentary scrutiny of EU affairs and the single constituency national list system adopted for EP elections. The extensive interest group networks associated with Austria's system of social partnership and linked to its two major parties have been a further factor. The significant decline since accession in public support for membership has also played a role. Furthermore, Austria's small size militates in favour of informal networks, not least since the number of the two categories of actors upon which we have focused (namely, EU specialists and party elites active at the supranational level) is comparatively small. In turn, this militates against organizational complexity and enhances the potential significance of the personality of individual actors.

The parties' variable organizational responses to European integration can in part be explained by party size: in the two largest, functional differentiation and thus EU specialization are intrinsically easier. Closely related to this point is the parties' relative entrenchment within Austrian neo-corporatism, proximity to which facilitates access to considerable EU-specific policy expertise. This again distinguishes the SPÖ and ÖVP on the one hand from the FPÖ and Greens on the other. The individual parties' traditional model of organization is also important.

The ÖVP's complex dual structure and very significant functional leagues militate in favour of what one might, at the risk of exaggeration, characterize as a
very pragmatic, or instrumental orientation to EU-related issues. By contrast, the
Greens comprise a 'new politics' party, in which the principle of the individual
mandate favours at times idiosyncratic behaviour on the part of holders of public
office, but the principle of internal democracy as yet militates against the consolidation of a party elite. A further factor is the parties' fundamental orientation to
European integration. European integration has had the most destructive effect on
the organization of the FPÖ, though it is possible that this has been due less to the
party's overall Euroscepticism than to the growing gap between the orientation of
the party on the ground and the party in public (and above all in governmental)
office. However, our study suggests the most significant determinant of individual
Austrian parties' organizational adaptation to European integration has been incumbency. Only incumbent parties participate in EU-level executive decision-
making. Incumbent parties are also more likely to see the strengthening of party
elites' intra-party power and the disaggregation of the party in public office that
comes with the executive bias of EU decision-making.

In conclusion, it is worth stressing that parties' organizational adaptation to
European integration is subject to change. For one, the future of European integration is itself uncertain. Moreover, as parties gain and lose incumbency status, the
relative significance of the various categories of EU specialists clearly alters, as
does the opportunity for party elites to engage in the supranational activities we
have demonstrated enhance their intra-party power.[27] Furthermore, the development of the FPÖ since 2000 has shown that there is a limit to the extent to which
EU specialists and party elites can expect to operate in respect of EU-level issues
in a manner that contradicts the sentiment of the party on the ground. Although
that room for manoeuvre might be especially constrained in respect of Eurosceptic parties, that does not detract from the general point that parties' structural and
procedural responses to European integration can be reversed.

Notes

1 The research underpinning this chapter includes 31 interviews, conducted between
   July 2004 and June 2005, with staff, functionaries and public office holders of the
   Social Democratic Party of Austria (*Sozialdemokratische Partei Österreichs* – SPÖ),
   Austrian People's Party (*Österreichische Volkspartei* – ÖVP), Freedom Party of Austria (*Freiheitliche Partei Österreichs* – FPÖ) and Greens (*Die Grünen – Die Grüne
   Alternative [Grüne]*). The prime target interlocutors were these parties' current or
   recent leaders; general secretaries; parliamentary party chairpersons; chief representatives on the parliamentary Standing Subcommittee for EU Affairs; European Parliament delegation leaders; EU-specialist staff; and international secretaries (where these
   exit). About 90 per cent of these persons were interviewed. The author appreciates
   their supporting his research in this way. Where not otherwise specified, this account
   of Austrian parties' organizational adaptation to European integration derives from
   information provided in these interviews. The chapter's empirical focus is limited to
   developments up to the end of 2005.
2 For relevant changes to Austria's constitution and parliamentary standing orders, see
   in particular the *Beitrittsermächtigungsgesetz* (*Bundesgesetzblatt* [BGBl] 1994/744),

Bundes-Verfassungsgesetz-Novelle 1994 (BGBl 1994/1013) and *Geschäftsordnungs-gesetz-Novelle* 1996 (BGBl 1996/438). See also Blümel and Neuhold (2001) and Pollak and Slominski (2003). Changes were also made to Bundesrat and Länder rights. Given the centralized nature of Austrian federalism, they will not be discussed further, but see for example the special agreement between the federation and Länder (BGBl 775/1992) regarding Länder and municipalities' rights in matters concerning EU legislation; *BVG-Novelle betreffend EU-Ausschuß des Bundesrates* (BGBl 1996/437); *Beschluß auf . . . Einführung des EU-Ausschusses* (BGBl 1997/65 I). Art. 23e(6) of the Constitution (BGBl 65/1997) permits the Bundesrat also to issue binding opinions to federal ministers due to act at the EU level in respect of the few matters over which the Bundesrat has a veto.
3 Regulated according to the following new constitutional provisions: BVG Art. 23 Abs. 1 and Art. 23 a–f, plus §29; 31, 31a; 31b; 31c; 31d; and 31e GOG-NR. As of mid-2005, ministerial reports on the business of the EU Council and Commission are discussed by the relevant specialist parliamentary committee and ministers have to produce detailed papers on the EU matters to be debated by the Main Committee on EU Affairs. Moreover, parliament now has plenary sessions (see Parliamentary Standing Orders §74b (GOG-NR)) devoted exclusively to EU themes. As the first was held only in September 2005, it is too early to tell what significance they might have.
4 In the first year this power existed (1995), the Main Committee issued 18 opinions, which is one more than the total for the subsequent ten years.
5 In the six years from its first meeting (7 December 1999), the Subcommittee issued only four binding opinions.
6 For the latest overviews of these parties (SPÖ, ÖVP, FPÖ and Greens), see Dachs *et al.* (2006). Two parties recently represented in Austria's parliament will be ignored: the LiF and the Union for the Future of Austria (*Bündnis Zukunft Österreich* – BZÖ). The former split from the parliamentary FPÖ in February 1993, dropped out of parliament in 1999 and is now organizationally largely defunct at the national level. In 2006, the SPÖ entered an electoral alliance with the LiF and granted its leader a safe place on its national election list. The BZÖ lacks organizational institutionalization and electoral support outside Carinthia. That it exceeded the 4 per cent national hurdle for parliamentary representation at the October 2006 general election was largely down to its strength in Carinthia. The party's long-term survival remains uncertain, however (Luther 2006b).
7 FPÖ, ÖVP and SPÖ: *Bundesparteitag*; Greens: *Bundeskongress*.
8 FPÖ, ÖVP and SPÖ: *Bundesvorstand*; Greens: *erweiterter Bundesvorstand*.
9 FPÖ and ÖVP: *Bundesparteipräsidium*: SPÖ *erweitertes Bundesparteipräsidium*; Greens: *Bundesvorstand*.
10 FPÖ: *Parteileitung*; Greens: *Bundestagung*; SPÖ: *Parteirat*.
11 See §27f of the ÖVP party statute. Formally, §14 of the Green party statute allocates that seat to one MEP elected by the party's EP delegation. That has to date been the leader of the – at most two-member – delegation.
12 See §§6 and 7 of *Statut des Klubs der sozialdemokratischen Abgeordneten zum Nationalrat, Bundesrat und Europäischen Parlament* (Sozialdemokratische Parlamentsfraktion), first introduced 13 March 1996.
13 See §5(3) of *Geschäftsordnung des freiheitlichen Parlamentsklubs*, as amended 13 October 1994.
14 Unlike the other parties, the Greens do not have a general secretary, but only a party manager (*Bundesgeschäftsführer*), whose prime responsibility relates to internal party organization.
15 The Austrian Chamber of Commerce (*Wirtschaftskammer Österreichs* – WKÖ); the Union of Austrian Industrialists (*Vereinigung Österreichische Industrieller* – IV); the Chamber of Labour (*Arbeiterkammer* – AK) and the ÖGB.

16   Indeed, over half the party's successful candidates at the 1996 election fitted this description.

17   During the first, which comprised the two years or so prior to membership, during which the final negotiations were taking place, EU expertise was at a premium especially for the party's provincial groups and three main leagues. In the early years of membership, that expertise was then applied above all within the provincial parties to help the Länder access the EU's various funding programmes.

18   This so-called 'Monday Circle' comprised the party's acting chair (and first delegation leader, who had retained a strong interest in EU policy), its general secretary and caucus chair, as well as former leader Haider.

19   In addition to the delegation leader and party leader, this body comprises the latter's two deputies (one of whom is caucus chair and the other a federal minister), the general secretary and the president of the Nationalrat.

20   Examples of issues whose greater salience have derived from their proximity to core party values include gene technology (ÖVP), the Benesch decrees (FPÖ) and the allegedly excessively neo-liberal thrust of the draft EU constitution (SPÖ and Greens). Examples of internally contested issues include Turkish accession (highly disputed within the SPÖ) and EU finances, including the Common Agricultural Policy, a classic bone of contention between the ÖVP's Farmers' and Business Leagues.

21   This comment refers to the period from 2000 to the EP election of June 2004, at which the party was reduced from five seats to one, which was won by an individual completely opposed to the national leadership. When the BZÖ was formed (April 2005), the FPÖ effectively left government.

22   One Green interviewee even suggested the Green delegation leader's internally unassailable position means national executive meetings should be regarded less as occasions on which he might be held to account than as opportunities for him to secure the national party's endorsement for positions he proposes to adopt.

23   Since 1995 there have been various attempts by FPÖ individuals and groups to forge transnational links. Interlocutors included Goldsmith's Referendum Party, de Villiers' group and the Vlaams Blok/Vlaams Belang (most recently in autumn 2005). Not only have such attempts all come to naught, but they have been internally highly divisive, especially after the party entered national office.

24   Federal chancellor from 1986 to 1997 and party leader from 1988 until 1997.

25   For example, during the 1995–99 SPÖ–ÖVP government, the minister of transport attended councils whose briefs included road traffic, even though this was not within his domestic portfolio. This lack of 'fit' was mitigated in 2000, when some Austrian ministries were re-organized.

26   All FPÖ respondents were interviewed before the BZÖ split in April 2005, which for reasons explained above further strengthened ministerial discretion.

27   Whilst the proofs for this chapter were being reviewed, the SPÖ won the general election of 1 October 2006 and appears likely to re-enter government. Should it do so, it would be interesting to investigate whether the expectation we have outlined regarding the likely impact of renewed incumbency upon the intra-party role of EU specialists and party elites active in EU-level executive bodies are borne out.

References

Blümel, Barbara and Christine Neuhold (2001) 'The Parliament of Austria: A Large Potential with Little Implications', in Andreas Maurer and Wolfgang Wessels (eds), *National Parliaments on their Way to Europe: Losers or Latecomers?*, Baden Baden: Nomos, pp. 313–34.

Dachs, Herbert (2006) 'Grünalternative Parteien', in Herbert Dachs, Peter Gerlich, Herbert

Gottweis, Helmut Kramer, Volkmar Lauber, Wolfgang C. Müller and Emmerich Tálos (eds), *Politik in Österreich. Das Handbuch*, Vienna: Manz, pp. 389–401.

Dachs, Herbert, Peter Gerlich, Herbert Gottweis, Helmut Kramer, Volkmar Lauber, Wolfgang C. Müller and Emmerich Tálos (eds), *Politik in Österreich. Das Handbuch*, Vienna: Manz.

Dolezal, Martin and Wolfgang C. Müller (2001) 'Die Mitgliedschaft in der Europäischen Union und die Rolle des Nationalrates', in Wolfgang C. Müller, Marcelo Jenny, Barbara Steininger, Martin Dolezal, Wilfried Philipp and Sabine Preisl-Westphal, *Die österreichischen Abgeordneten. Individuelle Präferenzen und politisches Verhalten*, Vienna: Universitätsverlag, pp. 479–520.

Fallend, Franz, Dagmar Aigner and Armin Mühlböck (2002) ' "Europäisierung" der lokalen Politik? Der Einfluss der Europäischen Union auf Politiknetzwerke und Entscheidungsprozesse in der lokalen Wirtschafts-, Beschäftigungs- und Arbeitsmarktpolitik in Österreich', in Europäisches Zentrum für Föderalismus-Forschung Tübingen (ed.), *Jahrbuch des Föderalismus 2002: Föderalismus, Subsidiarität und Regionen in Europa*, Baden-Baden: Nomos, pp. 563–76.

Fischer, Heinz (2002) 'Der Hauptausschuß des österreichischen Nationalrates als Instrument der Willensbildung in Angelegenheiten der Europäischen Union', in Bernd M. Kraske (ed.), *Pflicht und Verantwortung*, Baden-Baden: Nomos.

Gehler, Michael, Günther Bischof and Anton Pelinka (eds) (2003) *Österreich in der Europäischen Union. Bilanz seiner Mitgliedschaft. Austria in the European Union. Assessment of her Membership*, Vienna: Böhlau.

Höll, Othmar, Johannes Pollak and Sonja Puntscher Riekmann (2003) 'Austria: Structural Domestic Change Through European Integration', in Wolfgang Wessels, Andreas Maurer and Jürgen Mittag (eds), *Fifteen into One? The European Union and its Member States*, Manchester: Manchester University Press, pp. 337–54.

Karlhofer, Ferdinand, Josef Melchior and Hubert Sickinger (eds) (2001) *Anlassfall Österreich. Die Europäische Union auf dem Weg zu einer Wertegemeinschaft*, Baden-Baden: Nomos.

Katz, Richard S., Peter Mair, Luciano Bardi, Lars Bille, Kris Deschouwer, David Farrell, Ruud Koole, Leonardo Morlino, Wolfgang Müller, Jon Pierre, Thomas Poguntke, Jan Sundberg, Lars Svasand, Hella van de Velde, Paul Webb and Anders Widfeldt (1992) 'The Membership of Political Parties in European Democracies', *European Journal of Political Research*, 22(3): 329–45.

Lantis, Jeffrey and Matthew Queen (1998) 'Negotiating Neutrality: The Double-Edged Diplomacy of Austrian Accession to the European Union', *Cooperation and Conflict*, 32(2): 152–82.

Luther, Kurt Richard (1999) 'Must What Goes Up Always Come Down? Of Pillars and Arches in Austria's Political Architecture', in Kurt Richard Luther and Kris Deschouwer (eds), *Political Elites in Divided Societies: Political Parties in Consociational Democracy*, London: Routledge, pp. 43–73.

Luther, Kurt Richard (2003) 'The Self-Destruction of a Right-Wing Populist Party? The Austrian Parliamentary Election of 2002', *West European Politics*, 26(2): 136–52.

Luther, Kurt Richard (2006a) 'Die Freiheitliche Partei Österreichs (FPÖ) und das Bündnis Zukunft Österreichs (BZÖ)', in Herbert Dachs, Peter Gerlich, Herbert Gottweis, Helmut Kramer, Volkmar Lauber, Wolfgang C. Müller, and Emmerich Tálos (eds), *Politik in Österreich. Das Handbuch*, Vienna: Manz, pp. 364–88.

Luther, Kurt Richard (2006b) 'Strategien und (Fehl-)Verhalten. Die Freiheitlichen und die

Regierungen Schüssel I und II', in Emmerich Tálos (ed.), *Schwarz-blau. Eine Bilanz des „Neu-Regierens"*, Vienna: Lit Verlag, pp. 19–37.

Müller, Wolfgang C. (1994) 'The Development of Austrian Party Organizations in the Post-War Period', in Richard S. Katz and Peter Mair (eds), *How Parties Organize: Adaptation and Change in Party Organizations in Western Democracies*, London: Sage, pp. 51–79.

Müller, Wolfgang C. (2002) 'EU-Mitlgiedschaft und Regierungshandeln. Präferenzen, Strategien, Institutionen und politische Praxis', in Heinrich Neisser, and Sonja Puntscher Riekmann (eds), *Europäisierung der österreichischen Politik. Konsequenzen der EU-Mitgliedschaft*, Vienna: Universitätsverlag, pp. 101–32.

Müller, Wolfgang C. and Marcelo Jenny (2000) 'Abgeordnete, Parteien und Koalitionspolitik: Individuelle Präferenzen und politisches Handeln im Nationalrat', *Österreichische Zeitschrift für Politikwissenschaft*, 29(2): 137–56.

Müller, Wolfgang C., Marcelo Jenny, Barbara Steininger, Martin Dolezal, Wilfried Philipp and Sabine Preisl-Westphal (2001) *Die österreichischen Abgeordneten. Individuelle Präferenzen und politisches Verhalten*, Vienna: Universitätsverlag.

Neisser, Heinrich (1998) 'Die Mitwirkungsbefugnisse des Nationalrates in Entscheidungsprozesses der Europäischen Union', in Heinz Schäffer, Walter Berka, Harald Stolzlechner and Josef Werndl (eds), *Staat – Verfassung – Verwaltung. Festschrift anläßlich des 65. Geburtstages von Friedrich Koja*, Vienna: Springer, pp. 335–53.

Ogris, Günther (1995) 'Der Diskussionsprozeß vor der EU-Abstimmung', in Anton Pelinka (ed.), *EU-Referendum. Zur Praxis direkter Demokratie in Österreich*, Vienna: Signum Verlag, pp. 121–48.

Pelinka, Anton (ed.) (1995) *EU-Referendum. Zur Praxis direkter Demokratie in Österreich*, Vienna: Signum Verlag.

Plasser, Fritz and Peter Ulram (1995) 'Meinungstrends, Mobilisierung und Motivlagen bei der Volksabstimmung über den EU-Beitritt', in Anton Pelinka (ed.), *EU-Referendum. Zur Praxis direkter Demokratie in Österreich*, Vienna: Signum Verlag, pp. 87–120.

Pollak, Johannes and Peter Slominski (2002) 'Die österreichischen politischen Parteien und die europäische Integration: Stillstand oder Aufbruch?', in Heinrich Neisser and Sonja Puntscher Riekmann (eds), *Europäisierung der österreichischen Politik. Konsequenzen der EU-Mitgliedschaft*, Vienna: Universitätsverlag, pp. 177–99.

Pollak, Johannes and Peter Slominski (2003) 'Influencing EU Politics? The Case of the Austrian Parliament', *Journal of Common Market Studies*, 41(4): 707–29.

Puntscher Riekmann, Sonja, Roland Hierzinger, Monika Mokre and Johannes Pollak (2001) *Institutional Change and Problems of Democracy: State of the Art and Future Perspectives. Final Report*, Institut für Europäische Integrationsforschung, Österreichische Akademie der Wissenschaften, mimeo.

Tálos, Emmerich and Gerda Falkner (eds) (1996) *EU-Mitglied Österreich. Gegenwart und Perspektiven: Eine Zwischenbilanz*, Vienna: Manz.

3 Government change, organizational continuity

The limited Europeanization of British political parties[1]

Elisabeth Carter and Robert Ladrech

The question of the United Kingdom's (UK) relationship with, and role in, the European Union (EU) has been one of the most divisive and damaging issues in British party politics since the end of the Second World War. Furthermore, although it is perhaps less destabilizing than it once was, the question of the country's relationship with the EU continues to be a politically difficult one, not least because there is still no domestic consensus on the subject. Regardless of the views of the parties on the issue, however, and regardless of public opinion, growing European integration has brought pressure for institutional adaptation. For example, studies have demonstrated that the UK's institutions of government have successfully adapted to European integration (Allen 2005; Bulmer and Burch 2005). To date, however, little work exists that has examined the degree to which the parties themselves have adapted in response to increased levels of integration.

In light of this, this chapter investigates the impact of European integration on the internal workings of the three main British political parties – the Labour Party, the Conservative Party and the Liberal Democrats.[2] It investigates the ways in which these three parties have adapted their organizations so as to manage European issues and take part in European-level decision-making, and it considers whether those party actors who are concerned with the management of European affairs or who play a part in decision-making at the European level have gained power within their parties at the expense of actors who are not involved in European issues.[3]

Before turning to discuss the structural adaptation in which the British parties have engaged in response to European integration, and before assessing any changes to the internal balance of power within the parties, it is useful to devote a little time to examining the British experience of EU membership so as to better understand the context in which a Europeanization of British political parties might or might not be taking place.

Britain and 'Europe'

Historical background

The UK joined the European Economic Community (EEC) in 1973 although the question of whether to become involved in European integrationist moves had been debated within the three main political parties for many years before. In the 1950s, notwithstanding some early post-war enthusiasm for European unity, most actors inside the Conservative Party and the Labour Party rejected the idea that the UK should participate in any form of European integration. Many felt that the UK was still a world power, and that closer ties with West European nations would compromise the country's relation with the empire and the nations of the Commonwealth. They also worried that integration with Europe would jeopardize the 'special relationship' that the UK enjoyed with the United States. Involvement in the supranational projects of the 1950s, including the EEC, was therefore ruled out by the two main parties. The Liberal Party, by contrast, was generally more favourable to integrationist ideas, although some debate over the merits of joining these projects did exist within the party in the immediate post-war years (Clarke and Curtice 1998).

The attitudes of the Conservative Party and the Labour Party towards membership of the EEC began to change within the next decade, however. Driven by the knowledge that trade in Western Europe was fast outstripping the UK's trade with the Commonwealth, gradually realizing (especially after the Suez crisis) that the UK did not command the influence it once did in the international arena, and hoping that UK membership would bring Europe closer to the Atlantic Alliance, the (Conservative) Macmillan government sought entry into the Community in 1961. The Labour Party took slightly longer to see membership as attractive, but by the mid-1960s, in the face of severe economic difficulties, it too revised its earlier opposition to joining the Community, and in 1967 the (Labour) Wilson government once again applied for the UK to join the EEC. However, both the 1961 and the 1967 application for membership were unsuccessful, as both were vetoed by the French President, de Gaulle.

After the second veto, divisions within the Labour Party over the question of Europe resurfaced. The party leadership did resume accession negotiations in 1969, but by the time the UK became a member of the EEC, in January 1973, the left of the party had gradually become more influential, and the majority in the party had once again become increasingly hostile to membership. In the 1975 referendum the divisions worsened, with the party leadership campaigning hard in support of the UK remaining in the Community on the renegotiated terms, but a number of cabinet ministers, the majority of Labour MPs, and many others throughout the party supporting withdrawal from the EEC. The fall-out from this split was immense and it led to 'an intensification of anti-EC sentiment within the governing Labour party which helped plunge the party into civil war after its 1979 election defeat' (Geddes 2004: 186). From 1980 the party advocated withdrawal from the Community, and this move spurred the pro-European moderates within the Labour Party to break away and form the Social Democratic Party (SDP) in 1981. It was only after the devastating electoral defeat of 1983 that anti-European views were gradually sidelined and the party abandoned its outright rejection of membership, and it was not until the 1987 election that the party leadership began to develop a more positive approach towards the EEC.

In the same way that the Labour Party was torn apart by divisions over Europe in the 1960s, 1970s and 1980s, so the Conservative Party was ravaged by internal conflicts over Europe in the 1980s and 1990s. For more than a decade after accession the party leadership had been able to retain control of the party's policy on Europe, and had thus been able to manage internal tensions within the party, but by the mid-1980s it was becoming clear that many within the party were growing increasingly uneasy about the way in which European integration was progressing. Many were unhappy with the realization that the Single Market project was set to be far more 'social' in character than had been hoped, and many were troubled by the prospect that further economic integration would most likely be accompanied by further political integration. The prime minister, Margaret Thatcher, was particularly distrustful of the future direction of integration promoted by some in Europe, and in September 1988 she made her infamous Bruges speech in which she made it clear she would strongly oppose any moves aimed at turning the Community into an economic and political union in which the UK would have to cede power to the institutions of the EEC. The speech divided the already fractious cabinet, not only because of its content but also because of its uncompromising tone, and it effectively signalled the end of internal party consensus on the issue of Europe. It also legitimized factionalism within the party and allowed Euroscepticism to become a structured part of Conservative Party politics with the leadership unable to diffuse and neutralize it (Geddes 2004: 197). Divisions over Europe in the party worsened over the next two years and ultimately proved fundamental to Thatcher's departure from office in 1990. As Turner explains, 'by making the future of Thatcherism so dependent on such a critique of European integration, Thatcher was exposing her leadership to those in the party who did not see Europe as such a threat. Ultimately, it would mean a choice between Thatcher and Europe itself' (2000: 123).

Even after Thatcher left office Europe remained the most potent policy division within the Conservative Party (Garry 1995: 185). This was especially obvious during the ratification of the Maastricht treaty in 1992–93 when the prime minister, John Major, was first forced to threaten he would stand down and call elections if the government did not win a crucial vote in the House, and was then obliged to make the final vote on the Treaty a matter of confidence in the government. Tensions surfaced over a number of different matters during the Major premiership, but Europe was the one issue that rendered factionalism acceptable and that irrevocably split the party (Turner 2000: 167–8).

Throughout the Major premiership, the Labour leadership saw an advantage in exposing the divisions that were consuming the Conservative Party, and presented itself as both more united over Europe, and as progressively more pro-European. Once in government in 1997 it pursued this cautious pro-Europeanism, and in its first term in office in particular, it was quite proactive in its European policy, trying, and to some extent succeeding, to shed Britain's image as an awkward partner in Europe (Smith 2005). Differences of opinion do still of course exist within the Labour Party over issues such as the single currency and the European constitution, but the UK's general relationship with and place in the EU no longer cause division within the party. By contrast, despite attempts to unite around an anti-European agenda after the 1997 election defeat, the fundamental question of the country's role and position in the EU is still, to some extent, a fault-line in the Conservative Party, and one that exacerbates other internal rifts.[4]

This summary of the conflicts that have dogged both the Labour Party and the Conservative Party is important not only because it sheds light on the British experience of EU membership, but also because the conflicts go a long way to explaining why the two main British parties have resisted making Europe a significant electoral issue despite its potency (Allen 2005: 127). Indeed, all three main British political parties readily avoid debating the EU in public because the consequences of such a debate are, by and large, only negative: the media stirs up Eurosceptic feelings, any internal rifts are aggravated, and parties lose votes. Hence, rather than discuss the issue publicly, the debate on Europe has taken place within rather than between parties, and this, to some extent, helps explain why parties have been divided on the question of Europe. The failure to discuss Europe in the open is also explained, and indeed reinforced, by the public's distinct lack of interest in, and awareness of, European affairs, and by its Euroscepticism. The British public is distinctly unenthusiastic about the EU, as is reflected in regular surveys and in the extremely low turnout for European Parliament (EP) elections (see Table 3.1).[5]

The divisive impact of European integration and the consequences of this divisiveness have thus shaped the way in which the issue of Europe is treated and viewed in Britain. To some extent, these factors may also play a role in influencing the way in which the parties have adapted their organizations so as to manage European affairs. Before the chapter moves to address the central theme of the parties' adaptation, however, it is useful to briefly consider two further factors that may affect the way in which the parties have adapted their organizations in response to growing European integration, namely the general model of British party organization, and the institutional framework in which European policy is made in Britain.

The British model of party organization

The Conservative Party and the Labour Party have long been described as parties that have tended to be dominated by their parliamentary leaderships (McKenzie 1955). The Conservative Party developed out of a cadre-type party organization built around elected elites and, despite recent reforms designed to increase the level of intra-party democracy, the party remains a very hierarchical organization, in which the parliamentary leadership, and the party leader in particular, enjoy high levels of autonomy and influence. As Webb notes, to this day, 'formally, all authority and policy emanates from the leader' (2000: 192). Within this context

Table 3.1 Elections to the European Parliament in Britain: votes, seats and turnout, 1979–2004

	1979		1984		1989		1994		1999		2004	
	%	Seats	%	Seats	%	Seats	%	Seats	%	Seats	%	Seats
Labour	33.0	17	36.5	32	40.1	45	44.2	62	28.0	29	22.6	19
Conservatives	50.6	60	40.8	45	34.7	32	27.9	18	35.8	36	26.7	27
Liberal Democrats[a]	13.1	0	19.5	0	6.2	0	16.7	2	12.7	10	14.9	12
Others[b]	3.3	1	3.2	1	19.0	1	11.2	2	23.5	9	35.8	17
Turnout[c]/total seats	30.2	78	31.8	78	37.9	78	36.2	84	23.1	84	38.2	75

Sources: House of Commons (1999a, 1999b, 2004); Parties and Elections in Europe: www.parties-and-elections.de

Notes
Results are for Great Britain (i.e. they exclude Northern Ireland, which elects three MEPs).

a 1979: Liberal Party; 1984: Alliance between the Social Democratic Party and the Liberal Party (SDP–Liberal Alliance); 1989: Social and Liberal Democrats; since 1994: Liberal Democrats

b Others: 1979: Scottish National Party (SNP) won one seat with 1.9 per cent of the votes; 1984: SNP won one seat with 1.7 per cent of the votes; 1989: SNP won one seat with 2.6 per cent of the votes, the Greens won no seats but polled 14.9 per cent of the votes; 1994: the SNP won two seats with 3.1 per cent of the votes, the Greens won no seats but polled 3.2 per cent of the votes; 1999: the United Kingdom Independence Party (UKIP) won three seats with 7.0 per cent of the votes, SNP won two seats with 2.7 per cent of the votes; Plaid Cymru won two seats with 1.8 per cent of the votes, the Greens won two seats with 6.2 per cent of the votes; 2004: UKIP won 12 seats with 16.8 per cent of the votes, the Greens won two seats with 6.2 per cent of the votes, the SNP won two seats with 3.0 per cent of the votes, Plaid Cymru won one seat with 1.1 per cent of the votes, the British National Party (BNP) won no seats but polled 4.9 per cent of the votes.

c Turnout is calculated by dividing the total number of valid votes in Britain by the total number of eligible voters in Britain and multiplying this by 100.

then, the extra-parliamentary party is clearly subordinate to the party leadership at Westminster, and the primary task of the extra-parliamentary party is to serve the parliamentary leadership in securing electoral success and in winning power (Kelly 2004). Despite the wide-ranging *Fresh Future Reforms* introduced in 1998 by the then party leader William Hague, which brought the three wings of the party (parliamentary, organizational and voluntary) together under one single structure, and which saw the creation of a new extra-parliamentary leadership body (the Party Board), the balance of power between the Conservative parliamentary leadership and the extra-parliamentary party organization has remained fundamentally unchanged.[6]

As for the Labour Party, in spite of the democratic character of the party's constitution, and the fact that, formally, sovereignty lies with the party conference, in practice the parliamentary leadership has shown itself able to overlook parts of the conference-made programme, and 'has traditionally enjoyed considerable strategic freedom to devise election manifestos and to govern relatively unimpeded by the extra-parliamentary party once in office' (Heffernan and Webb 2005: 46). This autonomy grew from the mid-1980s onwards, as successive party leaders instituted new practices that made policy-making and campaigning more and more centralized and that saw the party's extra-parliamentary leadership body – the National Executive Committee (NEC) – become increasingly circumvented (Webb 1992; Shaw 1994).[7]

The Liberal Democrats differ somewhat from the other two in that, since they are a (territorially) federal party, a dispersal of power is designed into the structure of the party (Russell and Fieldhouse 2005: 53). The substantial incentives and opportunities afforded to Liberal Democrat party members – not only in the selection of candidates and election of leaders but also in the making of policy – further contribute to the diffusion of power within the party and further distinguish it from its two counterparts. In spite of the party's federal make-up and participatory character, however, and notwithstanding the fact that, formally, the party conference has the final say as regards party policy, the parliamentary party leadership has shown itself able to exert significant influence in policy-making and in the management of election campaigns. It has, for example, been able to limit the power of the party conference by making use of special policy committees (Webb 1994: 122). Furthermore, as well as sitting on the party's most important committee, the Federal Executive, the party leader is able to keep a firm grip on the direction of policy-making by virtue of the fact that he chairs the pivotal Federal Policy Committee (FPC), which develops party policy and drafts manifestos for both general and European elections.[8]

The institutional framework for European policy-making

The domination of parliamentary elites within British political parties is explained in large part by the fact that, within the Westminster system, the executive heavily dominates the legislature. As Webb argues 'from this perspective, parliamentary parties are almost entirely subservient to the needs of the elites occupying the executive offices of the state' (2000: 168). And this is very evident when one considers the way in which EU policy is made: as Bulmer and Burch (1998) explain, EU policy is coordinated by the Cabinet Office, with the Foreign and Commonwealth Office (FCO) and the UK's Permanent Representation to the EU (based in Brussels) playing supporting roles. EU policy-making therefore remains very much the domain of the executive, and in recent years this has become all the more so with the prime minister playing a growing role in EU affairs, and with the Cabinet Office's European secretariat being headed by the prime minister's personal advisor on EU matters (Allen 2005: 132).

The British legislature, and hence the parliamentary parties, are therefore not greatly involved in EU policy-making, and this despite the fact that 'on paper, Britain has the second most effective system for parliamentary scrutiny of EU legislation after Denmark' (Allen 2005: 134). Indeed, by contrast to other committees in the House of Commons that have only *ex post* control functions, the European Scrutiny Committee (ESC) was also given powers of control of the pre-legislative phase of the policy process (Carter 2001: 398). As well as examining EU documents and reporting its opinion on their legal and political importance and making recommendations for their future consideration, the Committee sees that a minister's policy position is cleared prior to negotiation in the Council of Ministers, and in doing so it may also try to exert influence over legislation. After the negotiations, ministers can then be called in front of the Committee to explain policy outcomes (Carter 2001: 402). As Allen notes, however, in spite of these powers, in practice the Committee is swamped by the sheer volume of EU legislation and suffers from the shortage of time it has to process it. In addition to being explained by these institutional pressures, the parliamentary parties' lack of involvement in EU policy-making is also a product of the fact that the vast majority of national MPs show little interest in the detail of this legislation anyway (Allen 2005: 134).

Having briefly considered the British experience of EU membership and the consequences of membership for the British parties, and having devoted a few words to discussing the general model of party organization in Britain and the institutional framework in which European policy is made, the chapter now turns to examining how the three main British parties have adapted their organizations in response to membership and to increased European integration. The next section considers the structural adaptation of the parties to European integration, while subsequent sections discuss the behaviour and influence of party actors involved in European affairs.

Structural adaptation of parties to European integration

The role of EU specialists in the management of European activities

In the run-up to accession, the issue of where responsibility for EEC matters should lie was discussed, and the decision was reached rather quickly that there would not be a separate ministry for Europe in the UK. The preference was for a coordinating machinery between key departments, similar to the one that had already begun to develop since the late 1950s in response to the foundation of the Community (Bulmer and Burch 1998: 610–12). Edward Heath, the prime minister at the time, was keen that each government department should consider Europe as integrally connected to domestic politics rather than as a foreign policy matter. In light of these arrangements, it was decided that it would be the foreign secretary who would represent the UK on the General Affairs Council (Geddes 2004: 165), and who would chair the cabinet committee in which the bulk of European business is discussed (Allen 2005: 132).

Even if there was not to be a ministry for Europe, however, there was to be a minister in charge of European matters, based in the FCO.[9] The role of the minister for Europe has varied considerably over time. Whereas early incumbents were concerned with the accession negotiations and then with the renegotiations of the terms of entry, as one senior Conservative interviewee explained, in more recent years the main task of this person has been to pass on information to colleagues and to develop a European angle on the government's position. Furthermore, since Labour came to power in 1997, as part of the government's 'step-change' programme, the minister for Europe has also taken on a public relations role, publicizing the government's European and domestic agenda to, and building relationships with, counterparts in other member states.[10] As is the tradition in the UK, the parties of opposition form an alternative, or 'shadow', cabinet to the government's, and in both the Conservative and the Liberal Democrat shadow cabinet there is a shadow minister for Europe, working under the leadership of the shadow foreign secretary.

Members of the House of Commons ESC may also be thought of as being EU specialists. The position of the chair of the ESC is not determined by the government and instead, as is the case with other parliamentary committees, it is MPs who vote to elect the incumbent. Traditionally, the ESC has been chaired by a member of the (main) opposition party so as to ensure its 'independence', yet, since 1997, this custom has been suspended, as the Labour MP who had chaired the Committee since 1992 has remained in post (Carter 2001: 403–4). As well as chairing the Committee, the chair of the ESC regularly travels to Brussels to visit all the British party delegations. He or she, along with other members of the ESC, also represents the House of Commons in COSAC (the Conference of Community and European Affairs Committees of Parliaments of the European Union).

In addition to serving on parliamentary committees such as the ESC, MPs also sit on committees within their parliamentary parties, commonly referred to as 'backbench committees'. Both the Labour Party and the Conservative Party have backbench committees on European affairs. Despite their existence, however, and even though the various posts within the committees are often contested (Norton 2000: 44), the committees have no decision-making power and really only act as a debating society for those (few) with an interest in European matters. When the party is in government, ministers do sometimes come to speak to these committees, and sometimes take notice of their mood, but in general the committees lack any real influence.

In addition to the EU specialists found in the party in public office – i.e. those who work within the government or the shadow cabinets of the opposition parties, and within parliament – British parties also employ EU specialists at their national headquarters. In the Labour Party's headquarters, until relatively recently, responsibility for the management of European matters rested with the international secretary, but in 2003 the position was replaced by that of the international manager. One of the duties of this person has been to liaise with the European Parliamentary Labour Party (EPLP), and hence to provide a channel of communication between the party leadership in government and the EPLP. This person also attends meetings of the Party of European Socialists (PES). In the Conservative Party, European affairs are handled by the head of the international office, and in the Liberal Democrats they fall under the remit of the international office director.

As well as having nationally based party personnel who deal with European matters, the British parties have also adapted their organizations to integrate their members in the EP. In the Labour Party, as a result of reforms introduced in 1993, Members of the European Parliament (MEPs) have a role in the election of the party leader: MEPs and MPs (together) now have one-third of the votes of the electoral college that elects the leader.[11] Furthermore, in all three British parties, MEPs are represented on their party's national executive committee. The leader of the Labour Party in the EP – who, like his or her counterparts in the other two British parties, is elected by fellow MEPs in a competitive contest – has statutory membership of the party's NEC. In the Conservative Party it is through convention rather than statutory right that the EP delegation leader is appointed to the Party Board. This system may be revised in the future, however, as there have been proposals within the party for the EP delegation leader to have statutory membership of the Board. In the Liberal Democrats, the MEPs vote each year to decide who amongst them will be their representative on the party's Federal Executive. Their representative on the Federal Executive is therefore not necessarily the delegation leader.

Although there has been some change over time in the role of the minister for Europe, and although slight changes have been seen within the Labour Party with both the downgrading of the position of international secretary and the involvement of MEPs in the selection of the party leader, no discernable pattern emerges in any of the parties that would suggest so-called EU specialists have become more visible or important in the face of growing European integration. Rather, as well as being minimal, changes in the role of EU specialists have simply reflected other concerns, be they an attempt to improve the perception of the UK's position in Europe, a desire to increase levels of internal party democracy, or a response to financial constraints.

Linkage mechanisms

In addition to examining specific positions within the parties that are concerned with European matters, it is useful to consider some of the broader mechanisms through which European issues are managed. One such mechanism in the Labour

Party is the 'link system', introduced by the Blair government in time for the EP elections of 1999. The link system brings MEPs into high-level policy development and decision-making and establishes a 'systematic relationship of policy coordination between [the Labour government] and [its] MEP delegation' (Messmer 2003: 202). It works by integrating each of the EPLP's official spokespersons in each EP committee into the government's relevant ministerial team.[12]

In return for MEPs being integrated so centrally into policy-making and decision-making, the EPLP is expected to lend its unequivocal support to the Labour government. When the system was first introduced, it was anticipated that the positive incentives offered by the link system (i.e. the increased influence and involvement in policy-making) would be backed up by sanctions that derived from the Labour Party's candidate selection mechanism for EP elections. Indeed, as will be seen below, the candidate selection procedure in place for the 1999 elections allowed the party leadership to punish disloyal or unruly MEPs by placing them further down the electoral list than they would otherwise be, hence cutting their chances of being re-elected. Unfavourable reaction from party members led to a change in the selection procedures, however, and since 2004, this sanction has effectively been removed.

The introduction of the link system reflects the desire of national party leaders to control their MEPs in a bid to gain greater influence in the EU policy-making process, especially given the increased powers of the EP after the treaties of Maastricht and Amsterdam. This system is also of particular appeal to a governing party such as Labour, as it enables the party leadership to try to avoid situations in which government ministers negotiate one position in the Council of Ministers, but MEPs support a different one in the EP (Messmer 2003: 202). Aside from these institutional incentives, the Labour Party leadership was also keen on the system because during much of the 1980s and 1990s the EPLP had been factional and detached from the party back home, and was perceived as damaging Labour's influence in the EP (Messmer 2003: 203).

The Conservative Party's system of policy coordination between its shadow cabinet and its delegation in the EP is not as developed as the Labour Party's link system, and instead resembles the system in place in the Labour Party before the link system was introduced. Individual Conservative MEPs are appointed by the party's EP delegation leader to be spokespersons on specific subjects, normally according to their interests. The delegation leader and the relevant spokesperson then together work out a position on each issue, and other Conservative MEPs are subsequently informed of the position taken and how they should vote in the EP should a vote arise. As concerns policy coordination with the party at Westminster, Conservative MEPs liaise with their policy counterparts in the shadow cabinet and also sit on the relevant shadow cabinet committee. Despite this coordination, however, the input of Conservative MEPs into policy-making is not as institutionalized as that of their Labour Party counterparts.

In the Liberal Democrats, the mechanisms through which EU issues are managed are much less well developed, owing, above all, to the fact that the party is still a small party, and only began to have a significant number of MEPs after the

1999 EP elections. To date there has been little or no structural adaptation in the party to deal with the formal management of European matters. Instead, European issues are mainly handled by the delegation leader, who liaises and cooperates with the party in Westminster. Other MEPs do also consult with the national party, but this is on a rather *ad hoc* basis. Interviewees did report that the party was gradually realizing that structural adaptation was becoming necessary, however; in this vein, one former delegation leader explained that there was a push to institutionalize a linkage between London and Brussels, with MEPs having the right to speak at Westminster.

The development of these linkage mechanisms does suggest that some changes have taken place in the ways in which European activities are formally managed within the three main British parties, and this is especially so in the case of the Labour Party. That said, these mechanisms are more a reflection of the desire of the national parties to increase their awareness of the activities of the EP, and in the case of the Labour Party to attempt to gain greater influence in the EU policy-making process, than a means by which EU specialists (in this case MEPs) may become increasingly important within their national parties. Furthermore, these mechanisms only go so far, in that they are much more of a carrot than a stick: while they offer MEPs the opportunity to be more involved in their party's policy-making, they do little to discipline or sanction unruly or rebellious MEPs.

Funding of European activities

Owing in large part to the fact that British political parties receive negligible public funding, most of the British parties' EU-related activities are not funded by the party organizations. Rather, the parties tend to rely on the salaries and allowances that their parliamentarians receive. Thus, while the minister for Europe, the shadow ministers for Europe, and the members of the ESC derive their salaries and may claim related travel costs from Westminster, the parties' MEPs claim their salaries and allowances from the EP, and employ assistants who are also paid for by the EP.

In addition to each MEP deriving a salary, claiming allowances and having funds to employ one or more assistant, each party's delegation benefits from further resources from the EP. The individual delegation's size (i.e. the number of seats it won in the last EP election) determines the size of the national section staff, and the number of seats won by the EP group to which each party belongs determines the size of the general group staff. There is also help with overheads, which is very crucial to the functioning of each delegation. The Labour Party delegation uses these funds to employ a person – the secretary-general of the EPLP – to assist in the organization and delivery of EPLP legislative actions, and to act as a link with the party in government (and its policy advisors) in London. The secretary-general of the EPLP is based in the offices of the EP in London. The office of the delegation leader of the Labour Party also employs an assistant who aids in liaising between the EPLP and the prime minister's office, where this individual is placed. Similarly, the Conservative delegation employs staff to coordinate its activities between London and Brussels, with one person based in each city. The Liberal Democrat delegation also employs an individual – the 'Director of Communications' – whose role it is to liaise between the party's MEPs on the one hand, and the Westminster parliamentary party and the party press office in London on the other. This person is based in Brussels. In all three parties, however, at the political, rather than the organizational level, coordination with the party leadership at Westminster rests firmly in the hands of the delegation leader or other MEPs.

In addition to relying on resources from Westminster and from the EP, the party in government is also able to make use of special advisors located in the European secretariat of the Cabinet Office, the FCO, and other ministries. Recalling the time when the Conservative Party was in power, one interviewee reported that these special advisors could exert significant influence, even affecting what the foreign secretary might say or do. Under Labour, the influence of special advisors has increased if anything, as the status of the leading officials in the European secretariat has been enhanced, and the overall size of the secretariat has increased (Bulmer and Burch 2005).

The national party organizations themselves have very limited resources for Europe-related activities. They provide no financial help at all to their MEPs, in the form of either money or staff support, and at party headquarters they only employ a very small number of people who work on European matters. Indeed, one senior Conservative interviewee reported that there were 'precious few' members of staff who work on European affairs within the party. He said that there have never been more than about three such people in Conservative Central Office: the European desk officer of the Conservative research department, and two or so others working on practical, organizational or operational matters. He argued that, in general, however, the party only really saw the need for organizational assistance in the run-up to EP elections, and for four and a half years out of five it was the MEPs (and their assistants) who were relied upon to deliver practical support. The situation is similar in the Labour Party, and in fact, in recent years, resources for EU-related activities in the party have become even more limited. As well as downgrading (and renaming) the position of international secretary, resources to the international section of the party have been cut, primarily because of the party's wider funding problem, which has come about, in large part, as a result of trades unions cutting back their contributions. As for the Liberal Democrats, they too only have a tiny number of party staff who work directly on EU matters, and they too rely heavily on MEPs and their staff.

On the basis of the above discussion, it is fair to conclude that British political parties have only engaged in minimal levels of structural adaptation in response to increased European integration. Very few posts have been created that deal specifically with European matters, and the majority have been established as a result of governmental or parliamentary obligations – for example the need to have a minister for Europe and representatives on the ESC. In addition, resources devoted to the management of European issues within national parties, and to any further structural adaptation, remain very limited.

Before turning to investigating the influence EU specialists might exert within their national parties, it is now useful to consider the methods the parties use to select their candidates for EP elections as this sheds further light on the extent to which British parties have adapted structurally to European integration.

MEP candidate selection procedures

Examining the ways in which parties select their candidates for EP elections is particularly relevant in the British case, as the change in the electoral system for EP elections announced by the Labour government in 1997, which saw the single-member plurality system replaced by closed list proportional representation based on 11 regions, has led the parties to alter the ways in which their candidates for EP elections are selected.[13]

The system used by the Labour Party for the 1999 EP elections began with local party units and (Westminster) constituencies nominating candidates. These were then subject to a ballot of party members in the (pre-1999) European constituency, and from this ballot a male and a female candidate were nominated. The sitting MEP was also subject to a ballot, but was in any event assured a place on the list. The two new candidates and the sitting MEP then went on to face a regional interview panel (made up of the party general secretary, NEC members, regional representatives and a few others) which established a pool of candidates from which a centrally appointed joint selection board made up the final list and rank-ordered the candidates (Ovey 2002: 180–1). It had been made clear from the start that the candidate selection system used in 1999 would be a one-off, however, devised to make the transition between the old electoral system and the new one as smooth as possible for the party and its sitting MEPs. The system was therefore altered quite significantly for the 2004 EP elections, and party members, unhappy with the degree of central party control in the 1999 system, exerted much pressure in the change.

In the 2004 system, incumbents and new candidates were selected separately, though simultaneously. Incumbents were guaranteed a place on the list if they were nominated by at least half the branches in their region. If they failed to receive this nomination (which no incumbent did), they would join the selection process for the new candidates. Successful incumbents were automatically placed on the top of the regional list, and their rank-ordering (at the top of the list) was decided by means of a ballot of individual party members. If the final rank-ordering of incumbents did not result in a woman being placed first or second on the list, then the best-placed woman was elevated to number two on the list. New candidates, by contrast, were interviewed by the regional executive of the party, which then drew up two shortlists (one male, one female), the combined length of which was equal to the number of seats not held by the party in the region. Party members then voted on each of these shortlists to decide the rank-ordering of the new candidates (www.meps.org.uk).

In 1999, therefore, the balance of power was very much with the central party, as the role of the party membership essentially involved nominating the candidates rather than having a say in the final selection and the rank-ordering of the lists. By 2004, however, the power of Labour party members in the selection of candidates for EP elections had increased significantly, although the system did make it rather difficult to remove sitting MEPs.

In the Conservative Party, since the introduction of the *Fresh Future Reforms* in 1998, party members have been accorded new rights in the process of selecting candidates for the EP elections (Webb 2000: 197). The party at central and regional level does remain in control of the early stages of the process, however, as prospective MEP candidates face a selection board, which places approved candidates on the 'Approved List' maintained by the Party Board. After this selection board, prospective candidates then face a regional sifting committee, made up of constituency and area chairs from within the region, which draws up a shortlist of prospective candidates (Webb 2000: 197). Sitting MEPs have a 'buy-out' through to the shortlist. After this shortlisting, it is up to party members to select and rank-order the candidates on the shortlist.

The balance of power in the selection of candidates for EP elections therefore lies very much with individual Conservative Party members, and other than 'weed out' potentially weak candidates and attempt to encourage a more representative base, the central and regional party has little influence over the final selection and rank-ordering of the candidates.[14] It can do little to ensure that favourable candidates are selected or non-favoured candidates are blackballed. Furthermore, although incumbent MEPs are automatically shortlisted, the party leadership can do little to ensure their re-election. As one senior Conservative MEP put it, 'the system is such that MEPs have to "sing for their suppers"'. It should be pointed out, however, that, although the new system of candidate selection for EP elections in the Conservative Party does confer new rights on party members, it would be misleading to conclude that Europe is any more or less important an issue than before. Rather the change in the system should be viewed as part of wider reforms, which were the outcome of a general push for greater levels of internal party democracy.

The selection procedure for candidates for EP elections used by the Liberal Democrats is similar to that of the Conservative Party, but incumbent MEPs are not guaranteed a place on the shortlist. In the Liberal Democrats the responsibility for drawing up a shortlist is discharged to a sub-committee approved by the regional executive of the Euro Region, or, in the case of Wales and Scotland, the state executive of the Euro Region. Candidates are shortlisted on the basis of their support for the values of the party and their previous participation and work in the party. Sitting MEPs thus have a high chance of being shortlisted, but they are not automatically assigned a place on the list. Once this shortlisting is complete, the selection committee holds one or more hustings meetings at which party members vote to select and order the candidates on the list. The makeup and ordering of the list can be changed to accommodate gender balance requirements specified by the selection rules of the state party (www.libdems.org.uk).[15] The federal party leadership therefore plays little part in the process. At best it can only indirectly influence the selection committee, through the regional or state executives of the Euro Region.

This review of the procedures used by the three main British parties to select their candidates for EP elections further suggests that they have engaged in limited structural adaptation in response to European integration. Not only have they failed to create many posts devoted to the management of European matters, and devoted few resources to the task, but they have also done little to alter existing traditions of candidate selection. Although the change in the electoral system for EP elections did prompt the parties to revise their candidate selection procedures, with the exception of the system employed by the Labour Party in 1999, the overall balance of power in candidate selection remains predominantly with party members rather than with party elites.

Acting nationally

Having examined the extent to which the British parties have engaged in structural adaptation in the face of increased European integration, the chapter now turns its attention to considering the power and influence of various party actors at the national level. Recalling one of the two hypotheses advanced in Chapter 1, this section investigates whether EU specialists have gained power and influence relative to other party actors. It first examines the general influence of the EU specialists identified above, and it then addresses their influence in the processes of manifesto formulation and policy-making.

The general influence of EU specialists within their national parties

Beginning with the minister for Europe, one has to conclude that the influence of this office has been rather limited, both in the incumbent's party and, for that matter, within the government. One reason for this is that responsibility and direction for European matters lies, in the first instance, with the foreign secretary. As Allen explains, foreign secretaries have been reluctant to cede power to the minister for Europe, remaining resistant to 'the idea that the post of minister for Europe should be elevated to cabinet rank [and being] reluctant to contemplate the downgrading of [their] own role that this might imply' (2005: 132). A senior interviewee confirmed this, stating that there was 'a tendency for the foreign secretary to curtail the minister for Europe's responsibilities so as to ensure that he (the foreign secretary) had the necessary room for manoeuvre'. In view of this, it is not surprising that the same interviewee described the position of minister for Europe as 'lacking prominence' and as being 'a difficult one', with incumbents finding it hard to 'make a mark on the job'. He also reported that other parliamentarians were often critical of the incumbent. This lack of influence is as acute in the opposition parties, if not more so. In the two opposition parties, the position of the shadow minister for Europe is also a junior front bench one, just as it is in the government, and the incumbent must work under the direction of the shadow foreign secretary.

As well as being curtailed by the dominance of the foreign secretary, Bulmer and Burch argue that the influence of the minister for Europe is also dependent on the incumbent's qualities and on the relationship he or she has with the prime minister. They explain that, under the Blair government, the office of the prime minister and the role of the prime minister's advisors on Europe have been significantly enhanced, and that, while the office of the minister for Europe has also been enhanced in this process, 'the significance of this post depends upon both the qualities of the incumbent and their relationship with the prime minister of the day' (2005: 882–3).

Indeed, the position of the minister for Europe has not always been filled by top party personnel or by people with a strong European vision. Smith quotes one former Labour MP as describing the minister for Europe as having '"no strong views" on the subject, [and as having no] particular qualifications for the job' (2005: 708), a sentiment that was echoed by a senior politician interviewed in the course of this project. In addition, the role of the minister for Europe (and the shadow ministers for Europe) has been made difficult by the high turnover in the post, with incumbents rarely staying long enough in the job to make a significant mark (Smith 2005: 711).

The lack of resources for Europe-related activities within the parties has also had an effect on the ability of the minister for Europe and the shadow ministers for Europe to exert influence within their national parties. One senior Conservative interviewee argued that the paucity of resources meant that it was really quite difficult for the shadow minister for Europe to keep abreast of developments in Europe, and that it was therefore difficult for him to accurately inform the party at Westminster of relevant issues. The interviewee summed up the situation by saying it was 'rather a case of the blind leading the blind'.

The chair of the ESC and other members of the committee also command little influence, both in their parties and indeed within parliament. As one member of the ESC noted, if the committee were to have real decision-making power, rather than simply an advisory or organizational role, then the position of chair would have a higher profile than it does, and selection would be more competitive. A senior Liberal Democrat interviewee also reported that there had been no contest in his party for membership of the committee, and he added that there was also no involvement from party leadership in the selection of its representative to the ESC. That said, he did add that, had the party leadership had reservations about its representative to the committee, then it would not have been unlikely that it would have intervened. In general, however, for all three parties, membership of the ESC is more a function of the members' interest in European matters than anything else.

It is therefore appropriate to conclude that elected EU specialists who work in the national arena command little influence within their parties. That is, being the minister for Europe, the shadow minister for Europe, or a member of the ESC does not make, and indeed has never made, an individual influential within his or her party.

The same is true for party staff members who work on European affairs. Not only are their numbers tiny, as was documented above, but, according to interviewees in both the Labour Party and the Conservative Party, these positions have also become less influential in recent years. As was mentioned above, in the Labour Party the position of international secretary was downgraded in 2003, while in the Conservative Party the activity of the international office has markedly declined since the early 1990s. It is no longer central to the party's management of European affairs and, perhaps in reflection of this, it has moved out of Conservative Central Office. Furthermore, in all three parties, these positions also include responsibilities for matters that relate to the rest of the world, despite some incumbents arguing for a differentiation of responsibilities between Europe and other international affairs. Indeed, the international office or unit of each party is heavily involved in managing projects that are aimed at supporting like-minded parties in newly emerging democracies, and in cooperating in these projects with sister parties in Western Europe.

Moving to party actors who operate at the European level, it would be misleading to conclude that delegation leaders and other MEPs have derived increased influence within their national parties as a result of the limited structural adaptation in which their parties have engaged. MEPs and delegation leaders have not gained influence within their national party by simply having membership of their party's national executive committee. Rather, if they do exercise power or influence within their parties, this comes from their expertise in, and experience of, European matters. Furthermore, the real power and influence of the Labour Party's NEC and the Conservative Party's Board should not be overestimated. In the Labour Party the NEC's influence in policy and decision-making has declined since the late 1980s (Webb 2000: 202–5), while in the Conservative Party, although the Board is 'the supreme decision-making body' in matters of organization and management, its remit does not encompass policy-making, nor does it have much influence over the selection of parliamentary candidates, as was illustrated above. In more general terms too, as Kelly argues, through 'imperious management', recent party leaders have shown little respect for the Board (2004: 401).

The influence of EU specialists in formulating manifestos

The extent to which EU specialists may exert influence within their national party organizations is further illustrated by the degree to which they may be involved in the formulation of manifestos, for both national and EP elections. In the Labour Party, although EU specialists do contribute to the formulation of both types of manifestos by offering advice on particular policies, their input only occurs at an early stage in the formulation process, and it is the party leadership that remains squarely in charge of matters. Even when the party decided to adopt the PES manifesto for the 1999 EP elections rather than draft its own, the leadership made sure that it exerted its influence, as the PES working group that drafted the manifesto was co-chaired by Robin Cook, the then foreign secretary. In more general terms too, the Labour leadership has kept a tight reign on manifesto formulation by routinely ignoring certain manifesto provisions put forward by the party conference.

In the Conservative Party the formulation of manifestos for national elections is a task for the manifesto committee, which is dominated by the party leadership and led by the party leader. Although it was the case that during the formulation of the 2001 general election manifesto the manifesto committee was chaired by the EP delegation leader, it was his expertise and his experience both as a former MP and as an MEP that led to him taking on this task, rather than the fact that he was EP delegation leader. Other MEPs were simply shown the Europe section of the manifesto, which in any case was very succinct and uncontroversial. In contrast, MEPs are centrally involved in the formulation of manifestos for EP elections, with the delegation leader and the deputy delegation leader being particularly heavily involved. In recent years the delegation leader has also taken over from the foreign secretary in chairing the EU manifesto committee.

In the Liberal Democrats, it is more or less the same team that puts together the manifesto for national elections and the manifesto for EP elections. Both are written by the national party leadership at Westminster and key actors in the formulation of the last national and EP election manifestos included the head of policy, the chair of the parliamentary party and the party's deputy leader and shadow foreign secretary. That said, however, EU specialists do have had an input into the formulation of both types of manifesto. In the case of manifestos for national elections this has been relatively modest, and has taken the form of the head of policy travelling to Brussels to consult MEPs on certain issues. By contrast, in the formulation of manifestos for EP elections, the involvement of the delegation leader and other MEPs has been quite significant. They have been heavily involved in all aspects of the manifesto and at all the stages of its formulation, and have played a proactive role in the manifesto's formulation by sending contributions to the drafting team on policies in which they have particular interest or expertise. As one senior national party politician was keen to point out, however, in spite of the involvement of MEPs, it is still very much the national party that remains in control of what goes in to the party's manifesto for EP elections, and it is party policy at the national level which informs its content.

The influence of EU specialists in policy-making

The dominance of the national party leaderships is even greater when it comes to policy formulation. For parties in government, the bulk of the technical input on policies related to Europe has come not from party actors or party EU specialists but from special policy advisors located in the European secretariat of the Cabinet Office and in other ministries, and from the UK's permanent representation to the EU. What is more, as was mentioned above, in recent years the influence of these special advisors has grown. The leader of the Labour Party delegation in the EP tends only to be involved in policy-making when policies may have political ramifications in the EU arena, and in the EP in particular. The influence of other MEPs in policy formulation is also limited. Indeed, although the Labour Party's link system might suggest that Labour MEPs are involved centrally in the development of policy, in practice, but for exceptional circumstances where EU policy expertise is not fully developed by the government ministry advisor, the link system is generally a way for the Labour Party in government to try to influence the EPLP rather than a means by which the EPLP may influence the government. As for the Conservative Party and the Liberal Democrats, decisions on policy also lie squarely in the hands of the parties' national leaderships, although, of course, policy formulation is less of a concern given that these two parties are not presently in government. The contribution of EU specialists is limited and tends to be sought only if it is in line with the national party leadership's policy preferences or if it is likely to help party strategy.

From the above discussion it is fair to conclude that the influence of EU specialists within their national parties is clearly limited. Nationally based EU specialists such as the minister for Europe, the shadow ministers for Europe, and members of the ESC command little influence within their parties and hence derive negligible power from their positions. As for MEPs, although they have been integrated into their national parties to some degree, and although they do have an input into their party's manifestos, and into the manifesto for EP elections in particular, this integration and involvement does not translate into them having increased influence or power within their national party organizations. Membership of their party's national executive committee does not endow MEPs with influence, and, similarly, involvement in the drafting of manifestos for EP elections is hardly a sign of power. EP elections remain second order elections, in which national issues dominate, and manifestos for EP elections must therefore address these national issues if they are to be relevant. This, by definition, means that the input of EU specialists is curtailed and that national party leaderships remain involved in the drafting of the manifestos and in control of the end product. The dominance of the national party leaderships is also plain to see in policy-making, where the involvement of MEPs and other EU specialists is very limited and is only sought if it supports the preferences of the leadership or if it may be of strategic value to the party.

Acting supranationally

EU specialists and party elites may not only (theoretically) derive power from the place they occupy in their party's formal structure and from their involvement in national party politics; they may also command influence as a result of being involved in decision-making at the European level. This section of the chapter focuses on this suggestion, and examines whether EU specialists and party elites have indeed acquired increased power and influence within their national parties as a result of the part they play in supranational-level decision-making. It begins by considering the influence MEPs may gain within their parties from their involvement in the EP; it then turns to examining the power that national party elites may accrue as a consequence of partaking in meetings of the Council of Ministers and the European Council; and finally it investigates what influence actors may gain within their national political parties from being involved in the activities of their Europarty.

Parties and their MEPs

Of the EU specialists identified above, it is really only MEPs who are active at the European level. The minister for Europe does not take part in any decision-making at the EU level, and, although the chair of the ESC (sometimes accompanied by other members of the committee) does represent the House of Commons in meetings of COSAC, that body has no decision-making power, and hence no real influence derives from it. By contrast, MEPs are, by definition, active in one of the EU's decision-making arenas – the EP – and the influence they exert in that arena may well make them more powerful within their national parties. What is more, they may well have become more influential in their national parties in recent years because, since the treaties of Maastricht and Amsterdam and the extension of the co-decision procedure, the EP now has a greater role in the European-level legislative process.

Recalling the discussion in the first chapter of this volume, two possible indicators of the power and influence that MEPs may derive from their activities in the EP are the degree to which they may engage in autonomous actions and the extent to which they may be held accountable for their decisions. Autonomy and accountability can be seen as indicators of power because they reflect the extent to which MEPs may be able to shape the party's activity at the European level, and the extent to which they may, in that process, develop a new power base within the party, of which the national party leadership will have to take account.

All the MEPs interviewed in the course of this project reported enjoying high levels of autonomy in their activities and low levels of accountability for their actions. Indeed, one MEP maintained that he had 'as much autonomy as he liked', while another argued that 'you set your own chains'. A third reported that 'London only knows what is happening if told'. Interviewees also explained that, although the national party might attempt to encourage its MEPs to behave in a certain way, it 'never sought to impose its will'. They said that there was no system of control from the national party, no reporting requirements and no sanctions, remarks that concur very much with the above discussion of the linkage mechanisms (including the Labour Party's 'link system') predominantly being ways in which the national parties may increase their awareness of the activities of the EP, rather than means by which MEPs may be controlled or disciplined.

This high autonomy and low accountability therefore appears to suggest that MEPs may well have gained power as a result of their activities in the EP, especially given the increased importance of EU decisions for national legislation. However, while this reasoning makes good sense, there is an important element missing from it, namely that national party leaderships need only take notice of this new power base if it is relevant to national party politics. The actions in which MEPs engage and the decisions that are made in the EP are not, by and large, relevant to national party politics, however. Although it is undeniable that legislation made at the European level has a great impact on domestic *policy*, it remains the case that the activities of MEPs and the legislative decisions of the EP do not greatly shape the contest for power at the national level (Krouwel 2004).

In short, they do not help win national elections. This is perhaps particularly so in the case of Britain since, as was mentioned in the early part of the chapter, Europe tends to be kept out of national politics and the British parties do not readily give prominence to the EU as an issue, except in rare situations where some electoral advantage may be gained.

The fact that party activity in the EU remains perceived as 'detached' from, and even irrelevant to, national party politics is reflected in, and indeed exacerbated by, the lack of interest that the majority of national party politicians have in the EU as a whole, and in the activities of their MEPs in particular. All MEPs that were interviewed reported that the national party had little interest in developments in the EP, that there was a lack of understanding within the national party of how the EP and its MEPs worked, and that there was even a certain level of distrust and resentment towards the institution and its members. They explained that this was the case in spite of increased efforts to improve communication between MEPs and MPs, such as meetings being set up between MEPs and MPs, reports being written by MEPs informing the national party of their activities, and regular emails being sent by the delegation to MPs. It is really only the national party leadership that takes notice of the actions of the national delegations in the EP, and even here attention tends only to be significant when specific legislative decisions may be of particular domestic importance.

The lack of interest by national politicians in the EP's activities also goes a long way to explaining why MEPs enjoy such high levels of autonomy. Indeed, uninterested national party politicians are unlikely to become acquainted with and involved in the activities of MEPs. High autonomy is also, to some extent, a product of the institutional logic of the EP that requires MEPs to work within their EP groups – the PES group in the case of the Labour Party; the EPP–ED group in the case of the Conservative Party, and ALDE in the case of the Liberal Democrats – if they wish to exert influence within the chamber and the EP's committees. The incentives to work with the groups are particularly relevant for the British delegations as all three delegations are large, and so can exert considerable influence within their respective groups. This sometimes means striking a balance between the wishes of the national party and the preferences of the EP groups, and at times this has put national delegations at odds with their national party's position. For example, one senior Conservative interviewee recalled that tensions between the party's EP delegation and the national party leadership were high during the 1980s at the time of the debate on the UK's contribution to the EEC budget. On the whole, however, disagreements between delegations and their national parties have been managed successfully, something which, according to one interviewee, has been helped by the fact that national party leaderships have come to better understand the institutional pressures of the EP in recent years and, no matter how foreign the concept, have gradually recognized that their MEPs are, after all, involved in coalition politics. Added to this increased understanding from national party leaderships, the autonomy of MEPs is also high because their anonymity is protected in many of the votes in the EP.

As for the low accountability of MEPs, this is also explained in part by the fact that national politicians have little interest in the EP's activities. Just as they are unlikely to inform themselves of the activities of MEPs if they are disinterested in European-level politics, national politicians are also unlikely to request that MEPs explain and justify their actions. Yet, even if national party politicians were interested in EU-level politics, there are no real ways in which they would be able to hold their MEPs to account. Indeed, in all three parties no institutionalized channels of control exist between the national party leadership and the EP delegation, mainly because, as was illustrated above, national party leaderships are unable to threaten MEPs with the ultimate sanction: de-selection. All national party leaderships can really do, much to their annoyance, is remain informed of the actions of their delegation, encourage MEPs to act in a certain fashion, and reprimand them if and when they do not.

Contrary to initial expectations, therefore, one must conclude that MEPs derive little power within their national parties as a result of their involvement in EU-level decision-making. Although they enjoy high levels of autonomy in their activities, and although they are not meaningfully held account for their actions in the EP, the fact that their activities are, by and large, not considered relevant in national party politics means that any influence MEPs may gain in the EP is not translated into them gaining power within their parties back home.

Paties and their ministers

For national party elites, the story might be different, however. Recalling the theoretical discussion of Chapter 1, it was suggested that party elites might gain considerable power from European integration because their involvement in European-level decision-making is likely to enable them to gain leverage over those party actors who do not partake in EU decisions, in particular the national parliamentary parties. The exclusive nature of European Council meetings and meetings of the Council of Ministers, by definition, gives national party elites a high level of autonomy: only those present know what really goes on. Furthermore, within limits, those present can then choose how the information gained in those meetings is fed back to the national party. In addition, the form of these meetings encourages a low level of accountability by the national party. Little detail is provided on how decisions are reached, and agreements (especially if reached under QMV) are often presented to the national party as the best possible achievable outcome.

The evidence gathered in the course of this study suggests that, as expected, national party elites do enjoy high levels of autonomy in their activities in the Council of Ministers and the European Council, and that they are also subject to low levels of accountability, both from parliament and from their parties, for the decisions they make. Indeed, on a parliamentary level, although the House of Commons is informed of the negotiating position of ministers before Council of Ministers meetings, it is not able to instruct ministers of what positions they should take. On a party level, the same is true: although national MPs can urge their cabinet members to adopt a certain stance, they cannot do anything to ensure they do. Similarly, when ministers return from Council of Ministers meetings, the House of Commons ESC can only ask for clarifications of the reasons for their voting behaviour; it has no power to apply any sanctions. As for the party, accountability mechanisms are also rather weak, if non-existent. Recalling the time when the party was in office, one senior Conservative politician reported that there were no formal mechanisms with which to hold ministers accountable for decisions reached in the Council of Ministers. Rather all that happened was that ministers occasionally appeared before the backbench foreign affairs or European affairs committees to brief MPs about decisions taken in the Council. In the Labour Party, the situation is similar: ministers do hold briefings for members of their parliamentary party, but there is little MPs can do other than air their opinions.

On the one hand the high autonomy and low accountability of ministers is explained, once again, by the lack of interest most national parliamentarians have in European-level politics. One interviewee reported that, although the foreign secretary does brief the Parliamentary Labour Party on EU-level deliberations, attendance at these meetings is usually very poor. On the other hand, many of the decisions reached in the Council of Ministers are either fairly uncontroversial, or are of a national rather than party political nature. This is reflected in the fact that the bulk of decisions are prepared beforehand by the government's representatives in the committee of permanent representative (COREPER). Party input, and indeed ministerial input, is often limited.

In general, therefore, national party elites do have wide latitude to negotiate in the inter-governmental bargaining that occurs in the European Council and the Council of Ministers. Although this suggests that they have indeed gained power within their national parties at the expense of other actors because of their involvement in the European arena, it is important to note that it is not only this involvement that explains why party elites may have come to dominate their parliamentary parties. Party elites may have become stronger vis-à-vis other parts of their party because of a whole range of other factors, including the weakening of their traditional bases, the pressures of globalization, and the growth in the size and complexity of the state (Poguntke and Webb 2005: 13–17).

Parties and their Europarties

Before drawing any final conclusions, it is worth considering one further EU-level arena in which national party actors participate, namely the Europarty. The Europarty is an institution that provides formalized links between national political parties and EU-level actors, facilitates communication between different EU-level actors, and generally encourages links between like-minded actors at the European level (Hix and Lord 1997: 57). The Labour Party is a member of Party of European Socialists (PES), and the Liberal Democrats are members of the European Liberal Democrat and Reform Party (ELDR). The Conservative Party does not belong to a Europarty. Although it is a member of the EPP–ED Group in the EP, it is not a member of the European People's Party (EPP), even though some members among its ranks have called for it to join.

National party politicians take part in the activities of the Europarties in a variety of ways. Senior national politicians sit on the executive committees, while
other party delegates make up the council, and others still attend the congress.
National party staff may also be engaged in Europarty activities. For example, the
Labour Party's international manager attends meetings of the PES coordination
team, the body that services the presidency of the PES. In addition, national party
leaders (whether in office or in opposition) are involved in the Europarties by
virtue of the fact that they attend party leader meetings, held two or more times
a year.

The suggestion that these national party actors drive power and influence within their national parties as a result of their activities in the Europarties very much
rests on the assumption that the Europarties are able to exercise power, and to all
intents and purposes there is little evidence that they do. Indeed, rather than being
a locus of important decision-making, Europarties are essentially transnational
coordinating mechanisms for like-minded parties that wish to 'upload' policy
ideas and transmit them to other parties. Even the Europarties' most high-profile
forum – the party leaders meetings – only goes as far as issuing resolutions and
recommendations. What decisions are made within the Europarties tend to be
reached by consensus. What is more, decisions are not binding in the sense that
sanctions can be levied against any member party that fails to implement them.

In reflection of this, and also on account of the general lack of interest in European-level politics and the divisive nature of the European issue in Britain, the
national leaderships of both the Labour Party and the Liberal Democrats have
tended to pay little attention to the activities of the Europarties. Even though
Robin Cook, Tony Blair's first foreign secretary, represented the Labour Party in
the PES for much of the 1990s, and then became its president from 2001 to 2004,
the Labour Party has taken little notice of the organization. If anything, it used
Cook's presidency to contain any ambitious organizational development within
the PES. As for national MPs, most are oblivious of the work of the Europarties,
and of the actions of their own representatives within them.

The above discussion therefore suggests that involvement in decision-making
at the supranational level can enable party actors to gain greater influence within
their national parties, and can thus change the balance of power within national
parties, but only if the arena in which they are involved is a locus of powerful
decision-making, and only if the activities of these actors are considered relevant
to national party politics. If the arena makes no binding decisions (as is the case
with the Europarties), or if the actions of party actors have no bearing on domestic
party politics (as is the case for most of the activities of MEPs), then involvement
in supranational politics does not translate into significantly greater power within
national political parties.

Conclusion

This chapter has illustrated that the three main British parties have undertaken
limited structural adaptation in response to growing European integration. Firstly,
they have created very few posts that deal specifically with European matters

and, what is more, of the handful that have been established, some have been created in response to governmental or parliamentary obligations rather than party needs. Secondly, and relatedly, the parties have devoted very limited resources to the management of European issues, and instead continue to rely on the salaries and allowances of their MEPs for this purpose. Thirdly, although some adaptation is evident in that the parties have developed mechanisms to better link their MEPs to their national party leaderships, the extent and impact of this adaptation should not be overestimated. As was argued above, rather than being a means by which MEPs may become more influential within their national parties, the linkage mechanisms in large part reflect the national party leaderships' desire to keep in touch with activities of the EP, and in the case of the governing Labour Party to try to influence policy-making in the EP. Finally, although EP delegation leaders (or other MEPs) do now sit on the national executive committees of their parties, this organizational adjustment does not amount to much, as these individuals have not derived increased influence within their parties in the process. Rather, if they are influential within their parties, it is because of their specific policy expertise or their prior political connections.

In addition to this limited structural change, further evidence that the main British parties have done little to adapt their organizations in response to growing levels of European integration lies in the fact that existing EU specialists have not become more visible or important within their national parties. Indeed, in the course of the above discussion it became clear that nationally based EU specialists command little influence within their parties and thus derive negligible power from their positions. As for MEPs, although they have been integrated into their national parties to some degree, and although they do have some input into their party's manifestos (especially those for EP elections), their integration and involvement does not translate into increased influence or power within their national party organizations.

Turning to the influence and power that party actors derive as a result of their activities at the supranational level, there is more evidence still to suggest that MEPs have not grown in importance and influence within their national parties. Although they may well enjoy high levels of autonomy in their activities in the EP, and although they may not be held accountable for their actions, as was argued above, this room for manoeuvre means little given that their activities are seldom relevant to national party politics. Similarly, there is reason to conclude that party actors involved in the Europarties derive little influence from their activities, since these are often also of limited relevance to national party politics. What is more, most decisions of the Europarties are merely non-binding recommendations anyway.

Crucially, however, the story is rather different when it comes to national party elites who are active at the EU level, be it in the Council of Ministers or in the European Council. Like MEPs, national party elites enjoy high levels of autonomy and low levels of accountability in their activities at the EU level, as they have the room for manoeuvre necessary to conduct negotiations and do not have their hands tied by actors in their national parliament or in their national party. In contrast to MEPs, however, national party elites *are* able to translate their involvement in

EU-level decision-making into greater power within their national parties because the decisions they take, and the deals that they make, are relevant to, and indeed contribute to, national party politics. One may therefore conclude that the 'executive bias' of EU decision-making does much to reinforce and enhance the power of national party elites within their own party organizations.

The question then is: how can the state of affairs just described be explained? Well, in the first instance, as was discussed early on in this chapter, there is a strong incentive for party leaderships to avoid bringing Europe into both inter- and intra-party discussion and debate because of the divisive nature of the issue. As a result, domestic legislation and policy concerns continue to dominate the agendas of the major parties and, in this environment, an expertise in EU affairs does little to enhance an individual's position or influence in his or her party. Secondly, the lack of any significant organizational adaptation on the part of the British parties may also be explained, to some extent, by the parties' finances. Not only are British parties comparatively modestly funded but, given that they do not receive any substantial state funding and that they depend instead on donations and membership dues, their income can fluctuate quite considerably. They must therefore watch their costs and prioritize their expenditures, and in this context it is unlikely that extra resources will be devoted to the management of European issues, especially as little attention is devoted to Europe anyway. Finally, and perhaps most importantly, the lack of adaptation on the part of the parties and the limited involvement of MEPs in the national party are explained by the fact that the party in central office and the parliamentary party are happy to delegate decision-making both on routine policy details involving the EU and on more highly politicized European issues to their executive in office. As Allen explains, British 'national parliamentarians do not seem to be that interested in tackling the detail of EU law at [the proposal] stage preferring instead to rely on the government to act in the Council' (2005: 134). In turn, the party in public office does not count on its supporting party for information on the details of EU policy-making, but relies instead on the civil service, the European secretariat of the Cabinet Office, and the UK's permanent representative to the EU, none of which are answerable to party bodies.

The purposeful lack of attention devoted to European issues, the weakness of the parties' extra-parliamentary organizations, and the low importance national MPs attach to EU policy-making all help explain why the Europeanization of British political parties has been only slight. These reasons also suggest that it is fairly unlikely that the British parties will undertake any further significant organizational adaptation in response to ever greater European integration.

Notes

1 We would like to thank Simon Bulmer, Martin Burch, Jane Green and Paul Webb for providing pieces of information included in this chapter. We are also very grateful to Thomas Poguntke for comments on earlier versions of this chapter.
2 Strictly speaking this chapter is about Great Britain, not the United Kingdom, since developments in the parties of Northern Ireland are not considered.

3 The empirical material on which this chapter is based comes from party statutes and documents (as referenced) and from 20 interviews with party politicians and staff members in the three main British parties. Interviewees included past and present party leaders, party chairs, ministers for Europe, members of the House of Commons European Scrutiny Committee, members of the House of Commons foreign affairs committee, European Parliament delegation leaders, other influential Members of the European Parliament, general secretaries of the European parliamentary delegation, other party staff in the European parliamentary delegation, and international secretaries. Interviews were conducted between spring 2003 and spring 2005.

4 Divisions in the Conservative Party over Europe were further aggravated by the rise of the United Kingdom Independence Party (UKIP), which won three seats (with 7 per cent of the vote) in the 1999 elections to the European Parliament, and 12 seats (with 16.8 per cent of the vote) in the 2004 contest.

5 In Eurobarometer surveys, the percentage of UK respondents who regard membership as a 'good thing' and who believe that the UK has benefited through EU membership has been consistently lower than the EU average. In spring 2004, for example, only 29 per cent of UK respondents considered membership to be a 'good thing' and only 27 per cent believed that the UK had benefited through EU membership, while 59 per cent thought that the country had not benefited as a result of membership (http://europa.eu.int/comm/public_opinion/index_en.htm).

6 The Party Board is made up of 15–20 members including the chairman of the party (i.e. the head of the extra-parliamentary party, who is appointed by the party leader), the chairman of the 1922 Committee (representing the parliamentary party), and the chairman of the National Conservative Convention (who represents the constituency associations). The party leader also attends meetings of the Board. It must meet at least six times a year, although in practice it tends to meet monthly (www.conservatives.com).

7 The NEC comprises about 30 members, including the party leader and the deputy party leader, a number of government ministers, members of the Parliamentary Labour Party and the European Parliamentary Labour Party, representatives of the trades unions, and representatives of the constituency parties (www.labour.org.uk). It meets every two months (Russell 2005: 183).

8 The Federal Executive is made up of about 35 members including the party leader, the party president, the party's chief executive, representatives of the parliamentary party, one MEP, representatives of the state parties, and representatives of local authorities (Liberal Democrats 2004). The Federal Executive carries out its duties by overseeing a number of other committees, including the FPC.

9 In the years prior to and just after accession, responsibility for Europe lay with the Chancellor of the Duchy of Lancaster (who is in effect a cabinet minister without portfolio), who was based first at the FCO and then in the Cabinet Office. From 1974 onwards, however, responsibility for Europe returned to the FCO and a new junior ministerial post was created within it (Bulmer and Burch 1998).

10 The 'step-change' project, launched in 1998, was concerned with shaping the perception of the UK's position on Europe both domestically and abroad. At home this was to be done by disseminating information on the EU, and by campaigning publicly on EU issues. As for the perception of the UK's European policy abroad, ministers and officials were encouraged to forge closer ties with governmental counterparts in other member states and with their counterparts in other centre-left parties to promote the UK's position on Europe and to gain a better understanding of the position of other member states (Bulmer and Burch 2005: 878; Smith 2005: 709).

11 The other two-thirds of the votes are shared equally between constituency Labour parties and affiliated organization members.

12 Each link member has either had membership of the relevant EP committee or at least been a substitute member of the relevant EP committee (see www.eurolabour.org.uk).

13 From 1999 the single-member plurality electoral system based on 84 single-member constituencies was replaced by a proportional representation system based on 11 regions (Northern Ireland continued to elect three MEPs by single transferable vote). In 1999 regions elected between four and eleven MEPs, whereas in 2004, because the total number of British MEPs was reduced from 84 to 75 in the light of EU enlargement, regions elected between three and ten MEPs. Seats are allocated at the regional level using the d'Hondt formula. There is no legal threshold.
14 In contrast to both the Labour Party and the Liberal Democrats, there are no formal mechanisms in the Conservative Party to ensure the representation of women candidates in EP elections.
15 In 1999 there was a 'zipping' of candidates, with a male candidate being followed by a female candidate on the list. In 2004, one of the top three on each list had to be of a different gender (ICPR 2003: 77).

References

Allen, David (2005) 'The United Kingdom: A Europeanized Government in a Non-Europeanized Polity', in Simon Bulmer and Christian Lequesne (eds), *The Member States of the European Union*, Oxford: Oxford University Press, pp. 119–41.

Bulmer, Simon and Martin Burch (1998) 'Organizing for Europe: Whitehall, the British State and European Union', *Public Administration*, 76(4): 601–28.

Bulmer, Simon and Martin Burch (2005) 'The Europeanization of UK Government: From Quiet Revolution to Explicit Step-Change?', *Public Administration*, 83(4): 861–90.

Carter, Caitríona A. (2001) 'The Parliament of the United Kingdom: From Supportive Scrutiny to Unleashed Control', in Andreas Maurer and Wolfgang Wessels (eds), *National Parliaments on their Ways to Europe: Losers or Latecomers?*, Baden-Baden: Nomos, pp. 395–424.

Clarke, Scott and John Curtice (1998) 'The Liberal Democrats and European Integration', in David Baker and David Seawright (eds), *Britain For and Against Europe: British Politics and the Question of European Integration*, Oxford: Clarendon, pp. 88–107.

Garry, John (1995) 'The British Conservative Party: Divisions over European Policy', *West European Politics*, 18(4): 170–89.

Geddes, Andrew (2004) *The European Union and British Politics*, Basingstoke: Palgrave.

Heffernan, Richard and Paul Webb (2005) 'The British Prime Minister: Much More than "First Among Equals"', in Thomas Poguntke and Paul Webb (eds), *The Presidentialization of Politics: A Comparative Study of Modern Democracies*, Oxford: Oxford University Press, pp. 26–62.

Hix, Simon and Christopher Lord (1997) *Political Parties and the European Union*, Basingstoke: Macmillan.

House of Commons (1999a) *European Parliament Elections – 1979 to 1994*, Research Paper 99/57.

House of Commons (1999b) *Elections to the European Parliament – June 1999*, Research Paper 99/64.

House of Commons (2004) *European Parliament Elections 2004*, Research Paper 04/50.

Independent Commission on PR (ICPR) (2003) *Changed Voting Changed Politics: Lessons of Britain's Experience of PR since 1997*, London: The Constitution Unit.

Kelly, Richard (2004) 'The Extra-Parliamentary Tory Party: McKenzie Revisited', *Political Quarterly*, 75(4): 398–404.

Krouwel, André (2004) *All Politics is National, but Policy is Supranational: A Decisive Discrepancy*, Europolity Virtual Conference Paper, www.fes.de/europolity/

McKenzie, Robert T. (1955) *British Political Parties: The Distribution of Power within the Labour and the Conservative Parties*, London: Heinemann.

Messmer, William B. (2003) 'Taming Labour's MEPs', *Party Politics*, 9(2): 201–18.

Norton, Philip (2000) 'The United Kingdom: Exerting Influence from Within', in Knut Heidar and Ruud Koole (eds), *Parliamentary Party Groups in European Democracies: Political Parties Behind Closed Doors*, London: Routledge, pp. 39–56.

Ovey, Joey-David (2002) *Between Nation and Europe: Labour, the SPD and the European Parliament 1994–1999*, Opladen: Leske and Budrich.

Poguntke, Thomas and Paul Webb (2005) 'The Presidentialization of Politics in Democratic Societies: A Framework for Analysis', in Thomas Poguntke and Paul Webb (eds), *The Presidentialization of Politics: A Comparative Study of Modern Democracies*, Oxford: Oxford University Press, pp. 1–25.

Russell, Andrew and Edward Fieldhouse (2005) *Neither Left nor Right? The Liberal Democrats and the Electorate*, Manchester: Manchester University Press.

Russell, Meg (2005) *Building New Labour: The Politics of Party Organisation*, Basingstoke: Palgrave.

Shaw, Eric (1994) *The Labour Party Since 1979: Crisis and Transformation*, London: Routledge.

Smith, Julie (2005) 'A Missed Opportunity? New Labour's European Policy 1997–2005', *International Affairs*, 81(4): 703–21.

Turner, John (2000) *The Tories and Europe*, Manchester: Manchester University Press.

Webb, Paul (1992) 'Election Campaigning, Organisational Transformation and the Professionalisation of the British Labour Party', *European Journal of Political Research*, 21(2): 267:88.

Webb, Paul D. (1994) 'Party Organizational Change in Britain: The Iron Law of Centralization', in Richard S. Katz and Peter Mair (eds), *How Parties Organize: Change and Adaptation in Party Organizations in Western Democracies*, London: Sage, pp. 109–33.

Webb, Paul (2000) *The Modern British Party System*, London: Sage.

4 Continuity amidst political system change

Why French party organization remains immune to EU adaptive pressures

Robert Ladrech

This chapter analyses French political parties in order to detect evidence of organizational change that has resulted from the increased influence of the European Union.[1] The parties considered in this analysis are the *Parti Communiste Français* (French Communist Party, PCF), *Les Verts* (the Greens), the *Parti Socialiste* (Socialist Party, PS), the *Union pour la Démocratie Française* (Union for French Democracy, UDF) and the *Union pour un Mouvement Populaire* (Union for a Popular Movement, UMP), which incorporates the former *Rassemblement pour la République* (Rally for the Republic, RPR).[2]

In order to evaluate whether or not European integration dynamics have engendered organizational change in French political parties, it is necessary to first understand the extent to which the wider political system has adjusted to being a member state of the European Union (EU). National institutional adaptation, or Europeanization, is stimulated more often than not by legal commitments and adjustment of domestic policy-making practices to better process EU legislation and in turn to influence Brussels. Political parties are to a large extent goal-seeking (i.e. office, votes, policy), and incentives to adapt their structures or behaviour that emanate from Brussels, and/or significant changes in their domestic operating environment, may account for change (see Chapter 1). It is clear that national political parties do not derive significant resources directly from EU institutions that in any way account for domestic office-seeking or policy-influencing advantages. Therefore, the most likely cause for change in political party organization – if it has occurred – must be a consequence of institutional change in the national political system, their primary operating environment, now transformed by the growth in the influence of the EU. A brief background description of the EU and the French Fifth Republic will suffice before focusing discussion on change inside French parties. Attention is drawn, in particular, to the points at which parties operate in the Europeanized architecture of the national state.

France and Europe

Historical and institutional background

Since France was a founding member state of the European Economic Community (EEC), successive French governments have paid particular attention to the policy and institutional evolution of what has now become the EU. French governments have been critical to the development of the EU, playing 'a central role in determining the direction, scope and shape of the integration process' (Kassim 1997: 171). Together with (West) Germany, often referred to as the Franco-German tandem (Cole 2001), French governments have been actively involved in setting agendas leading to further EU advances (or even setbacks, as in the 2005 EU constitution referendum). In the 1960s, President de Gaulle's European policy towards the EEC emphasized the primacy of the nation state vis-à-vis supranational institutions. His actions that resulted in the Luxembourg Compromise effectively secured a national veto within the Council of Ministers, thereby placing a check upon Commission ambitions and shaping the nature of EU decision-making as well as that of successive French governments until the late 1980s.

Coinciding with the development of the EEC in the 1960s was the institutionalization of the new Fifth Republic. The important change in terms of regime structure from the Fourth to the Fifth was the creation of a strong executive led by a directly elected president, and a weakened parliament vis-à-vis the executive. As the Fifth Republic's first president, de Gaulle included reshaping Europe in his project for France, and foreign policy, including European policy, was considered to be a *domaine reservé* of the president. Until 1986, the line or direction of governmental power and influence was clear: a parliamentary majority supported the government, led by a prime minister appointed by and accountable to the president. Foreign policy, including attention to the European integration process, continued to be a special interest of the president. In 1986 and again in 1993 (for two years on each occasion), and again in 1997 (for five years), a type of power-sharing, dubbed cohabitation, occurred, represented by a partisan disjuncture between the majority in parliament and the president. During periods of cohabitation, the prime minister, though still technically appointed by the president, now represented the parliamentary majority, and consequently enhanced the prime minister's policy agenda influence and independence from the president. As more domestic policy areas became intertwined with EU competences by the 1990s, the prime minister became much more engaged in EU affairs.

As regards the machinery of government in the area of EU matters, the president dominates the more public engagements such as EU summits, though throughout the 1990s the EU impact on an increased number of domestic issues strengthened the weight of the prime minister in daily or routine decision-making. The executive coordinates EU administrative matters between the various ministries through the General Secretariat of the Inter-ministerial Committee for Questions Relating to European Economic Cooperation (French acronym: SGCI), under the direct authority of the prime minister. The SGCI also has responsibility for liaising with relevant parliamentary groups – national and European – as well as with the French permanent representation in Brussels. In 2005, the prime minister announced the creation of a new inter-ministerial committee on Europe in addition to the SGCI, ostensibly to focus more on the policy and political ramifications of EU matters in response to a public perception of a loss of influence by Paris to Brussels. Larger political issues and treaty negotiations include the president, and the two heads of the executive keep in communication on critical EU issues, though this may be more problematic during periods of cohabitation. A minister for Europe, placed within the foreign ministry, is involved in this coordination, although the specific duties of this position have fluctuated in importance since the late 1980s (see below).

As noted above, the parliament, the Senate and the National Assembly, is much weaker in the Fifth Republic's 'semi-presidential' regime (*inter alia*, Elgie 1999). Although a 1992 constitutional amendment – Art. 88-4 – had as its intent to bring the National Assembly more fully into the sphere of deliberating EU matters, in particular through its National Delegation for the European Union (the French equivalent of a European affairs committee), in practice the Assembly remains dependent on information from the executive and has virtually no power to hold the executive accountable (Rozenberg 2004). It has even been suggested that information on government EU policy and negotiating positions is better gleaned through personal specialist networks than formally through the prime minister (Szukala and Rozenberg 2001). The dynamics of government and opposition ensure party discipline and therefore party support for the government, so that legislating on EU matters is practically never a cause for concern for the government. Additionally, French governments are able, constitutionally, to avoid parliamentary debate on delicate issues by invoking Art. 49-3, which allows the government to make one of its own bills an issue of confidence (Elgie 1993).

French parties and the EU

It would be fair to state that the EU has been more a source of conflict within the main parties of government than between them. That being said, the conflict is not about staying in or pulling out of the EU as it is in some quarters in Britain; rather it is about what type of EU would be best for France. Consequently, broadly put, it is a debate between those who believe in maintaining nation state control of the EU, and thereby constraining the development of the European Parliament (EP) and the Commission, and those for whom some degree of federalism ought to be part of the 'finality' of the European integration process. It has, therefore, not been a right versus left issue in France for most of the period under study. In the event of referendums on EU matters, for example on the Maastricht treaty in 1992 or the constitutional treaty in 2005, this conflict is expressed most clearly in the breakdown of party unity (see Aylott 2002 for a discussion of national referendums and party unity over Europe). On the other hand, based upon evidence from the 2005 referendum on the EU Constitution, Ivaldi (2006) suggests that the EU issue is becoming integrated into left versus right competition in France, and perhaps in future domestic electoral contests we may see more widespread evidence of this. The main party on the right, the UMP (consisting of the former RPR, the neo-liberal wing of the UDF, *Démocratie Libérale*, and a majority of the UDF), and on the left, the Socialist Party, have experienced the greatest internal debate, though until recently it has been more pronounced on the right (Shields 1996). The other parties, the PCF, the Greens and what remains of the centre-right UDF, have been fairly consistent in their orientation towards European integration. The

Communists have been wary of the market liberalizing policies of the EU, while the Greens and the UDF have been supportive of supranational developments.

Elections to the EP have also served as an outlet for intra-party tensions over the direction of European integration. Conflict within the Socialist Party over the Maastricht treaty referendum led to the departure of a government minister, Jean-Pierre Chevènement, who went on to form his own party, the *Mouvement des Citoyens* (Movement of Citizens), dedicated to defending French sovereignty. The 1994 European elections produced a centre-left list that attracted some socialist voters, enough to produce the worst election result for the Socialists and prompting the resignation of the party leader (see Table 4.1). On the right, sovereigntists within the RPR and UDF left to form their own party, *Rassemblement pour la France* (Rally for France), which contested the 1994 and 1999 European elections. The institutional context of European elections, although second-order, can therefore provide opportunities for intra-party conflict that have the potential to produce change in both the French national party system as well as the French component of the European party system (Evans 2003; Mair 2000).

Finally, before we turn to analysing French parties for evidence of organizational change, it is necessary to understand the general structural attributes of French parties. Knapp succinctly summarizes the state of French party organization: the 'salient point about French parties . . . is that aside from the pre-1980s PCF, they have tended to organisational weakness' (2004: 21). Relatively low levels of party membership (apart from the PCF), a tendency for party splits (especially on the right), an organizational profile reflecting a cadre party model (also on the right), an emphasis on personality due to competition for presidential candidacies, etc., all combine to suggest that '[p]olitical parties do not find a natural breeding ground in France' (Cole 2003: 11).

It is relevant for the discussion below to note that the balance of influence between the parliamentary and extra-parliamentary wings of French parties leans in the direction of the extra-parliamentary party (Thiébault and Dolez 2000). This fact may not be too surprising given the weakness of the parliament in relation to the executive. The Communist and Socialist Parties' organizational structures resemble classic party models of their respective party families, though in the case of the Socialists it is much less of a mass party than its continental cousins. On the right, the Gaullist party has gone through several name changes and rebirths since the founding of the Fifth Republic in 1958. Although the UDF (the main non-Gaullist moderate right party since 1978) is more clearly so, the RPR (UMP since 2002) has resembled a cadre party in the sense of Duverger. The UMP declared its goal to strengthen its organization as part of a self-declared 'modernization' of centre-right politics, aiming to build a more membership-based party. The UDF, was in reality of confederation of smaller parties, essentially Christian democratic and liberal, organized in order to contest national elections together and thereby magnify its weight in electoral politics (and balance the strength of the Gaullists). Since 1998, with the departure of the liberal party component to form the UMP along with the RPR, the UDF is now a much smaller but unified party.

Table 4.1 Elections to the European Parliament in France: votes, seats and turnout, 1979–2004

	1979		1984		1989		1994		1999		2004	
	%	Seats	%	Seats	%	Seats	%	Seats	%	Seats	%	Seats
PCF	20.5	19	11.2	10	7.7	7	6.9	7	6.8	6	5.3	3
Les Verts	4.4	0	3.4	0	10.6	9	5.0ª	0	9.7	9	7.4	6
PS	23.5	22	20.7	20	23.6	22	14.5	15	22.0	22	28.9	31
RPR/UMP	16.3	15							12.8	12	16.6	17
UDF	27.6	25							9.3	9	12.0	11
RPR+UDF			43.0	41	28.6	26	25.6	28				
Others	7.7	0	21.7	10	29.5	17	48.0	37	39.4	29	29.8	10
Turnout/total seats	60.7	81	56.7	81	48.7	81	52.7	87	46.8	87	43.1	78

Sources: France Politique: http://francepolitique.free.fr/frElections.htm; European Parliament: http://www.elections2004.eu.int/ep-election/sites/en/results1306/turnout_ep/turnout_table.html

Notes

a Two ecology parties, Les Verts 3 per cent and Génération Ecologie 2 per cent

For the 1984, 1989 and 1994 elections, the RPR and UDF ran together in an electoral alliance.

The RPR became the UMP in 2002.

'Others' includes parties and protest movements. 'Others' that won seats: 1984 *Front National* (FN) won ten seats with 11.0 per cent of the vote; 1989: FN won ten seats with 11.7 per cent of the vote; a separate UDF list (entitled *Le Centre pour l'Europe*) headed by Simone Veil won seven seats with 8.4 per cent of the vote; 1994: a list headed by Philippe de Villiers (entitled *Majorité pour l'Autre Europe*) won 13 seats with 12.3 per cent of the vote; a left-wing list – *Mouvement des Radicaux de Gauche* (MRG) – headed by Bernard Tapie won 13 seats with 12.0 per cent of the vote; the *Chasse, Pêche, Nature, Traditions* list won six seats with 6.8 per cent of the vote; 1999: the *Rassemblement pour la France* (RPF) won five seats with 5.7 per cent of the vote; and the *Lutte Ouvrière et Ligue Communiste Révolutionnaire* won five seats with 5.2 per cent of the vote; 2004: the FN won seven seats with 9.8 per cent of the vote; and the *Mouvement pour la France* (successor to the RPF) won three seats with 6.7 per cent of the vote.

Another feature of French parties, one that also contributes to the continuing cadre-party model characteristics, is holding multiple offices. It is common for French politicians to be an MP *and* a mayor, or an MP and a Member of the European Parliament (MEP), etc. In some cases, party organization statutes specify that a proportion of the membership of their party councils must be made up of the party's holders of local public office. The fact that a politician may have more than one political base contributes to the relative weakness of the central party office, as more options exist for elected office outside direct party candidate selection. With the parties on the right especially, local party 'barons' have enormous influence on the upper echelons of the party (Hanley 2002).

Finally, and especially important for this study of organizational change and the prevalence of EU specialists (see Chapter 1), the extra-parliamentary wings of French parties have functionaries who are generally referred to as national secretaries. They are divided into thematic and functional responsibilities, and in most cases are elected by the parties' mid-level leadership bodies or congresses. In the case of the two biggest parties, the PS and UMP, the individuals occupying these posts are themselves elected politicians, whether in local, national or European arenas. If the prominence of the EU is reflected in new or more powerful posts within parties directly related to EU issues, then we may expect to see this represented in the position of national secretary.

Parties do play important roles in the French political system, providing the basis of governmental stability. But, given the relative power of the executive, parties – whether the parliamentary group or extra-parliamentary party – are marginal to the detail of policy-making. To give further proof of this situation, one has only to note that MPs are required to give up their parliamentary seats if taking up a ministerial position, and also that a not insignificant minority of cabinet ministers are not even party politicians. Consequently, when we turn our attention to the possible impact of European integration on French political parties, their distance from the central levers of national governance would lead us to expect that, although French political institutions may have adapted structures and activities to the logic of EU policy and decision-making, French parties' organization are likely to have remained basically unaffected.

Structural adaptation to European integration

One of this volume's main hypotheses suggests that, in response to the growth in importance of the EU in domestic policy-making and politics, parties may have created more EU-specific positions, whose holders we have labelled EU specialists. We also assume an increase in resources for EU specialists. These EU-related positions are identified below.

Formal management and funding of Europe-related activities

The international secretariat of the PS is a substantial section of the party organization, second only to that of the party leader. This, according to one senior informant, is a legacy of Mitterrand's restructuring of the party in the 1970s. The national secretary for international relations acts in general as the party's foreign representative, representing the party in venues abroad. The national secretary for international relations is usually an elected politician, though his or her prominence has fluctuated over the past 10 to 20 years. The responsibilities of this position include maintaining relations with other sister parties, including the Party of European Socialists (PES), representing the party to the media on current international issues, etc., and in regards to European Union matters, this person is assisted by a full-time staff member who is specifically charged with organizing the detail of the party's EU affairs. In practice, this individual prepares the EU briefs for the national secretary for international relations as events dictate, and acts as a liaison between the PS delegation in the EP and the national party organization. This particular post is appointed, but after interviews of prospective candidates. The selection of this individual has not been related to the relative weight of the party's internal factions. In the post-Mitterrand leadership era of the PS (i.e. since 1995), and in particular under the party leadership of Hollande (1997 to the present), the political visibility of the national secretary for international relations has risen, especially with the return to opposition in 2002. (From 2002 onwards this post has been occupied by the former minister for European affairs.) Opposition status for the PS means that the national secretary for international relations is also the party's senior policy advisor on EU matters (whereas in government this responsibility would be less significant). In the period after the 2004 EP elections, the national secretary for international relations was joined by a spokesperson on specifically European affairs, referred to as the national secretary for Europe. This person was a member of the party's EP delegation, though not the delegation leader.

The RPR handled international relations with a division between a staff international relations director, based in the party's secretariat, and a national secretary for international relations, usually an elected politician. For the most part, European affairs were absent from the brief of the national secretary, as the party leader and/or president held the reins of decision-making. With the formation of the UMP in 2002, the international relations secretariat was divided between international relations and Europe. A national secretary for European issues was also elected. The staff director essentially coordinates the activities of UMP individuals in the Commission, the EP and the National Assembly. The national secretary for Europe, an MEP, however, is dependent upon EP resources in order to discharge duties for the national party. This person is essentially an expert advisor. A new UMP leader elected in 2004, Nicolas Sarkozy, set about restructuring the party organization – especially in terms of personnel. As part of this re-design, the European and international relations secretariat were briefly abolished, and then revived in late 2005 with a director combining Europe and international relations again.

The UDF does not have a national secretary for international relations, as the party leader, Mr Bayrou, holds the international and specifically European affairs portfolios himself. The party provides an individual staff member to coordinate and liaise with the party's EP delegation and national actors. As the UDF has in the past ten years lost a substantial proportion of its votes, financial resources have become critical, and the party is not capable of maintaining a separate department for international affairs. In fact, the senior advisor on EU affairs – especially relating to constitutional issues – is an MEP, and informal communication between this individual and the party leader is frequent. In 2004, Mr Bayrou instructed the UDF EP delegation to leave the European People's Party and European Democrats (EPP–ED) group and join with the smaller renamed Liberal group, the Alliance of Liberal and Democrats for Europe (ALDE). According to an interviewee, membership of the smaller group (and affiliated transnational party federation, the European Liberal and Democratic Reform party, ELDR), translates into a proportionally greater voice, and perhaps resources, for the UDF.

The Greens have had an international relations spokesperson, and European matters were part of the portfolio. This individual was the party's representative to the European Federation of Green Parties (EFGP). In January 2005, after elections for a new executive committee, the party created a separate position of spokesperson on European matters. Responsibilities include acting as the party's representative to the newly created European Green Party.

The PCF has long had a national secretary for international relations, and in the pre-1989 period relations with the Soviet Union and other national Communist Parties were high on the list of responsibilities of this position (although the party leader maintained high-level and more intimate relations with Moscow). The party formally organizes its activities or thematic areas according to commissions of the National Council, and it is here that a commission named 'World, Europe, Globalization' is located. This should be considered more of a working group, with a chair, than an executive branch of the party organization. As for the Executive College of the party (i.e. the national executive), it is divided into four sectors, each dealing with many specific themes. The smallest sector is 'Europe and the World', comprising 'Europe: Battle of the Party for another European Construction' and 'International Relations'. The individuals responsible for these areas act as national spokespersons for the party.

What is apparent is that French parties have devoted some organizational resources and posts to matters involving the EU. First, liaising with their elected members in the EP has usually been a responsibility of a member of staff. Second, the parties have spokespeople for a variety of thematic areas, and a national secretary for international relations appears in all parties but the UDF (in which the party leader exercises that responsibility). All parties have created a more specific responsibility for representing the party's position on Europe, but only in the PS and the UMP has this been reflected in a position of national secretary. In the PS, the greater attention given to European matters as represented in positions may be linked to the long-standing prominence of the international secretariat. In the end, though, the number of these positions is roughly one per party, not enough to warrant serious organizational change.

The leader of a party's delegation to the EP is a figure that may wield more influence with the growing prominence of the EU. The delegation leader of the PS is elected by MEPs. The weighting of factional influence does not play a part in the election of the delegation leader. The delegation leader does sit on the party's national executive (political bureau), but this is not a statutory right. Rather, this person is voted onto the national executive. Yet a delegation leader has never failed in this vote. Over the past ten years, a couple of MEPs have sat on the national executive along with the delegation leader, mostly because they were well-known personalities in the party. However, since 2002 the national executive has included five MEPs, suggesting the rising profile of EU issues in the party (or higher status of MEPs in the party). This fact should be kept in perspective, however, as there are approximately 50–55 members of the national executive.

The background of MEPs is covered in more depth below in the section on MEP candidate selection. Suffice it to say that, since the mid-1980s, RPR lists to the EP have been assembled in negotiation with the RPR's coalition partner, the UDF. From 1994 to 2004, the RPR–UDF group held a dual delegation leadership (the RPR joined the EP EPP–ED group, alongside the UDF). Delegation leaders are elected by their respective, fellow MEPs, although the party leadership will have signalled its preference. However, in the 1984, 1989, 1994 and 1999 EP elections, the first name on the RPR list was the party president, even though upon election the person was replaced by their *suppléant* (or stand-in; a practice shared with other French parties). In the UMP, created in 2002, the delegation leader is now a statutory member of the party's national council.

The UDF delegation elects its leader, the choice and preference of the party leader being crucial in this respect. The delegation leader sits on the party's executive committee, but all of the MEPs have statutory membership on mid-level executive bodies in the party. The central role of the UDF party leader since the departure of the liberal component to the UMP means that personal networks are more important than formal positions in terms of influence.

The Greens do not have a delegation leader per se. The size of the delegation has been so small – six as of 2004 – as to obviate the need for a formal leader in any case. The party's executive committee also follows a non-hierarchical structure, and its members, including the national secretary, are elected by the party's congress. However, prominent elected individuals, including those who have stood for president in the past, have been MEPs (e.g. Dominique Voynet, who was also environment minister in the Jospin government).

The Communist Party does not have a delegation leader, and its delegation, like the Greens, is small enough to dispense with such a structure. However, a French Communist is the president of the EP parliamentary group to which the Communist delegation belongs, the European United Left/Nordic Green Left (GUE/NGL). Consequently, this individual reports on EP matters as they impact Communist Party concerns.

In sum, therefore, the delegation leader has a position that varies in its statutory position in national leadership bodies. We have also seen that prominent MEPs may in reality be the main source of policy advice to the national party leadership rather than or in addition to the delegation leader (this is the case in all parties except the PCF).

Although not a party position per se, the position of minister for Europe has been filled most of the time by a party actor (see below). This position has grown in stature in the French governmental system, although with occasional lapses. Originally an advisory post in the presidential office, it became a junior foreign ministry position involved in the coordination of European policy with the main government ministries. In the period from the early 1990s until 2002, the appointment of this individual involved negotiation between the president and the prime minister, as cohabitation occurred between 1993 and 1995 and again between 1997 and 2002. The PS occupant of this position between 1997 and 2002 was a member of the party elite (from the younger generation). Reporting to parliament or the party was generally absent. The party had no mechanism to affect his actions, as he took instruction from government leaders. Nevertheless, as a member of the PS national executive, he could answer questions on broad topics such as the single currency, but party policy on European matters was understood to be a preserve of the PS prime minister during this period. During the cohabitation of 1993 to 1995, the post of minister for Europe was occupied by a member of the UDF, as part of the coalition agreement between the RPR and UDF. From 1995 to 1999, a member of the RPR, Michel Barnier, a confidant of the newly elected president, Jacques Chirac, held the post, acting also as the chief negotiator during the 1996–97 intergovernmental conference (IGC). Barnier then went on to become a European Commissioner and, after the 2002 national elections, left this post to become French foreign minister. His trajectory is marked by proximity to the president. After 2002 and the re-election of Chirac and his now renamed party the UMP in the parliamentary elections, the role of the minister for Europe in French policy-making was downgraded, no doubt to the advantage of the foreign minister. It was in fact occupied by a non-partisan individual, whose background was not in EU affairs. After the defeat of the EU constitution referendum in May 2005, a close associate of Chirac, who was secretary of the presidential office, became Europe minister. Selection of the post-holder is evidently not dictated by the parties.

The position of chair of the National Assembly's European affairs committee may also be considered an EU specialist position, although it does not translate into any particular statutory position on national party bodies. The European affairs committee (there is also one in the Senate) is not a full standing committee, and its powers are limited. However, after constitutional changes in line with the Maastricht and Amsterdam treaties, the delegation has increased its visibility somewhat, as the government is now obliged to send to the parliament all propositions it has received from the European Commission. The delegation is to evaluate the significance of this material and propose any resolutions to be debated. Since 2002 the chair of the National Assembly delegation has held the position of UMP national secretary for European affairs as well as the UMP representative to the transnational party the European People's Party (EPP). He was replaced in his party organization post in 2005.

In addition to having specific EU specialist positions, all of the parties under study have also created working groups on European issues at one time or another.

These are usually determined by the party leadership and approved at a party congress or next higher level of decision-making. They are subject to budgetary approval, so they usually have a specified shelf life. In some parties, such as the Greens, non-members may also participate in their deliberations. Reports are the usual output of such working groups, and their recommendations are not binding.

French parties receive state funding depending on prior election results. In addition, the parliamentary groups in the National Assembly and Senate receive resources depending on their size. As noted above, the PS international secretariat is relatively well resourced. The international secretariat in the RPR has not been as relatively well resourced as the PS, owing in part to both government involvement and party leader control of EU policy. The smaller parties are more dependent on additional financial resources because of their size. The Communists, more than any other French party, continue to receive a noticeable amount of funding from party members, though this has been in decline as membership has shrunk over the past ten years. Elected Communist politicians also contribute their salary to the party, which then determines their individual annual financial support. Additionally, resources are also available to parties through institutional sources such as personal MP budgets and parliamentary group staff and supplies. In this respect the Greens suffer most, as they have been too small (since they first entered the National Assembly in 1997) to constitute a formal parliamentary group. The Greens are therefore, again more than the other parties, dependent upon their MEPs to engage in activities – conferences, etc. – that benefit the party as a whole. After the 2004 European elections, the Greens created an office which they defined as an 'autonomous structure of interface' between their MEPs and the national party, the goal being facilitating the exchange of knowledge and views in both directions. It is financed by the Green MEPs (six as of the 2004 elections), and located in the EP representation headquarters in Paris. In reality, it is routine for MEPs' assistants to be engaged in party activities, an activity that is crucial for smaller parties. The larger parties also devote some financial resources to a range of publications, some of which will at times cover European issues, though not exclusively. The major parties also hold specific 'Europe' conferences, usually as part of the process of drafting a new party programme. In these circumstances, the logistical help of MEPs is part of the planning. In sum, it is the main parties, the PS and the UMP, that have sufficient funds for Europe-related activities, and the minor parties that find EU funding much more crucial.

In the end, apart from a slightly heightened visibility of national secretaries for Europe (and this visibility derives from the nature of events, not anything inherent in the position itself), the overall extent of change in terms of structures that have been created to deal with Europe has been modest.

MEP candidate selection procedures

Until the 2004 EP elections, the electoral system for EP elections in France was proportional representation, based upon a national list (this shifted to regional lists for the 2004 election). In the PS, selection of candidates and their place on the list was negotiated between the party leadership and the factions, or *courants*. The first dozen places were usually assured of election. Additionally, from 1984 to the 1994 EP elections, party leaders headed the list, it being understood that upon election their 'second' would take their place. Negotiation regarding position on the list was also the case for the RPR but, rather than a priority amongst RPR personnel, it was in negotiation with the party's coalition partner, the UDF. In the 1989 and 1994 EP elections, the RPR allowed the UDF to have most of the top positions, for reasons of domestic coalition politics. The RPR/UMP list has also included non-party individuals, or representatives from what was dubbed 'civil society'. The RPR delegation leader since 1999 is one of these individuals. The UDF, having shrunk since 1999 when component parties left it, and having become even smaller since 2002 as many of its elected politicians left to join the new UMP, is a more unified, if compact, party organization, and the leader takes a special interest in EU matters, to the degree of influencing MEP selection (Mr Bayrou, the party leader, is also a former MEP). Candidate selection for the Greens takes place officially at a party national general assembly, the different sensibilities of the party therefore having to strike compromises as to candidacies. The Communist party has since the mid-1990s – i.e. after a leadership succession – opened up the party list to non-party members, or 'personalities from civil society', as a strategy to engage independent left-wing activists and rebuild its domestic political fortunes (Bell 2003). A council is set up by the national leadership to determine candidacies and places on a list. In all of these cases except the Greens, the parties' central leadership is in control of the selection and positioning of candidates on party lists. The nomination of names is a combination of co-optation and local/regional proposals. Apart from the shift away from a national list to eight regional lists for the 2004 EP elections, and the subsequent complexities this introduced, one cannot say that candidate selection procedures have been affected by the growing influence of the EU.

Acting nationally

Having considered structural change in French parties, we can now turn to the question of how EU specialists may have influenced some of the classic functions of parties such as manifesto formulation, policy development, etc.

For the PS, manifesto formulation, both national and European, is controlled by the party leadership, which constructs a final document from the contributions of the various factions. MEPs sitting on the national executive make political contributions early in the drafting process. As the document is finally a compromise, the degree of detail is usually left at a fairly general level as regards strictly European initiatives. The national secretary for international relations – depending on interest – and specific European advisors are key members in the final drafting, again subject to approval by the party leader. Where a domestic policy is heavily influenced by EU legislation, for example directives affecting public services, MEPs with expertise in the issue are involved in the drafting of the manifesto for national elections as well as for the European elections. The RPR has followed pretty much the example set by the PS, only the national secretary for international relations has been a much more modest position, and thus not an independent contributor in terms of manifesto items. Since 2002, the UMP national secretary for Europe has played a more critical role in manifesto formulation, owing to his expertise and experience in EU matters. In the UDF, the party leader, in consultation with EU specialists, especially certain MEPs, has the final word on manifestos. The Greens' manifesto is subject to a wide assortment of contributions, but the EU component of national and European manifestos is heavily influenced by MEPs. Finally, the Communist party's references to EU matters in national and European manifestos are brief and very general. They more elaborate for party programmes but still contain very little actual proposal details.

In all of these cases, parties in government have policy advisors who also contribute to manifesto formulation by virtue of their expertise and closeness to relevant ministers. Additionally, presidential election manifestos are often drafted independently of the party, despite the fact that the presidential candidate is a candidate of a party. It is nevertheless a fact that as the EU has loomed larger in French domestic politics, EU specialists such as key MEPs have become more integrated into the manifesto formulation process.

As regards European policy formulation of major political institutional issues, when the party is in government, this is the responsibility of experts within the president and prime minister's office. In opposition, those individuals who were Europe minister continue to wield influence in the area of EU issues, but it should be remembered that they were part of the party elite/leadership in the first place. The Greens and the Communist Party have never held more than a few ministries when acting as a junior coalition partner, though some of these portfolios were very much EU-related: transport (PCF) and environment (Greens). In general, government policy-making that involves the EU – especially in respect of 'low politics' issues – is heavily reliant on experts located in ministries as well as the French Permanent Representatives in Brussels. As the government is composed of individuals not occupying a parliamentary seat, there is no direct connection between the parliamentary party and its government in the policy formulation stage. This is not to say that the prime minister may not 'sound out' his or her parliamentary party in order to maintain positive relations. Nonetheless, parties, both the parliamentary and extra-parliamentary wings, are supportive of their government as government–opposition dynamics demand.

Acting supranationally

What is the influence on national party internal dynamics of those who act at the European level? In other words, do expertise and participation in European level arenas endow those actors with added influence in national party power rivalries and other activities? In this section, the focus is upon those party actors involved in the EP, the Council of Ministers and the European Council, and Europarty activities.

Parties and their MEPs

We hypothesize that, because of the growing significance of the EU in domestic policy-making, specialists in EU matters such as MEPs may have greater power within their respective national parties. Evidence for this would lie in high autonomy and low levels of accountability. The first point to note is that the influence of French party delegations in the EP has not been equal to their overall number, thanks to the multiplicity of different groups brought about by splits in the major domestic parties at EP elections. The number of national parliamentary parties between 1994 and 2004 was five, that is, the PCF, the Greens, the PS, the UDF and the RPR/UMP. However, there were almost double this number in the two European Parliaments elected during this time. Naturally, the use of proportional representation facilitated the ability of smaller groups to get elected. Spread out in this manner in the EP, a large member state such as France has wielded less influence within the EP than it might have been able to do (Bertoncini and Chopin 2004). On the eve of the 2004 European election, President Chirac – fearing a loss of French influence in Brussels – went so far as to publicly urge the soon-to-be-elected MEPs to consolidate their presence in as few EP groups as possible, in order to concentrate French influence in EP decision-making. This indirect acknowledgement of insufficient French influence itself suggests that EP participation does not confer any notable domestic influence, as the EP has not been perceived as instrumental for French interests.

National politicians pay little attention to the activities of the national delegations of the major parties in the EP. This is for a number of reasons. First, there is a long-standing French preference for intergovernmental action at the European level, so the EP has never attained much of a profile in France, for either the public or politicians. Second, in the Fifth Republic, the national parliament has been demoted to the advantage of the executive. This has caused something of a heightened sense of national parliamentary primacy vis-à-vis the EP, which many MPs, notably in the RPR, regard as an unwelcome competitor for legitimacy. This has been the case especially during IGC negotiations when the EP has argued for more power, as in the Maastricht and Amsterdam treaties. The PS delegation is nominally under national party discipline, the MEPs normally do not veer away from high priority national interests, such as agriculture (and reform of the Common Agricultural Policy). The same is true for the RPR.

Although a number of French MEPs have attained high-level positions in the EP since the beginning of the 1990s, this has not translated into added power within their national party. Examples of such positions would be the Socialist Group president from 1989 to 1994, and the chair of the EP Committee on Economic and Monetary Union in the 2004 EP. Also in the 2004 EP, the former PS Europe minister was elected a vice-president of the EP, and another MEP became spokesperson for the Socialist Group on economic issues as well as national secretary for Europe. The RPR has been virtually invisible in the EP's leadership positions. The fact that the RPR delegation leader is not a party politician denotes how little value this position carries in the domestic party.

French MEPs, then, have not wielded power in their national parties. Despite individual high standing in the EP itself, this prominence does nothing to enhance their position within their national party organization. Autonomy has been high mostly because their activities in the EP have been considered marginal, thanks to the long-standing French emphasis on intergovernmental action. We could go so far as to say that the activities of MEPs have been ignored, at least among the party membership and mid-level leadership bodies. Mechanisms to make MEPs accountable to their parties are also undeveloped, as nominal party discipline, combined with only infrequent reports of activities, means national parties have not considered MEPs' activities relevant to their main goals.

Parties and their ministers

Following the French tradition favouring intergovernmental European tactics, the Council of Ministers (for more routine matters) and the European Council (for more critical or strategic matters) have been the preferred EU institutions for focusing French political energies. Bearing in mind the weak position of the National Assembly in the Fifth Republic, it should not be a surprise to report a high degree of autonomy for government ministers from both parliament and their respective parties. This applies to all parties of government (including the Greens in regards to their occupancy of the environment ministry in the Jospin government). As deliberations in the Council of Ministers are not transparent and open, domestic audiences, whether MPs or other party actors, are completely dependent on whatever information about negotiations the minister in question wishes to divulge. It is more accurate to state that participation in Council of Ministers and European Council meetings has an institutional effect – adding to executive autonomy from parliamentary scrutiny – than to argue that it increases the standing of any individual minister. As ministers do not belong to a parliamentary party, there is no institutional obligation to report to such a parliamentary party. Furthermore, according to one senior Green party source, extra-parliamentary party members are not interested in the detail of what has occurred in Council of Ministers meetings, and so only general reports at long intervals are submitted to the party.

As for European Council summits and the occasional IGC, the key actors are the president and, during periods of cohabitation, the prime minister. They are assisted in the planning and coordination with other government ministries by the Europe minister, but the nature of summits and IGC negotiations, that is, high politics, excludes parties in the development of bargaining positions. The prime minister will afterwards report to the National Assembly as a whole, with no further reporting to a solely parliamentary party audience.

Parties and their Europarties

Membership in a Europarty obliges the member national party to maintain an ongoing liaison with the secretariat of the Europarty. In most cases, the Europarties routinely communicate with a party's national secretary for international relations, or another individual for whom EU affairs is part of his or her brief. This means that maintaining relations with the Europarty is a secondary responsibility, for none of the French parties has an individual whose role is devoted exclusively to maintaining linkage with a Europarty.

The PS belongs to the PES. The PS has articulated a doctrinal support for the PES for a number of years, represented in manifestos both European and national. According to one senior PS informant, the party, or at least its potential role in stimulating Europe-wide social democratic action, has an almost 'mythic' place in the collective PS mind. The PS supplied a secretary-general for the PES from 1997 to 1999, and again beginning in 2004. Jacques Delors, as Commission president, gave active support to the PES, taking part in some of its congresses. Along with other party leaders, the PS has taken part in PES party leaders' summits. In 2004, the PS shifted strategy, and became an active supporter in reforming the PES. In this respect, it gave crucial support to the former Danish prime minister, Poul Nyrup Rasmussen, as president of the PES, in the first competitive election for this position. The former Europe minister Pierre Moscovici also chaired a PES working group on organizational change, seeking to make the PES more relevant to national member parties.

The RPR, although joining the EPP–ED group in the EP in 1999 as an affiliated member, did not join the transnational EPP party. It did so only – as the UMP – in 2002. Apart from the fact that one of the EPP's vice-presidents is the UMP chair of the National Assembly delegation for the EU, there is not much evidence of interaction with this Europarty, especially as former UDF members were, from the early 1990s, the sole French conservative representatives in the EPP. Component parties of the UDF were in two different EP groups and parties in 1979. The *Centre des Démocrates Sociaux* (Christian Democratic Party, CDS) was a member of the EPP party and group, and the liberal and republican parties were members of the liberal EP group and Europarty, the ELDR. During the 1989–94 EP legislature, all of the UDF components placed themselves in the EPP–ED group and the EPP. The UDF then left the EPP–ED group and the EPP to join a new Liberal group and party in 2006, the ALDE. Both of these moves were directed by the party leader, so we cannot say that the actions actually enhanced the leader's position within the national party, as both EP group and Europarty activities are, as in all parties, far removed from the attention of national members.

What is clear, then, is that involvement with an affiliated Europarty does not bring any added influence in a national party. The value of membership is mostly symbolic for the national parties as a whole; and party leader summits are, by definition, attended by those already endowed with power, and Europarty activities do not add to this.

Minor parties

The PCF and the Greens were not included in the above sections because of their limited presence in European arenas. The PCF did not belong to a Europarty before the creation of the European Left (EL) in 2004 and neither the PCF nor the

Greens had more than one or two ministers participating in Council of Ministers deliberations. Nevertheless, some findings bear reporting, if only to amplify the conclusions reached in regard to the major parties. The Greens were first a *European* parliamentary party, and only then a national parliamentary party. The prominence of their MEPs is therefore related not to the influence of the EU but to the origins of the party itself. The small number of MPs, eight elected in 1997 and six in 2002, has meant that formal, bureaucratic structures have not evolved. The Greens' international secretary was the liaison to the European Federation of Green Parties (EFGP), but according to a senior European Green source concerned herself with more with non-European issues. As long as the French Greens were in government not much attention was given to the green Europarty (Dietz 2002) but when the EFGP reinvented itself as the European Green Party this received enthusiastic support from the French Green leadership. To conclude, although French Green MEPs are indeed influential in the party, this prominence derives from their prior national stature, not the European-level position they occupy.

The PCF, of the French parliamentary parties, has been the most reticent about the nature of European integration. Suspicious of the neo-liberal character of European integration, especially since the Single Market launch, it did not involve itself with EU policy-making in the national arena. In the EP, especially from the mid-1990s onward when its new leadership attempted to broaden the base of the party, and in so doing 'de-stalinize' the party's structures, it went so far as to recruit non-party members onto its EP list. Its MEPs are allowed a large amount of autonomy from the party, and some have established respectable credentials inside the EP for their contributions. The leader of the Left group in the EP comes from the PCF. However, PCF MEPs are virtually unknown in French domestic politics.

Conclusion

The EU has certainly had an impact on French politics and institutions, contributing to constitutional change, party system fragmentation, developments in subnational politics, etc. The EU has been a divisive issue in the two main parties of government, on the centre-left and centre-right. Yet, throughout the period of the Fifth Republic, coinciding almost exactly with the history of European integration, the EU has not been a force stimulating organizational change in these parties or a cause in shifting the balance of power within these parties in favour of EU specialists. Why have French parties not internalized these changes through organizational adaptation? Four interconnected reasons are suggested. First, there is the weakness of French party organization. Second, there is the overwhelming orientation towards presidential leadership. Third, there is the near total control of foreign – including European – and defence policy by the executive, especially the president. Fourth and last, expertise in the EU does not translate into influence within parties because it does not add any new element into traditional patterns of competition. These four points are elaborated below.

Why should the comparative weakness of French party organization be a factor explaining the absence of adaptive EU pressures? In all of our cases, including the Communist party since the mid-1990s, French parties have been in continuous change, even schizophrenic (Machin 1989) owing to the pressures of the Fifth Republic institutional context, namely bipolarization and direct elections for the presidency. This has determined coalition strategies and has elevated the electoral orientation of party organizations: i.e. they increasingly serve as campaign machines for capturing the presidency, and this puts a premium on individual or personal attributes of leaders/presidential aspirants. In fact, parties do not control presidential candidacies, a fact that has had more striking consequences for the Gaullists (Knapp 2002: 135). Especially on the right, party organization has been adapted for the sake of achieving power at the summit of French politics. Organizational dynamics have been affected by these calculations (Haegel 2004), and it therefore serves the interest of party leaders to have a flexible organization that can be altered easily. One of the adaptive changes we have hypothesized – the creation of additional and permanent EU specialist positions that may include a degree of autonomy – goes against the logic of personalized party leadership (Gaffney 2002).

The second point follows directly from the first regarding party organizational flexibility. Presidential leadership or dominance, as constitutional experts on the Fifth Republic are quick to point out, is not explicitly stated in the constitution. It evolved out of de Gaulle's leadership and personal standing in the early years of the new regime. It is the active interest of successive presidents that has led to the 'presidentialization' of French European decision-making (Guyomarch *et al.* 1998). By definition, a strong party leader is also his or her party's presidential candidate in opposition, and in government relatively detached from formal party organization (upon election, presidents have resigned their party organizational position). Presidential leadership, *effective* leadership, ensures a degree of autonomy in decision-making from competing centres of power in the party (Clift 2005). The image of authority while in opposition is necessary for presidential campaign strategy as well.

Third, the French executive, the president and the prime minister and his or her cabinet, effectively control EU policy and decision-making. Whether one characterizes the French policy-making approach as statist or 'statist under EU pluralist pressure' (Schmidt 2004), it is certainly the case that, as regards EU decision-making, the parliament is an outsider trying to look in. With parliament, in particular the National Assembly, so demoted in this regard, parliamentary parties cannot exert pressure to keep the government accountable. There is then very little incentive for parliamentary groups to create their own expertise, or EU specialists. There is also the common feature found in other national parliaments that EU policy competence is so widespread that specific policy expertise has more value than generalist knowledge on major EU political issues or EU institutional familiarity, i.e. expertise on the EU and agriculture or the EU and defence is more important for standing committees than being the chair of the National Assembly delegation for the EU.

Lastly, we hypothesized that EU specialists may be able to influence their parties' internal balance of power. This would suggest that expertise on EU matters is a highly sought after commodity, and therefore translates into potential influence. Is this the case? It has been noted above that MEPs enjoy a certain degree of autonomy from their national parties. Is this autonomy, i.e., freedom from constraints in decision-making, and ignorance of or little to no interest in one's activities from colleagues, one and the same thing? Is it not more credible to believe that an MEP who wishes to climb the career ladder in his or her party by moving into national politics will more likely than not be a conformist to the party leadership? In one study of French MEPs expertise and how this structures their relationship with their national party, it was noted that the only audience for an MEP was the party leadership, and not the electorate (Beauvallet 2003). Autonomy is therefore not necessarily an indicator of power in this arrangement, because this autonomy is reserved to deciding matters in the EP not within the national party. Also, becoming a party's national secretary for international relations (where this is a post filled by an elected politician) does not signal power, as in most parties this position has been filled by both high and low profile individuals. The best that can be suggested is that a big party in opposition needs to provide some platforms for its senior and mid-level elites and, given personal interest, it may be that the position of national secretary for international relations may be filled by a member of the party's elite.

We have seen that a party in government has a role to play in support of its government, especially in government–opposition dynamics. This promotes party discipline in parliament but not much else in the normal pursuit of governance. French party government does not include much 'party' on account of the weakness of parliament. The party actors in the governing executive have at their disposal other means to collect information on EU matters, and no attempt to develop a British Labour Party 'link system' has been attempted (this is not to say that an individual whose past government experience combined with expertise may not play an important liaison role between party, government and EP delegation, but this is exceptional, not routine). Parties' extra-parliamentary organization includes MEPs on leadership bodies, sometimes in an *ex officio* capacity, but a French party in opposition is not as concerned with routine EP/EU legislation as with exceptional issues which may have some political capital. In this case, the EU specialist plays only an advisory role, and regular party politicians take the lead in debate. Indeed, debates in 2006 over the EU Commission's directive on liberalizing services witnessed a large number of non-specialist comments from politicians in all French parties – and suddenly everyone became an EU specialist. EU specialists gain a higher profile in parties when the EU becomes an issue in domestic politics because their expertise is demanded by the media as well as in party debates. But this attention does not 'stick' in the sense that this attention accrues over time into power or influence.

In the end, French parties are insulated from Europeanization influences on their organization because they are themselves insulated from government activities by the lack of an assertive parliament and the constitutional prerogatives of the executive. Party elites are therefore enhanced in their power vis-à-vis their respective parties, but as a by-product of the overall strengthening of the national executive in relation to the legislature. It is clear from most analyses that French 'policy paradigms, policy instruments and policy rules have considerably evolved under the influence of the EU over the last two decades' (Balme and Woll 2005: 115; see also Cole and Drake 2000). Despite this, the detachment of parties from policy-making – though not from political recruitment, interest articulation, etc. – explains why French party organization has only experienced marginal change in regard to EU influences. In other ways the EU has certainly become a challenge to the functioning of French party politics in general (Meunier 2004), bringing parties such as the Socialists to the verge of major internal turmoil by splitting the party leadership in two over the referendum on the EU constitution. Our study has had a narrower focus; in terms of a greater number and more influence within their parties, French EU specialists – and by extension, the EU policy-making process itself – remain far removed from the internal balance of power in parties. Indeed, in terms of restructuring the internal balance of power within the French state, 'the vast majority of the representatives and citizens of this state still fail to recognize the transformation in the locus and form of political power' (Smith 2005: 121).

Notes

1 The empirical material on which this chapter is based comes from party statutes and documents and from 13 interviews with party politicians and staff members in all of the parties cited (no interviews with the PCF). Interviewees included past and present party leaders, ministers for Europe, European Parliament delegation leaders, other influential Members of the European Parliament, other party staff in the European Parliament delegation, international secretaries and other party staff in the party central office.
2 In 2002, following successful presidential and legislative elections, the RPR, a majority of the UDF and *Démocratie Libérale*, a smaller centre-right party, merged to form this new party.

References

Aylott, Nicholas (2002) 'Let's Discuss this Later: Party Responses to Euro-Division in Scandinavia', *Party Politics*, 8(4): 441–61.

Balme, Richard and Cornelia Woll (2005) 'France: Between Integration and National Sovereignty', in Simon Bulmer and Christian Lequesne (eds), *The Member States of the European Union*, Oxford: Oxford University Press, pp. 97–118.

Beauvallet, Willy (2003) 'Institutionnalisation et professionnalisation de l'Europe politique: le cas des eurodéputés français', *Politique Européenne*, 9: 99–122.

Bell, David S. (2003) 'France: The Left in 2002: The End of the Mitterrand Strategy', *Parliamentary Affairs*, 56(1): 24–37.

Bertoncini, Yves and Thierry Chopin (2004) *Le Parlement Européen: un défi pour l'influence française*, Paris: Fondation Robert Schuman.

Clift, Ben (2005) 'Dyarchic Presidentialization in a Presidentialized Polity: The French Fifth Republic', in Thomas Poguntke and Paul Webb (eds), *The Presidentialization of Politics: A Comparative Study of Modern Democracies*, Oxford: Oxford University Press, pp. 221–45.

Cole, Alistair (2001) *Franco-German Relations*, London: Longman.

Cole, Alistair (2003) 'Stress, Strain and Stability in the French Party System', in Jocelyn Evans (ed.), *The French Party System*, Manchester: Manchester University Press, pp. 11–28.

Cole, Alistair and Helen Drake (2000) 'The Europeanization of the French Polity: Continuity, Change and Adaptation', *Journal of European Public Policy*, 7(1): 26–43.

Dietz, Thomas (2002) 'European Federation of Green Parties', in Karl Magnus Johansson and Peter Zervakis (eds), *European Political Parties between Cooperation and Integration*, Baden-Baden: Nomos, pp. 125–59.

Elgie, Robert (1993) 'From the Exception to the Rule: The Use of Article 49-3 of the Constitution since 1958', *Modern and Contemporary France*, 1(1): 17–26.

Elgie, Robert (ed.) (1999) *Semi-Presidentialism in Europe*, Oxford: Oxford University Press.

Evans, Jocelyn (2003) 'Europe and the French Party System', in Jocelyn Evans (ed.), *The French Party System*, Manchester: Manchester University Press, pp. 155–70.

Gaffney, John (2002) 'Protocol, Image, and Discourse in Political Leadership Competition: The Case of Prime Minister Lionel Jospin, 1997–2002', *Modern and Contemporary France*, 10(3): 313–24.

Guyomarch, Alain, Howard Machin and Ella Ritchie (1998) *France in the European Union*, Basingstoke: Palgrave.

Haegel, Florence (2004) 'The Transformation of the French Right: Institutional Imperatives and Organizational Changes', *French Politics*, 2(2): 185–202.

Hanley, David (2002) *Party, Society, Government: Republican Democracy in France*, New York: Berghahn.

Ivaldi, Gilles (2006) 'Beyond France's 2005 Referendum on the European Constitutional Treaty', *West European Politics*, 29(1): 47–69.

Kassim, Hussein (1997) 'French Autonomy and the European Union', *Modern and Contemporary France*, 5(2): 167–80.

Knapp, Andrew (2002) 'France: Never a Golden Age', in Paul Webb, David Farrell and Ian Holliday (eds), *Political Parties in Advanced Industrial Democracies*, Oxford: Oxford University Press, pp. 107–50.

Knapp, Andrew (2004) *Parties and the Party System in France: A Disconnected Democracy?*, Basingstoke: Palgrave.

Machin, Howard (1989) 'Stages and Dynamics in the Evolution of the French Party System', *West European Politics*, 12(4): 59–81.

Mair, Peter (2000) 'The Limited Impact of European National Party Systems', *West European Politics*, 23(4): 27–51.

Meunier, Sophie (2004) 'Globalization and Europeanization: A Challenge to French Politics', *French Politics*, 2(2): 125–50.

Rozenberg, Olivier (2004) 'La perfectible adaptation des parlements nationaux à l'Union Européenne', in Olivier Costa, Eric Kerrouche and Paul Magnette (eds), *Vers un renouveau du parlementarisme en Europe?*, Brussels: Editions de l'Université de Bruxelles, pp. 73–87.

Schmidt, Vivien (2004) 'Europeanization of National Democracies: The Differential Impact on Simple and Compound Polities', *Politique Européenne*, 13: 113–40.

Shields, James (1996) 'The French Gaullists', in John Gaffney (ed.), *Political Parties and the European Union*, London: Routledge, pp. 86–109.

Smith, Andy (2005) 'The Europeanization of the French State', in Alistair Cole, Patrick Le Galès and Jonah Levy (eds), *Developments in French Politics 3*, Basingstoke: Palgrave, pp. 105–21.

Szukala, Andrea and Olivier Rozenberg (2001) 'The French Parliament and the EU: Progressive Assertion and Strategic Investment', in Andreas Maurer and Wolfgang Wessels (eds), *National Parliaments on their Ways to Europe: Losers or Latecomers?*, Baden-Baden: Nomos, pp. 223–50.

Thiébault, Jean-Louis and Bernard Dolez (2000) 'Parliamentary Parties in the French Fifth Republic', in Knut Heidar and Ruud Koole (eds), *Parliamentary Party Groups in European Democracies: Political Parties Behind Closed Doors*, London: Routledge, pp. 57–70.

5 Europeanization in a consensual environment?

German political parties and the European Union[1]

Thomas Poguntke

Political consensus, cooperative federalism and an active role in European integration have been the hallmarks of post-war German politics, and not even the upheavals following the fall of the Berlin Wall and German unification have changed this significantly. Yet the political environment of German political parties has been transformed considerably by the fundamental changes in the size and the powers of the European Union (EU) following the end of the Cold War. As a growing proportion of national legislation is now predetermined by the institutions of the EU, we would expect national political parties to feel pressures to adapt their formal structures and internal processes to the growing relevance of the supranational level of governance. Following the questions raised in the introduction to this volume, this chapter will investigate formal and informal changes within German political parties in response to the growing relevance of the EU. We expected that those who are directly involved in the European institutions of governance, such as Members of the European Parliament (MEPs), members of national governments and EU specialists will benefit from processes of organizational adaptation, while those confined to national or sub-national politics are likely to have suffered a loss of influence and power. The analysis covers all relevant German parties including the Christian Democratic Union (CDU) and its Bavarian sister party the Christian Social Union (CSU), the Social Democrats (SPD), the Liberals (FDP), the Greens and the post-Communist Left Party, which called itself the Party of Democratic Socialism (PDS) until the 2005 Bundestag election campaign when it decided to join forces with the pro-welfare protest party WASG (Election Alternative for Jobs and Social Justice) and chose a name which would be less reminiscent of its Communist past.[2]

Germany and Europe

The relevance of history

A founding member of the European Economic Community (EEC), Germany has traditionally been among the most pro-integrationist member states of the innovative and unique political edifice that is now known as the European Union. Marred by the responsibility for the worst crimes in human history, the German political class regarded European integration as a means of rebuilding international respectability (Anderson 2005: 79). It is little exaggeration to argue that European integration became a substitute for a national identity that had been destroyed so completely by Nazi Germany. Much of this was, however, elite driven, and the famous 'permissive consensus' on European integration was as prevalent in Germany as elsewhere in the mass publics of the founding member states of a united Europe (Haas 1958; Lindberg and Scheingold 1970). In contrast to many other member states, however, there is to this day a very strong and active elite consensus not to debate the institutional politics of European integration in a controversial way (Niedermayer 2003: 142). Attempts to put European integration on the agenda of national political debate have been rare, and they have usually been met by widespread rejection by the vast majority of established German politicians. A few leading politicians with populist instincts have attempted to test the waters in this way but their attempts have always met with considerable distaste from across the political spectrum (Sloam 2003: 71). Little can exemplify the widespread consensus so well as the explicit commitment shared by politicians of all traditional German parties to keep the introduction of the euro out of the German federal election campaign of 1998. Even the German Greens, who were sceptical about the democratic credentials of the EU in their early years, never questioned the desirability of European integration as such. Similarly, the Left Party is largely united in its principled support for the idea of European integration even though the party remains sceptical about the concrete *Gestalt* of the EU.

For many years, public support for European integration was solid and higher than in most other European countries but this has significantly declined since the mid-1980s. Arguably, the growing economic difficulties in the aftermath of German unification at least partially account for this (Niedermayer 2003: 138). While erosion of popular support for the advancement of European integration has created the potential for Eurosceptic mobilization, the elite consensus has so far held. None of the Bundestag parties has reconsidered its generally supportive stance on European integration, nor have there been credible challenges from non-established political entrepreneurs to mobilize on an anti-European ticket (Niedermayer 2003). That said, there was a modest but noticeable shift of the German federal government's general approach to European affairs when power changed from the Christian–Liberal government headed by the arch-European Helmut Kohl to the red–green coalition led by Gerhard Schröder in 1998. Germany has become a more openly assertive actor on the European scene, prepared to punch its weight and more concerned with the way its European action might generate domestic political capital (Hyde-Price and Jeffery 2001: 700–2). Significantly, in the legislative term following the 2004 elections, the two largest parliamentary groups in the European Parliament (EP) were chaired by Germans: the Socialist group by Martin Schulz and the People's Party group by Hans-Gert Pöttering. Furthermore, Chancellor Schröder repeatedly made it clear that he did not agree with certain EU policy initiatives and fought openly for changes. Although the corrections to the stability and growth pact in spring 2005 are among the most relevant examples

(Wagener *et al.* 2006: 558–90), this changing approach to European affairs first became apparent when the Schröder government started insisting on the use of German language translation in technical negotiations where previous governments had followed a more pragmatic line.

Arguably, this shift in style and emphasis owes much to the mounting economic difficulties of the Federal Republic at the beginning of the new millennium. For many years, Germany has been the biggest net contributor to the EU budget, and in a climate of domestic economic hardship, this situation is becoming increasingly unpopular. In addition, thanks to geographic proximity, eastward enlargement has more direct repercussions on the German labour market than on that of many other old EU member states. To a certain degree, however, this shift also needs to be understood as an expression of a generational change among German elites. The Schröder cabinet was the first truly post-war government in that most of its leading members had no personal recollection of National Socialism and World War II, something that makes them somewhat less concerned with the (possible) sensitivities of their European partners.

The institutional framework and European integration

Within government, European competencies are traditionally split between the foreign office and the ministry for economics. Given that European integration was traditionally driven by economic integration, the latter tended to have a leading role until the 1980s.[3] This began to change in the wake of the Maastricht treaty when the foreign office gradually assumed a more dominant role. The extension of EU competencies did not, however, result in the creation of a specific portfolio within the cabinet. Instead, an increasing number of government departments created European divisions to deal with their individual Europe-related affairs. As a result, the executive management of European affairs in Germany is very fragmented, or 'sectorized' (Derlin 2000; Bulmer *et al.* 2001: 182), which tends to weaken German influence in everyday European policy-making (Pehle and Sturm 2005: 885–91).

Institutionally, Germany has become a somewhat more cumbersome European partner. In order to ensure the necessary consent of the Länder in the ratification of the Maastricht treaty, the federal government agreed to grant the Länder direct co-determination rights at the European level. In theory, the Länder can take over from the federal government if the negotiations in the Council of Ministers or the European Council concern matters in which they have exclusive legislative powers (Goetz 1995: 106; Anderson 2005: 87; Pehle and Sturm 2005: 898). Given the natural diversity of Land interests, however, the practical consequences of the formal strengthening of Land powers in EU-level policy-making have been limited (Jeffery 1997: 72–3). More consequential has been the growing involvement of the Länder alongside the federal government in European-level negotiations, an established practice for which the Länder achieved formal recognition in exchange for giving up some of their powers as a result of the European treaty revisions (Börzel 1999: 584, 2005: 55; Anderson 2005: 88). Where Land interests are concerned, and this has become more frequent as a result of the widening scope of the EU, the Länder are part of the delegation in the Council of Ministers (Goetz 1995: 107). Many Länder now run their own 'embassies' in Brussels and have become active players in EU politics (Moore 2006).

Traditionally, parliamentary scrutiny of European affairs has been weak in Germany, which can be explained by the strong elite consensus favouring European integration (Hansen and Scholl 2002). Before the first direct elections to the European Parliament in 1979 there was no special Bundestag sub-committee for European affairs and it was only after the ratification of the Maastricht treaty that a fully-fledged European affairs committee was created in 1994.[4] The creation of the European affairs committee was intended to strengthen the role of the Bundestag vis-à-vis the government in European policy-making. Reflecting the increasing scope of EU policy-making, the remit of the European affairs committee of the Bundestag cuts across the competencies of other Bundestag committees. This also has repercussions on its schedule because it often needs to wait until other, specialized committees have considered certain pieces of legislation. Constitutionally, the government needs to keep the Bundestag informed about all EU-related initiatives but, in reality, the Bundestag suffered from an informational disadvantage vis-à-vis the Bundesrat in that it received relevant documents later than all other relevant actors (see also Auel and Benz 2005: 389). There is an intention to improve the situation through opening a Bundestag office in Brussels. Moreover, in September 2006 the Bundestag and the federal government reached an agreement which will ensure the provision of the same information to the Bundestag and the Bundesrat. There are, however, also practical impediments to a closer connection between the Bundestag and the EP: although some MEPs are also members of the Bundestag European affairs committee they are rarely able to attend because of the overlapping parliamentary calendars (Auel and Benz 2005: 386).

In any case, the inherent executive bias of European politics has prevented the committee from seriously constraining executive action (Saalfeld 2003: 86; Pehle and Sturm 2005: 893–5) and German government actors are not confronted with *ex ante* guidelines from the Bundestag European affairs committee concerning their negotiations in Brussels. MPs who belong to the governing majority avoid binding mandates and use informal cooperation which takes place largely within the parliamentary parties (Holzhacker 2002: 467; Fuchs 2004: 19; Töller 2004: 39–41; Auel and Benz 2005: 388–9).

German parties and the EU

German politics is now almost entirely dominated by politicians who lack the unreserved, emotionally grounded support for European integration that was the hallmark of Helmut Kohl and many of his contemporaries. While the current German elite still shares a strong consensus favouring European integration, its members are more willing than their predecessors to ask questions about the limits to integration and, above all, the magnitude of the German contribution to the EU. However, this shifting emphasis has not led to a discernible conflict within the

German party system over European integration. Hence, one crucial source of variation when it comes to analysing the impact of European integration on the internal dynamics of national political parties is virtually missing in Germany (Lees 2002; Niedermayer 2003). Whereas fierce intra-party conflict over EU policies has had important repercussions on the internal power distribution within parties elsewhere (Chapter 3 above; Chapter 7 below), this variable can largely be disregarded in Germany.

This does not mean that German parties agree on each and every issue that concerns European integration. The Greens rejected the institutional reforms of the Maastricht treaty, although they have come a long way since and now support the constitutional treaty (Rüdig 1996: 263–5). Their initial scepticism somewhat resembles the current attitude of the Left Party, which emphasizes its principled support for European integration but remains critical of the lack of internal democracy within the Union and its alleged bias in favour of a neo-liberal economic philosophy. The introduction of the euro and, to a greater degree, the issue of opening accession negotiations with Turkey are clear indications that issues of European integration are becoming more relevant and potentially divisive in German party politics. However, the fault-lines are mainly between the elite on the one side and the rank-and-file and the mass public on the other. So far, the elite consensus not to turn issues concerning European integration into campaign themes has held: what was evident in the non-debate about the euro was repeated to a considerable degree over Turkish accession, which has the potential of splitting the memberships of the German parties and their electorates down the middle. The leadership of the CDU and the CSU responded to the substantial scepticism about Turkish accession among its own rank-and-file and electorate by calling for a 'privileged partnership' before the 2005 elections but, significantly, refrained from turning this into a campaign issue. This could have created considerable problems for the SPD, whose rank-and-file had grudgingly accepted Schröder's pro-Turkish stance. Similarly, the FDP and the Left Party officially support Turkish accession without being able to really count on solid support from either the party faithful or the electorate. The motives of the party leaderships differed somewhat and included strategic considerations in the post-9/11 world and electoral tactics (SPD, FDP), while the Left Party was mainly motivated by its traditional commitment to internationalism. This leaves the Greens as the only relevant German party in which leadership and grass roots are largely united in their support for Turkish accession.

Similarly, the constitutional treaty was not entirely uncontroversial in all German parties. The Left Party rejected it after considerable internal debate and, while the CDU was mainly in favour, there was considerable scepticism in some sections of the Bavarian CSU. This was related to the specific role of the CSU as a regionally based party with a seemingly permanent claim to Bavarian government, which makes it particularly sensitive to the allegedly insufficient recognition of the principle of subsidiarity in the constitutional treaty. Yet, it also reflected a growing concern about the geographical and political limits to European integration, which is increasingly giving rise to discussions in all German parties.

However, the strong role of cooperative federalism with its perpetual pressures to achieve compromise between the national government and the Bundesrat, in conjunction with the fact that national governments are normally supported by coalitions, mean that all relevant German parties normally participate in the multi-level policy-making process. This creates very strong pressures for consensual politics, which have acted as an important constraint against (arguably still moderate) temptations to mobilize Eurosceptic sentiments. As one interviewee put it, it might be possible to win an election on a Eurosceptic ticket but it would be impossible to govern Germany with such an agenda.

Since European integration has been largely consensual between parties, and since elites have agreed to keep the few potentially controversial issues out of election campaigns, European Parliament elections have remained second order national elections (Reif and Schmitt 1980; van der Eijk *et al.* 1996) which are mainly fought over national policies while European topics tend to play only a minor role. They are regarded as a test of the national political mood even though a poor result in European Parliament elections will normally not create serious difficulties for a party's leadership. Furthermore, they offer an important platform for smaller parties to (re-)establish their credibility as a national political force and boost their finance through election reimbursement. Hence, it was particularly important for the Left Party to be returned to the EP in 2004 after it had lost all but two seats in the 2002 Bundestag elections. Similarly the extreme right-wing *Republikaner* crossed the 5 per cent hurdle in a nationwide election only in the 1989 EP elections (see Table 5.1).

The German model of party organization

As a result of the very high degree of state regulation of internal party affairs, territorial constraints and functional needs (Poguntke 1998), the formal organizational structure of all German parties is very similar. They are required to have a party congress or a general assembly as a main rule-making body, and this then elects several more selective bodies: the party council (*Parteirat* or *Länderrat*) is often referred to as a small party congress and deals with issues that need to be addressed between regular party congresses. All German Bundestag parties have a national executive that leads the party organizationally and politically and, with the exception of the Left Party, a smaller executive committee which runs the party on a daily basis. The territorial units of German parties follow the federal structure of the German polity. The smallest organizational unit is usually the local branch, followed by district (regional) and Land organizations. National parties are essentially federations of Land organizations, and the formal powers of the national leadership to control lower units are very limited. Rather, the national leadership derives its power from its role in coalition building and from the force of its arguments. Again, this is largely the result of party legislation which requires all German parties to comply with a relatively detailed set of requirements that guarantee a formal bottom-up flow of power in internal party affairs (Poguntke 1994, 2002; Herzog 1997).

Table 5.1 Elections to the European Parliament in Germany: votes, seats and turnout, 1979–2004[a]

	1979		1984		1989		1994		1999		2004	
	%	Seats	%	Seats	%	Seats	%	Seats	%	Seats	%	Seats
CDU	39.1	32	37.5	32	29.5	24	32.0	39	39.3	43	36.5	40
CSU	10.1	8	8.5	7	8.2	7	6.8	8	9.4	10	8.0	9
FDP	6.0	4	4.8	0	5.6	4	4.1	0	3.0	0	6.1	7
SPD	40.8	34	37.4	32	37.3	30	32.2	40	30.7	33	21.5	23
Greens	3.2	0	8.2	7	8.4	7	10.1	12	6.4	7	11.9	13
Left Party							4.7	0	5.8	6	6.1	7
Others	0.8	0	3.7	0	10.9[b]	6	10.2*	0	5.4*	0	9.9*	0
Turnout/total seats	65.7	78	56.8	78	62.3	78	60.0	99	45.2	99	43.0	99

Source: www.Bundeswahlleiter.de

Notes

a Seats for West Berlin were elected by the West Berlin legislature before German unification: 1979: CDU two, SPD one; 1984: CDU two, SPD one; 1989: CDU one, SPD one, Alternative List (Greens) one. Upon German unification the Bundestag delegated 18 observers from the new Länder to the EP on 21 February 1991: CDU eight; SPD five; Left Party two; FDP one; Greens one; *Deutsche Soziale Union* (DSU) one (see Schindler 1994: 1240).

b Includes extreme right-wing *Republikaner*: 1989: 7.1 per cent (six seats); 1994: 3.9 per cent (no seat); 1999: 1.7 per cent (no seat); 2004: 1.9 per cent (no seat).

All German parties are characterized by a formally strict separation between parliamentary and extra-parliamentary party, which again is required by party legislation and party finance legislation (Arnim 1991; Gunlicks 1995; Naß-macher 2002). Although parties may differ in their traditional understanding of whether the party in parliament or the extra-parliamentary party should be politically dominant, they are all, *de facto*, now dominated by their parliamentary parties to a considerable degree. In large part, this domination flows from the superior resources available to parliamentary parties, which give them a clear lead in detailed policy formulation. Still, extra-parliamentary parties are powerful and distinct organizational entities based on the concept of a mass membership party (even though membership has been declining), and the leader of the extra-parliamentary party is the party leader who oversees the development of basic party programmes and leads coalition negotiations. Having said this, there is a considerable overlap between the party in public office and the party in central office in that virtually all those who hold elected positions in national leadership bodies will also sit in a Land parliament, the Bundestag or the EP. Only the Green Party restricts the number of parliamentarians in its executive committee to one-third of its members.[5] Depending on the political constellation, the offices of parliamentary and extra-parliamentary leader may also be held by the same person (except in the Green Party). But they remain clearly distinguishable functions and with separate chains of accountability attached to them. When a party is in government, the leader of the parliamentary party remains outside the cabinet and assumes a crucial role in ensuring parliamentary discipline and, depending on political circumstances, in keeping the government in check (Schüttemeyer 1998; Saalfeld 2000). Unlike in pure Westminster systems there is no full fusion of parliamentary frontbench and government (Lijphart 1992). The parliamentary party remains a separate entity and the government needs to keep a watchful eye on the political preferences of its members.

The CDU and the CSU are fully independent parties that traditionally sit in a joint parliamentary party in the Bundestag. Similarly, they form a joint delegation in the EP headed by a CDU/CSU delegation leader although there is also a CSU group leader. Given that the CSU is essentially a Land party, it sometimes struggles to match its national and European ambitions with sufficient qualified personnel.

Structural adaptation to European integration[6]

Formal management and funding of Europe-related activities

As a result of the constraints of party finance, all German parties depend to a very large extent on the resources of their parliamentary parties. Members of the Bundestag and the Land parliaments have access to funds that allow them to employ personal assistants. Also, parliamentary parties obtain additional funding for researchers. As a result, the overwhelming majority of detailed substantive work tends to be done by the parliamentary parties at the different levels of the political system while the extra-parliamentary organization tends to have a strong orientation towards organizing campaigns and elections. To be sure, there is some variation that is related to the ideological traditions of individual parties but this owes more to cherished myths than to bare facts: the Social Democrats, the Greens and the Left Party would find it harder to admit to this than the Christian parties and, particularly, the FDP, but when we look at the number of political staff employed by extra-parliamentary party organizations, all parties are very similar, and this extends to resources devoted to European politics.

German parties employ no (FDP, Greens), one (CSU), two (Left Party) or three (SPD, CDU) political staff in their party headquarters who cover European affairs, although normally they also deal with international affairs in general. Their remit includes liaising with relevant party actors and drafting relevant policy documents. Unsurprisingly, there has not been any change worth reporting, as this represents the bare minimum, but it is evident that European issues have tended to demand more time and attention. Those who specialize in European matters in party headquarters have experienced a noticeable increase in demand for their expertise as a result of the growing encroachment of European policy-making upon the national political process. This offers opportunities for influence based on specific expertise in limited issue areas, but very little general influence in intra-party power games.

Much of the detailed, policy-oriented work is covered by parliamentary researchers, who work for MPs in the Bundestag or the Länder who specialize in EU matters and are normally members of the relevant European affairs committees. The number of these researchers has fluctuated according to electoral fortunes, especially as the smaller parties are not always returned to Land parliaments. Since these researchers will often also cover the other political activities of their MPs, it is difficult to provide precise figures. In 2004, a Green politician estimated that about six or seven parliamentary researchers in Land parliaments and one in the Bundestag were working on European issues amongst other tasks. These figures are reasonable estimates for the other smaller parties. About 15–20 researchers working on European and international affairs may be employed by the SPD and a similar number by the Christian parties together.

The post of party spokesperson for European affairs is usually a junior one in most parties and the role is often combined with that of a spokesperson for international affairs. For all practical purposes those who cover this area within the parliamentary party are politically far more relevant. Two functions need to be distinguished here: the member of the executive of the parliamentary party with an EU brief, and the senior member of the parliamentary party in the European affairs committee of the Bundestag. While smaller parties have combined these roles, the SPD created a special deputy leader of the parliamentary party for EU affairs in 2002 in order to recognize the increased importance of this policy area. All parties have regular working groups specializing in EU affairs which bring together relevant parliamentary researchers, party head office staff, MPs and, of course, MEPs. The European working group (*Europakommission*) of the SPD is jointly chaired by a senior MEP and the relevant deputy of the parliamentary party of the Bundestag and involves between 20 and 30 politicians specializing in

Europe. It meets about every two months. In addition the EP delegation meets for a joint session with the Bundestag parliamentary party twice a year. Similarly, the FDP European working group (*Bundesfachausschuß Europa*) meets two or three times a year and the Greens have similar fora which are designed to provide communication and networking opportunities for those working on European matters in the Länder, at the federal level or in Brussels. One regular three-monthly meeting assembles parliamentarians and invites the chairs of the federal party working group on European politics, while another series of meetings brings together party activists interested in European matters. Likewise, the CSU has a bi-monthly meeting for all relevant parliamentarians and their staff, and CDU/CSU MEPs meet with their counterparts in the Bundestag on a regular basis. In addition, the CDU/CSU delegation leader in the EP liaises regularly with Christian Democratic Land prime ministers in order to coordinate legislation relevant to Land interests. As a result of losing all but two seats in the 2002 Bundestag elections, Left Party MEPs lacked sufficient linkage to the national parliament between 2002 and 2005. However, the party has developed a number of ways of formally integrating its EP delegation into national party politics: the EP delegation leader participates in the regular meetings of leaders of parliamentary parties of the Länder and the Bundestag, a member of the EP group staff participates in the weekly telephone conferences of parliamentary managers (*parlamentarische Geschäftsführer*), and about every two months the party organizes coordination meetings on relevant European topics which include European spokespersons from all party arenas and members of the EP delegation.

Generally speaking, all parties have attempted to strengthen the links between national, sub-national and European politics and this has also been documented by the introduction of *ex officio* seats for leading MEPs in national leadership bodies. The CDU/CSU delegation leader is an *ex officio* guest of the CDU national executive (since 2003) and the European People's Party (EPP) group leader (if a CDU member) has been an *ex officio* member of the CDU executive committee since 1981. Similarly, the CSU EP group leader has been a member of the Land executive since 1982, and an FDP MEP (usually the delegation leader) holds an *ex officio* position in the party's national executive and executive committee (since 1978).[7] The Social Democrats are traditionally averse to full *ex officio* seats on their leadership bodies but the EP delegation leader has always been invited to meetings of the national executive. It is a reflection of the increased weight of EU politics that these invitations were extended to executive committee meetings (initially for specific meetings only) and that by 2005 two leading MEPs were elected to the SPD executive committee. The Greens, by contrast, who until recently have adhered to a strict separation of party office and parliamentary mandate, admit two members of the EP delegation only to their Land council, which functions like a small party congress (Poguntke 2003). The Left Party has no *ex officio* representation of its EP delegation in the national executive and has invited representatives of its EP delegation to meetings of the national executive only in times of acute crisis, that is, when matters of European integration became conflictual within the party as in the debate over the constitutional treaty.

Another important mechanism to ensure linkage between the parliamentary delegations in the EP and the German Bundestag is the existence of a special liaison officer employed by MEPs who is located within the Bundestag parliamentary parties. All German parties use EP funding to employ a permanent member of staff charged with maintaining everyday contact between the party's delegation in the EP and the national parliamentary party.

The linkage mechanisms described above are intended to guarantee the flow of information between Land, federal and European levels of party activity and to ensure that party actors coordinate their political positions both on matters of institutional politics and, increasingly importantly, on the broad range of policies that are now pre-determined by the EU. However, the increased communication and coordination have not moved EU specialists substantially closer to the centres of decision-making power within their parties.

MEP candidate selection

Candidate selection procedures are strictly regulated under German electoral law and leave relatively little flexibility for parties to write their own rules. Lists need to be decided upon by a special or general assembly of delegates (or a party assembly) and the requirement is that the party rank-and-file control the composition of the list either directly or through elected delegates (Europawahlgesetz 1994 §10). All relevant parties select their list candidates through special assemblies. As a result of these legal constraints and the strongly federal nature of German parties, the influence of national party leaderships is limited. There is substantial variation, however, which is directly related to the size of the parties. The CDU, CSU and SPD can normally expect to win enough EP seats to obtain representation in all German regions. Hence, the regional power base is by far the single most important criterion for individual candidates to be placed in a good position on the list. In the larger parties this base is normally the party district (*Bezirk*), which is the territorial sub-unit below the Länder. This regional influence is particularly strong in the case of the CDU, which runs with separate Land lists, as this effectively cuts out any substantial influence by the national leadership. Where pre-selected Land lists need to be combined into one national list, as it is the case for the SPD, the Greens and the Left Party, the national leadership can, in principle, play a moderating role in the negotiations between Land parties. Nevertheless, the influence of the SPD leadership is relatively limited because the principle of regional representation is paramount and rare attempts by the national leadership to place candidates in favourable positions on the list are strongly resented by regional power brokers (see also Ovey 2002: 129–35). The same logic applies to the regionally based CSU, where the influence of the districts is paramount and severely limits the influence of the Land leadership.

The situation is somewhat different for the smaller parties. Since they cannot reasonably expect to win enough seats to achieve territorial coverage, other aspects than a regional power base tend to be relatively more important. The FDP leadership, for example, took a strategic decision before the 2004 EP elections to place a media-friendly young female candidate at the top of the list who, as intended, played a central role in the party's media-based EP election campaign and achieved a public visibility hitherto largely unknown for leading candidates for EP elections. The FDP invested particular energy in this campaign because the party had not been represented in the EP during the previous two legislatures. The importance of such strategic considerations, which are not directly related to the relevance of European integration, is also demonstrated by the Left Party. In their struggle for survival as a credible national political force, 'electability' was the central criterion in 1994, whereas the regional power base became somewhat more important in 1999. The Left Party is also the only German party in which the inner national leadership in consultation with incumbent MEPs plays a strongly proactive role in the composition of a national list. This was particularly apparent in 2004 when particular attention was given to the EP elections because the party had lost all but two Bundestag seats two years earlier. The national leadership formulated a set of required qualifications for those who wanted to be selected and also consulted with the Land parties. Even then, however, the leadership's proposal did not pass the party congress unchanged, a fact that testifies to the structural limitations to leadership control over candidate selection in Germany.

As in some other aspects, the Greens have come a considerable way since their days of radical grassroots democracy. Since 1994, there have been regional assemblies that bring together several Land parties, and these assemblies pre-select candidates for a national list. Since the Greens cannot hope to cover all Länder, the regional power base of prospective candidates is not decisive. However there is an attempt to make sure that all relevant German areas (e.g. the new Länder or North Rhine–Westphalia) have a chance of sending an MEP to Brussels, and the national party leadership has attempted to coordinate these efforts. The candidates' qualifications play a much stronger role now than in the past when largely unknown activists could hope that a convincing performance at the national party congress might win them nomination – with at times disastrous consequences for the performance of the Green delegation in Brussels (Bomberg 1998: 86, 96). Unsurprisingly, attempts by the national executive to influence the composition of the list are normally not entirely successful, as Green party conferences still tend to be allergic to obvious elite control. In addition, it is noteworthy that very little attention was given to the 1999 EP election list because all political energies were absorbed by the party's newly assumed national government responsibilities.

If we wanted to identify commonalities in the candidate selection procedures of the different parties, it is evident that regional power base is the paramount selection criterion for the larger parties whereas the strategic situation of the smaller parties has varied over time, hence providing differential opportunities for national leaderships to exert influence (see Table 5.2). Overall, it is fairly evident that the attention given to the process of candidate selection has grown in all parties even though this has been confined primarily to party elites who have become aware of the need to have competent political personnel in Brussels. However, this has not led to national party leaderships trying to seriously influence the selection of delegation leaders in the European Parliament, which is decided by a (usually)

Table 5.2 Candidate selection for European Parliament elections in Germany

	CDU	CSU	FDP	SPD	Greens	Left Party
Selection level	Regional	Regional	National	National	National	National
Influence of regions	Very strong (districts)	Very strong (districts)	Important (Land executives)	Very strong (districts)	Moderate	Moderate
Influence of national leadership	Weak	Weak	Moderate/ strong	Weak	Moderate	Strong
Intra-party attention	Increased	Increased	No change (always high)	Increased	Increased	No change (always high)

secret vote within the delegation to the EP. Although the choice of delegation leader is sometimes a foregone conclusion because a certain MEP has been able to gain a strong position over the previous legislature(s) or because he or she has been specifically selected as the frontrunner (as in the case of the FDP in 2004), the autonomy of MEPs is usually respected and, in any event, the self-confidence of elected parliamentary representatives would be sufficiently strong to rebuff attempts at outside interference.

Acting nationally

The guiding theme of our investigation relates to potential shifts in the balance of power within national parties as a result of increased European integration. We have seen in the previous section that the growing relevance of the EU as a locus of political decision-making that is immediately relevant to national politics has not resulted in a noticeable increase in the number of specialists working on European issues within national party organizations or national and sub-national parliaments. At the same time, the number of those in national politics whose remit is somehow affected by European decision-making has clearly grown. The question then is whether this has led to those who specialize in European politics becoming more powerful as a result of their relevant knowledge and, potentially, their useful networks. In others words, has the influence of MEPs, MPs special-izing in Europe, and EU specialists within party head offices grown as a result of the increasing importance of European integration? If we want to answer this question first for national activities, we need to focus on two essential dimensions of intra-party power, namely the ability to influence the selection of personnel and the formulation of programmatic positions.

Clearly, a precondition for such a shift of power would be a growing aware-ness among relevant political actors that European integration has indeed become more important. By and large, all interviewees agreed that the awareness of the importance of the EU has grown. However, the perception that European integra-tion has become more important is greater among party elites than it is among the rank-and-file, something that clearly limits the weight of EU specialism in intra-party power games. We have already seen that the decisive players in candidate selection for EP elections are regional party organizations. With the partial exception of the Left Party, in which sitting MEPs have been involved in pre-selecting the list for the EP elections, there is no specific influence of EU specialists in personnel selection within German parties. When it comes to personnel decisions, all politics is regional in Germany.

Unsurprisingly, the situation is different when it comes to programme formulation. Those who have specialist knowledge of the EU usually play an important role in the drafting of European election manifestos and the relevant sections of national election manifestos. However, there is no clearly discernible trend; rather the influence in manifesto formulation usually depends on the overall influence of certain individuals within their party, and their specifically European role is normally only one element of it. In general, it is fair to conclude that all those who have a senior role in EU politics tend to be involved in the drafting stage of European election manifestos. More precisely, this includes senior MEPs, the senior member (*Obmann*) of a party in the Bundestag European affairs committee, the party spokesperson on EU affairs (if this separate position exists) and the specialists in the party head office. Often this means, in the first instance, that a parliamentary assistant or a junior person in the party head office will be charged with writing a first draft of the manifesto based on previous programmatic documents. This will then form the basis of editorial sessions, which involve all relevant politicians including the party leadership. As mentioned already, who exactly takes the lead in this process depends more on individual personalities, their overall political clout and their specific expertise than on incumbency of a specific parliamentary or party position. There is, however, one noteworthy trend in the way manifestos for EP elections are drafted: as a result of the increasingly pervasive scope of European legislation, politicians' special knowledge of particular policy areas is becoming more important when it comes to involvement in the process of manifesto writing. While expertise in the big issues such as enlargement, the constitutional treaty and the general trajectory of the EU remains important, this has also been complemented by demand for more specific knowledge. Finally, it is indicative of the low importance attached to European election manifestos that both large German parties have in the past decided to simply adopt the manifesto of their respective Europarty as their own: the CDU used the EPP manifesto in 1989, and the SPD campaigned with the Party of European Socialist (PES) manifesto in 1989, 1994 and 1999 (Poguntke and Pütz 2006). Clearly, this can also be read in another way: it is also a reflection of the strong position of these German parties within their Europarties, which has enabled them to prevent anything from being written into these manifestos that could have damaged their electoral prospects back home.

National election manifestos are, in principle, written in a similar fashion but the involvement of EU specialists tends to be mainly limited to the specifically European sections of the document, even though there is a tendency to recognize the ever more cross-cutting nature of European integration, which leads to an increasingly broader involvement of European specialists in manifesto writing. To be sure, these changes are slow, and the dominant mode of national manifesto formulation still follows the principle of 'departmental' specialism in which EU specialists are consulted on specific questions instead of being involved through-out. Again, there is considerable fluctuation as regards the exact configuration of people involved in the process but the common denominator is that the control over drafting the manifesto is in the hands of the party leadership. In times of governmental incumbency, a considerable part of this control rests either with the chancellor's office or with the most important government members of the junior coalition partner.

Eventually, manifestos are usually approved by a party congress that has the right to change the documents as it wishes, but it is indicative of the comparatively unimportant role of election manifestos in German election campaigns that parties have no clear rules on manifesto writing other than that the final document needs the approval of a party conference. After all, under conditions of coalition politics, manifestos are inevitably less binding than in two-party systems.

Beyond influence on basic programmatic documents, EU specialists might also influence specific policy positions of their party as a result of their expertise. However, the record is mixed, to say the least. Those EU specialists who are located in the national arena agree that their general political influence is largely independent of their EU specialization. Political influence and power is depend-ent on other, better-known intra-party factors such as regional power bases or positions of factional leadership, and a special expertise in European affairs adds little or nothing to this. The case of MEPs underlines this point: notwithstanding their EU specialism, MEPs find it difficult to maintain a power base within their party, and hence an influence, precisely because of their (geographical) distance from domestic centres of power. The dense schedule of the EP exacerbates this too, making regular attendance at national meetings, for example, rather difficult. That said, faced with a choice between securing a regional power base (which is crucial for re-selection) and maintaining or even enhancing their standing in the national party, MEPs may opt for the former and thereby sacrifice national power. The situation is somewhat different for delegation leaders who have become in-creasingly more integrated into national party politics and have therefore gained political weight within their national parties.

Although EU specialization does little to enhance career prospects within na-tional political parties, it could, in principle, provide members of the Bundestag European affairs committee and their aides with substantial influence over na-tional legislation. In response to the wide scope of EU legislation that needs to be translated into national law, the remit of the European affairs committee cuts across the competencies of other Bundestag committees. However, as indicated above, the Bundestag European affairs committee has so far not been able to function as a genuine focal point of EU politics in the national political arena. To a degree, this flows from a still substantial lack of awareness on the part of Bundestag MPs of the fact that considerable control over national legislation has now been transferred to Brussels – a lack bemoaned by many interviewees. More crucially, however, the Bundestag seems to suffer from an informational disadvantage concerning new initiatives by the Commission or ongoing negotiations by the national government. To some extent, the regular liaison meetings between national and European politicians compensate for this but the Bundestag is often in danger of not fully knowing about relevant legislative initiatives in Brussels. Furthermore, members of the executive are largely unconstrained by previous opinion formation (or even instruction) by the legislature when they participate in meetings of the Council of Ministers or the European Council (see above).

To conclude, the different categories of EU specialist have gained influence over their parties' programmes and, to a lesser extent, their policies but they have not gained new decision-making power, nor have they been able – with the partial exception of delegation leaders – to increase their weight in intra-party power games.

Acting supranationally

Parties and their MEPs

Members of the European Parliament are the only category of party politicians who are full-time members of a European institution. This sets them apart from members of national governments, whose involvement in the Council of Ministers, the European Council or the leadership bodies of the Europarties derives from their primary positions as national party politicians or government members. This lies at the heart of the frequently made assumption that MEPs might have a tendency to 'go native' as they are exposed to the supposedly socializing effects of working full-time in a European institution. While it is reasonable to expect that the values and norms prevalent in an institution will eventually leave a mark on the belief systems of those working within it, the evidence is at best mixed (Raunio 1997; Scully 2001). There are, however, also institutional factors that might explain why MEPs are often seen as being more pro-European than their peers back home. After all, national delegations also need to attempt to act within the general political guidelines of their multinational EP group and this may sometimes require going against the wishes of their national party. Furthermore, it cannot be assumed that MEPs always know the preferences of their national party. There may be a lack of permanent communication between national party bodies and the EP delegation, or national debates may lag behind European decision-making processes and hence leave MEPs without clear orientation. What exactly is the situation for German MEPs, and how has it changed over time?

All MEPs interviewed would welcome more attention by national party politicians (and the public) to European matters in general and their activities in the EP in particular. At the same time, they report that the interest in Europe has grown over time, and that there is greater awareness that many relevant policies are now determined in Brussels, but they all would like to see more linkage between national and supranational activities. By and large, the regular meetings of politicians engaged in EU politics across regional, national and supranational levels (see above) are not sufficient to cope with the sheer mass of detailed EU legislation that is now initiated in Brussels and that sets the boundaries for national law-making. While exchanges over the big issues like the constitution or the budget are usually fairly intense, MEPs often struggle to draw the attention of their national colleagues to less spectacular issues that may nevertheless have a substantial impact on national politics. The service directive and the directive on old cars are but two fairly recent examples where national politics entered the debate rather late.

This lack of national public attention furnishes MEPs with a very considerable autonomy in their own decision-making. Rather than being held accountable by their national parties, MEPs follow a 'supply-side logic of accountability': they actively engage in creating and strengthening their linkage to national party arenas in order to achieve closer coordination between their legislative behaviour and the preferences of their national party. One example is that delegation leaders reported that they are more likely to request European issues be put on the agenda of national executive meetings instead of being asked to report on the activities of the EP delegation. To be sure, this might reduce their autonomy, although, in exchange, increased national visibility might actually strengthen their influence in the national party arena, and hence in national politics. The importance of public attention applies more generally in that the autonomy of MEPs is inversely related to the degree of attention their actions attract from national politicians and the public at large. Party conferences are also of limited value in this respect: whereas all parties routinely expect their EP delegations to report on their activities at regular party conferences, these reports normally attract little attention and are clearly not a tool to raise intra-party attentiveness to European issues or to hold MEPs accountable for specific decisions made in the EP.

Unsurprisingly, the degree of linkage between parties and their EP delegations varies between parties and it is fair to say that contacts are more regular and specific between national and European parliamentarians than they are between MEPs and relevant extra-parliamentary EU specialists. By the end of the last decade, the CDU/CSU delegation in the EP introduced a method of coordination that monitors all policy initiatives by the Commission and attempts to ensure that the delegation and the national party agree on a common position. This institutionalization of cooperation with the national parliamentary party superseded 16 years of a fairly personal European regime under Chancellor Kohl who regularly invited the delegation to the chancellor's office in order to issue instructions. Similarly, the SPD and Greens attempt to maintain fairly close contacts between national and European parliamentarians but the intensity of these links varies across policy areas. The Left Party also attempts to integrate the activities of its EP delegation closely into an overall political strategy, which reflects the party's organizational philosophy that the extra-parliamentary organization should control the action of parliamentary delegates. The Left Party EP delegation is integrated into a weekly telephone conference of all parliamentary managers with the national party manager. Arguably, the FDP has so far developed somewhat less efficient mechanisms for connecting its EP delegation to national party arenas but this may be because the party was not represented in the EP between 1994 and 2004. Overall, therefore, there has been a clear tendency to strengthen the coordination and integration of national and supranational parliamentary action across all German parties.

Despite these linkage mechanisms, German MEPs report that they enjoy a very high degree of independence and autonomy, which is, first and foremost, rooted in the paramount importance of their regional power base for re-selection. Since national leaderships have very little leverage in influencing candidate selection, they lack a crucial instrument for ensuring discipline and holding MEPs accountable. Institutionally, this autonomy is amplified by the multinational nature of EP parliamentary groups, which represent a second reference point of political loyalty for national delegations. Furthermore, EP groups need not keep a government in power, which is the single most important institutional imperative for maintaining voting discipline and party coherence in parliamentary democracies. Consistently, the autonomy of German MEPs tends to be more limited when their party is in national government, because it becomes politically more difficult (not least due to higher public attention) to vote against decisions reached in the Council of Ministers or the European Council that have previously been agreed by members of their 'own' government.

Parties and Europarties

All German parties are members of their respective Europarties.[8] As a result of the size of the country and its comparatively generous rules for public party finance, German parties have also tended to play a leading role in these extra-parliamentary European party organizations which have only recently acquired an independent legal status (Johansson and Raunio 2005) and are beginning to become a somewhat more important locus of European party politics (Bardi 1996, 2002; Hix and Lord 1997; Poguntke and Pütz 2006). This important role has been reflected in German politicians chairing several Europarties, including the PES and the European Liberal Democrat and Reform (ELDR) Party. When it comes to smaller and more recent party families, the influence of German parties has been even more conspicuous. The German Greens have always been the driving force behind the various incarnations of the European Greens who transformed themselves into a European Green Party in spring 2004 (Dietz 1997, 2002) and the Left Party has been pivotal in creating the European Left Party which was launched in May 2004.

The political significance of Europarties for pre-structuring European-level decision-making varies significantly between party families. Europarty meetings, in particular the party leader meetings on the eve of European summits, represent important opportunities for national opposition politicians to build up a European network. Reportedly, both Helmut Kohl and Angela Merkel have actively used these structures for that purpose. Party leader meetings have sought to coordinate political strategies at the European level and their relevance has grown over the past decade even though national interests often override such efforts of party political coordination. In the end, the significance of such meetings depends strongly on incumbency, and this is why PES meetings have not functioned particularly well in the late 1990s and the early years of the new millennium: Tony Blair and Gerhard Schröder tended to show little inclination to attend. The relevance of incumbency also explains why these meetings have tended to be less important for the smaller Liberal party family (ELDR), which is less likely to have prime ministers among its ranks. In contrast to the other Europarties, the European Greens have traditionally not organized leader meetings.

Besides these attempts to coordinate intergovernmental action along party political lines, Europarties play a potentially important role in working towards a common political platform and agenda which could provide a political point of reference for their respective EP parliamentary groups and indeed their member parties. So far, however, national parties devote little attention to the activities of their representatives within Europarty leadership bodies. There is no institutionalized mechanism to hold these representatives accountable although all report that they will normally communicate back to their respective national bodies and act within the boundaries of their national party programmes and policy decisions. Again, it is a reflection of the different organizational culture of the Left Party that it is unique in discussing important Europarty matter *ex ante* in the national executive but this may be partly because the Left Party had a leading role in creating the European Left Party. All this said, however, with the partial exception of the Left Party, having a leading role in a Europarty adds little to a German party politician's national political stature. Rather, the chain of causality runs in the opposite direction: politicians tend to be elected to senior Europarty positions because they have previously held (or still hold) senior positions in national politics.

Parties and their ministers

When German cabinet members negotiate in meetings of the Council of Ministers, they are normally not constrained by specific party political instructions. As indicated above, the Bundestag European affairs committee is not a central player in EU-related politics and many MPs are not sufficiently aware of the immediate relevance of EU decisions for national politics to be inclined to attempt constraining the government anyway. To be sure, the attention of national MPs to what governments do in Brussels has grown considerably over time. Furthermore, cabinet members know the political preferences of the party or parties that support their government and important issues are discussed before crucial meetings in the relevant meetings of the parliamentary parties. Hence, they know the scope of their discretion when they are involved in decisions in the Council of Ministers and are able to anticipate potential resistance by their MPs. There are, however, no specific *ex ante* guidelines by either the relevant parliamentary parties or the Bundestag European affairs committee that would constrain a German cabinet member to a similar degree to that known from Scandinavian countries such as Denmark. German cabinet members are largely unconstrained by the Bundestag when they take part in decisions at the European level, which are, eventually, binding for national parliaments. Effectively, this gives ministers the power to shift the policy position of their own party as it will eventually have to follow the lead of its cabinet members unless it wants to exit government (see for example Bomberg 2002: 39).

Although linkage to parliamentarians is based on communication and anticipation, this does not mean that individual ministers act entirely without constraints in Council of Ministers negotiations. On the contrary, communication back into the cabinet and the higher levels of the federal bureaucracy is fairly intense. Still largely absent, however, is a comparably strong linkage to the legislature. Again, this is beginning to change as a result of the gradually growing awareness of the importance of EU decisions. Furthermore, we also need to distinguish between policy areas: whenever a particular issue attracts strong public attention or is particularly close to the heart of a specific party or organized interest, the concomitant heightened awareness reduces the freedom of manoeuvre for the executive. The debate over the service directive in 2005 is indicative here: SPD government ministers first hailed the liberalization of Europe-wide competition but were quickly forced to backtrack when other SPD politicians began to emphasize the risk for the domestic labour market.

Arguably, the infamous democratic deficit reaches its nadir when chief executives meet in the European Council or for summit meetings of an Intergovernmental Conference (IGC). Structurally, there are no effective mechanisms short of a governmental crisis to constrain the freedom of manoeuvre of a German chancellor in a European Council meeting. The constitutional right of a German chancellor to determine the 'guidelines of politics' (*Richtlinienkompetenz*) plays only a minor role in this regard. Primarily, the very considerable autonomy of the German chancellor flows from two causes.

First, it is inherent in the logic of a parliamentary system that the majority normally supports its government, and this extends to the relationship between the cabinet and the chancellor and his or her foreign secretary who also attends these meetings. Furthermore, Germany is usually governed by coalitions, and the foreign secretary is typically a member of the smaller coalition party, which removes a potential fault-line within the coalition. As long as chancellor and foreign secretary agree, they can normally expect their parties to support their decisions in the European Council or at an IGC summit. This logic is augmented by a very strong norm of unified majority government that is deeply rooted in post-war German political culture. The Weimar experience of unstable majorities and the subsequent collapse of democracy still makes governing with uncertain majorities, or even relying on the opposition in certain policy areas, virtually inconceivable in Germany. Hence, the pressure to support a chancellor even if his or her decisions go against party lines is stronger in Germany than in most other parliamentary democracies.

Second, the European Council usually deals with those problems that have not been resolved either by previous Council of Ministers meetings or during the preparatory negotiations at lower levels preceding a summit. In other words, it is the difficult, controversial issues that are left for the big beasts to resolve, and inevitably this requires a considerable freedom of discretion and autonomy to strike bargains.

Consequently, German chancellors enjoy a very high discretion when participating in European summit meetings. Essentially, they act largely according to the logic of foreign policy where governments control the negotiation process (including the information about it) and where national parties and parliaments are normally confronted with agreements that they are asked to approve *ex post*. To a degree, this is also due to personality and leadership style. European integration was always very close to the heart of Chancellor Kohl and he therefore tolerated very little interference with his European leadership. Similarly, Gerhard Schröder quickly began to emulate the presidential style of his predecessor and single-handedly imposed some European decisions on his party (Poguntke 2005). To be sure, a substantial portion of this considerable freedom of action can be attributed to the still prevalent consensus among German elites. Across the different elite groups, there is strong agreement that European integration is generally desirable and that the good cause justifies a strong German contribution.

Conclusion

In the light of the pervasive Europeanization of all aspects of national politics German party organizations have remained remarkably unaffected by the indisputable growth of the powers of the EU institutions of governance. There has been virtually no formal adaptation beyond the creation of *ex officio* seats for EP delegation leaders in national executives or executive committees in recognition of the increased relevance of the European Parliament. The considerable expansion of EU competencies in the wake of the treaties of Maastricht, Amsterdam and Nice has not been mirrored by an expansion of European policy competence at party headquarters. It has, however, led to changes in parliamentary committee structures and, concomitantly, more resources for those who specialize in European affairs in national or Land parliaments.

To be sure, there can be little doubt that the attention given to what is going on in Brussels has grown, but this has hardly led to those who know most about this, that is the broad category of EU specialists, gaining intra-party weight. Above all, MEPs are still operating in a manner largely detached from national politics. There is a considerable linkage deficit between national and supranational parliamentary politics although the awareness is growing that cooperation between national and European members of parliament needs to be strengthened.

All interviewees agreed that the most conspicuous power shift within national parties is a result of the executive bias of European decision-making that gives party elites – when in government – considerable freedom of action that can be used to re-position their party on major issues. This is particularly pronounced in the European Council, where the head of government has very considerable room for manoeuvre. The logic of majority government simply means that the majority in the Bundestag has little choice but to agree *ex post* to whatever a German chancellor has signed up to in a summit meeting. Individual government ministers, by contrast, tend to be more closely monitored by the Bundestag but even they enjoy very significant room for manoeuvre.

If we want to assess long-term trends, the picture is not entirely unambiguous. On the one hand, the executive bias means that members of government have experienced an increase in their power vis-à-vis national party arenas – simply because they participate in decisions at the European level which pre-determine the political positions of their parties back home. Clearly, this applies, first and foremost, to parties of national government (and, to a lesser extent, Land government). On the other hand, countervailing trends are beginning to make themselves felt. The growing awareness of the fact that European politics shape a substantial portion of national legislation means that national parliamentarians are beginning to invest more time and energy in monitoring what their MEPs – and their governments – are doing in European decision-making arenas. As a result, the traditionally very large freedom of manoeuvre is beginning to be narrowed.

With regard to the widespread debate about how parties hold their agents in the EP to account (Müller 2000; Strøm *et al.* 2003), German parties generally follow a supply-side logic of accountability: instead of attempting to avoid control by their principals, German MEPs actively try to strengthen the link to national politics because they want to improve policy coordination and reduce their detachment from national politics. While a stronger integration into national politics will entail a reduction of their autonomy as legislators (which would suggest considerable power reduction), the greater visibility brought about by integration into national politics may actually mean they gain additional power, both in national politics generally and, more specifically, within the party. Hence, MEPs may want to trade policy-making power at the European level for political power at the national level.

So far, however, European integration has left German national parties relatively unaffected. There are few structural changes, and the overall distribution of power has not changed significantly on account of the growing importance of European politics. In contrast to our suggestion in the introductory chapter, EU specialization, be it by party staff or by parliamentarians, has not become a significant resource in German national power games. Our first hypothesis, however, is corroborated by the analysis of the case of Germany: essentially, the major effect of European integration is that it further amplifies the effect of governmental incumbency, which tends to shift power towards party elites.

Clearly, this is largely because the logic of intergovernmentalism still dominates European governance. To a degree, this may be a false perception given the considerable expansion of the co-decision powers of the European Parliament. However, as far as the adaptive pressures on national party organizations are concerned, perception seems to matter more than the formal distribution of competencies. Furthermore, the (still) strong consensus among German political elites favouring European integration tends to muffle or even suppress debates over European politics and policy in Germany; this lack of public debate slows down the process of growing public and elite awareness of the relevance of the EU for domestic politics.

The fact that the main adaptive pressures flowing from the EU strengthen party

elites, particularly when in government, explains why parties needed little structural adaptation: except for the Greens, German parties are traditionally geared
towards elite domination and have therefore been well equipped for a further shift
in power in favour of their elites. There are, however, clear indications that the
realities of the increased role of the EP are beginning to catch up with German
parties in that their senior MEPs are beginning to acquire a greater stature in national politics. That said, it is fair to conclude that the Europeanization of German
political parties has not fully realized its potential yet.

Notes

1　My special thanks go to Elisabeth Carter for helpful comments on earlier versions of
this chapter.
2　The WASG (*Wahlalternative Arbeit und soziale Gerechtigkeit*) attracted some senior
members from the SPD, including the former party chairman Oskar Lafontaine, who
had become increasingly disaffected with the neo-liberal turn of the SPD under Chancellor Gerhard Schröder. It ran candidates on an open Left Party list for the Bundestag
and entered into merger negotiations with the Left Party after the 2005 Bundestag
elections. The name Left Party will be used throughout this chapter in order to avoid
confusion.
3　In 1998, the first red–green government moved the European division of the ministry
of economics to the ministry of finance because the then SPD leader Oskar Lafontaine
wanted to have a particularly strong position with the cabinet.
4　This was the result of a change in Article 45 of the German Basic Law (*Grundge-
setz*).
5　§14.4 party statute of December 2005.
6　Unless stated otherwise, the following is based on 24 interviews with relevant politicians and members of staff in all parties that are covered in this chapter. The positions
of the interviewees included the following (past and present): government minister,
party chair, general secretary, leader or deputy leader of Bundestag parliamentary
party, deputy general secretary of the Europarty, member of the executive of the Europarty, delegation leader, MEP, senior member of the European affairs committee of
the Bundestag. Several interviewees have held multiple positions. Interviews were
carried out between spring 2004 and spring 2006.
7　See also relevant party statutes and Poguntke and Boll (1992).
8　CDU and CSU: European People's Party (EPP); SPD: Party of European Socialists
(PES); FDP: European Liberal Democrat and Reform Party (ELDR): Greens: European Green Party (EGP), Left Party: Party of the European Left (EL).

References

Anderson, Jeffrey J. (2005) 'Germany and Europe: Centrality in the EU', in Simon Bulmer
and Christian Lequesne (eds), *The Member States of the European Union*, Oxford: Ox-
ford University Press, pp. 77–96.
von Arnim, Hans-Herbert (1991) *Die Partei, der Abgeordnete und das Geld*, Mainz: v.
Hase and Koehler.
Auel, Katrin and Arthur Benz (2005) 'The Politics of Adaptation: The Europeanisation of
National Parliamentary Systems', *The Journal of Legislative Studies*, 11(3/4): 372–93.
Bardi, Luciano (1996) 'Transnational Trends in European Parties and the 1994 European
Elections of the European Parliament', *Party Politics*, 2(1): 99–113.

Bardi, Luciano (2002) 'Parties and Party Systems in the European Union: National and Supranational Dimensions', in Kurt Richard Luther and Ferdinand Müller-Rommel (eds), *Political Parties in the New Europe: Political and Analytical Challenges*, Oxford: Oxford University Press, pp. 293–321.

Bomberg, Elizabeth (1998) *Green Parties and Politics in the European Union*, London: Routledge.

Bomberg, Elizabeth (2002) 'The Europeanisation of Green Parties: Exploring the EU's Impact', *West European Politics*, 25(3): 29–50.

Börzel, Tanja A. (1999) 'Towards Convergence in Europe? Institutional Adaptation to Europeanization in Germany and Spain', *Journal of Common Market Studies*, 37(4): 573–96.

Börzel, Tanja A. (2005) 'Europeanization: How the European Union Interacts with its Members States', in Simon Bulmer and Christian Lequesne (eds), *The Member States of the European Union*, Oxford: Oxford University Press, pp. 45–69.

Bulmer, Simon, Andreas Maurer and William Paterson (2001) 'The European Policy-Making Machinery in the Berlin Republic: Hindrance or Handmaiden?', *German Politics*, 10(1): 177–206.

Derlin, Hans-Ulrich (2000) 'Germany', in Hussein Kassim, B. Guy Peters and Vincent Wright (eds), *The National Co-ordination of EU Policy. The Domestic Level*, Oxford: Oxford University Press, pp. 54–78.

Dietz, Thomas (1997) *Die grenzüberschreitende Interaktion grüner Parteien in Europa*, Opladen: Westdeutscher Verlag.

Dietz, Thomas (2002) 'European Federation of Green Parties', in Karl Magnus Johansson and Peter Zervakis (eds), *European Political Parties between Cooperation and Integration*, Baden-Baden: Nomos, pp. 125–59.

van der Eijk, Cees, Mark Franklin and Erik Oppenhuis (1996) 'The Strategic Context: Party Choice', in Cees van der Eijk and Mark Franklin (eds), *Choosing Europe? The European Electorate and National Politics in the Face of the Union*, Ann Arbor, MI: Michigan University Press, pp. 332–65.

Europawahlgesetz (1994) *Gesetz über die Wahl der Abgeordneten des Europäischen Parlaments aus der Bundesrepublik Deutschland (zuletzt geändert am 15. August 2003)*.

Fuchs, Michael (2004) 'Der Ausschuss für die Angelegenheiten der Europäischen Union des Deutschen Bundestages', *Zeitschrift für Parlamentsfragen*, 35(1): 3–24.

Goetz, Klaus H. (1995) 'National Governance and European Integration: Intergovernmental Relations in Germany', *Journal of Common Market Studies*, 33(1): 91–116.

Gunlicks, Arthur (1995) 'The New German Party Finance Law', *German Politics*, 4(1): 101–21.

Haas, Ernst B. (1958) *The Uniting of Europe: Political, Social and Economic Forces 1950–1957*, London: Stevens.

Hansen, Troels B. and Bruno Scholl (2002) 'Europeanization and Domestic Parliamentary Adaptation: A Comparative Analysis of the Bundestag and the House of Commons', *European Integration Online Papers (EIoP)*, 6(15) <http://eiop.or.at/eiop/texte/2002-015a.htm>.

Herzog, Dietrich (1997) 'Die Führungsgremien der Parteien: Funktionswandel und Strukturentwicklungen', in Oscar W.Gabriel, Oskar Niedermayer and Richard Stöss (eds), *Parteiendemokratie in Deutschland*, Opladen: Westdeutscher Verlag, pp. 301–22.

Hix, Simon and Christopher Lord (1997) *Political Parties in the European Union*, New York: St. Martin's Press.

Holzhacker, Ronald (2002) 'National Parliamentary Scrutiny over EU Issues: Comparing

Goals and Methods of Governing and Opposition Parties', *European Union Politics*, 3(4): 459–79.

Hyde-Price, Adrian and Charlie Jeffery (2001) 'Germany and the European Union: Constructing Normality', *Journal of Common Market Studies*, 39(4): 689–717.

Jeffery, Charlie (1997) 'Farewell the Third Level? The German Länder and the European Policy Process', in Charlie Jeffery (ed.), *The Regional Dimension of the European Union: Towards a Third Level in Europe?*, London: Frank Cass, pp. 56–75.

Johansson, Karl Magnus and Tapio Raunio (2005) 'Regulating Europarties: Cross-Party Coalitions Capitalizing on Incomplete Contracts', *Party Politics*, 11(5): 515–34.

Lees, Charles (2002) ' "Dark Matter": Institutional Constraints and the Failure of Party-Based Euroscepticism in Germany', *Political Studies*, 50(2): 244–67.

Lijphart, Arend (1992) *Parliamentary versus Presidential Government*, Oxford: Oxford University Press.

Lindberg, Leon N. and Stuart A. Scheingold (1970) *Europe's Would-Be Polity: Patterns of Change in the European Community*, Englewood Cliffs, NJ: Prentice-Hall.

Moore, Carolyn (2006) ' "Schloss Neuwahnstein"? Why the Länder Continue to Strengthen their Representations in Brussels', *German Politics*, 15(2): 192–205.

Müller, Wolfgang C. (2000) 'Political Parties in Parliamentary Democracies: Making Delegation and Accountability Work', *European Journal of Political Research*, 37(3): 309–33.

Naßmacher, Karl-Heinz (2002) 'Parteienfinanzierung in Deutschland', in Oscar W. Gabriel, Oskar Niedermayer and Richard Stöss (eds), *Parteiendemokratie in Deutschland*, Wiesbaden: Westdeutscher Verlag, pp. 159–78.

Niedermayer, Oskar (2003) 'The Party System: Structure, Policy, and Europeanization', in Kenneth Dyson and Klaus Goetz (eds), *Germany, Europe and the Politics of Constraint*, Oxford: Oxford University Press, pp. 129–46.

Ovey, Joey-David (2002) *Between Nation and Europe. Labour, the SPD and the European Parliament 1994–1999*, Opladen: Leske and Budrich.

Pehle, Heinrich and Roland Sturm (2005) 'Die Europäisierung des politischen Systems', in Oscar W. Gabriel and Everhard Holtmann (eds), *Handbuch politisches System der Bundesrepublik Deutschland*, third edition, Munich: Oldenbourg, pp. 883–904.

Poguntke, Thomas (1994) 'Parties in a Legalistic Culture: The Case of Germany', in Richard S. Katz and Peter Mair (eds), *How Parties Organize: Change and Adaptation in Party Organizations in Western Democracies*, London: Sage, pp. 185–215.

Poguntke, Thomas (1998) 'Party Organisations', in Jan W. van Deth, (ed.), *Comparative Politics: The Problem of Equivalence*, London: Routledge, pp. 156–79.

Poguntke, Thomas (2002) 'Parteiorganisationen in der Bundesrepublik Deutschland: Einheit in der Vielfalt?', in Oscar W. Gabriel, Oskar Niedermayer and Richard Stöss (eds), *Parteiendemokratie in der Bundesrepublik Deutschland*, Wiesbaden: Westdeutscher Verlag, pp. 253–73.

Poguntke, Thomas (2003) 'Die Bündnisgrünen nach der Bundestagswahl 2002: Auf dem Weg zur linken Funktionspartei?', in Oskar Niedermayer (ed.), *Die Parteien nach der Bundestagswahl 2002*, Opladen: Leske and Budrich, pp. 89–107.

Poguntke, Thomas (2005) 'A Presidentializing Party State? The Federal Republic of Germany', in Thomas Poguntke and Paul Webb (eds), *The Presidentialization of Politics: A Comparative Study of Modern Democracies*, Oxford: Oxford University Press, pp. 62–85.

Poguntke, Thomas and Christine Pütz (2006) 'Parteien in der Europäischen Union. Zu den Entwicklungschancen der Europarteien', *Zeitschrift für Parlamentsfragen*, 37(2): 334–53.

Poguntke, Thomas with Bernhard Boll (1992) 'Germany', in Richard S. Katz and Peter Mair (eds), *Party Organizations: A Data Handbook on Party Organizations in Western Democracies, 1960–90*, London: Sage, pp. 317–88.

Raunio, Tapio (1997) *The European Perspective: Transnational Party Groups in the 1989–94 European Parliament*, Aldershot: Ashgate.

Reif, Karlheinz and Hermann Schmitt (1980) 'Nine Second-Order National Elections: A Conceptual Framework for the Analysis of European Election Results', *European Journal of Political Research*, 8(1): 3–45.

Rüdig, Wolfgang (1996) 'Green Parties and the European Union', in John Gaffney (ed.), *Political Parties and the European Union*, London: Routledge, pp. 254–72.

Saalfeld, Thomas (2000) 'Bureaucratisation, Coordination and Competition: Parliamentary Party Groups in the German Bundestag', in Knut Heidar and Ruud Koole (eds), *Parliamentary Party Groups in European Democracies. Political Parties Behind Closed Doors*, London: Routledge, pp. 23–38.

Saalfeld, Thomas (2003) 'The Bundestag: Institutional Incrementalism and Behavioural Reticence', in Kenneth Dyson and Klaus Goetz (eds), *Germany, Europe and the Politics of Constraint*, Oxford: Oxford University Press, pp. 73–96.

Schindler, Peter (1994) *Datenhandbuch zur Geschichte des Deutschen Bundestages*, Baden-Baden: Nomos.

Schüttemeyer, Suzanne S. (1998) *Fraktionen im Deutschen Bundestag 1949–1997*, Opladen: Westdeutscher Verlag.

Scully, Roger (2001) 'Voters, Parties and Europe', *Party Politics*, 7(4): 515–24.

Sloam, James (2003) 'Responsibility for Europe: The EU Policy of the German Social Democrats since Unification', *German Politics*, 12(1): 59–78.

Strøm, Kaare, Wolfgang C. Müller and Torbjörn Bergman (eds) (2003) *Delegation and Accountability in Parliamentary Democracies*, Oxford: Oxford University Press.

Töller, Annette Elisabeth (2004) 'Dimensionen der Europäisierung – Das Beispiel des Deutschen Bundestages', *Zeitschrift für Parlamentsfragen*, 35(1): 25–50.

Wagener, Hans-Jürgen, Thomas Eger and Heiko Fritz, (2006) *Europäische Integration. Recht und Ökonomie, Geschichte und Politik*, Munich: Vahlen.

6 European integration and Spanish parties

Elite empowerment amidst limited adaptation[1]

Luis Ramiro and Laura Morales

In this chapter we analyse how European integration has (or has not) exerted an impact on the internal life and organization of the five main Spanish parties: PSOE, PP, IU, CDC and PNV.[2] We examine to what extent these parties have transformed their organizations in order to incorporate the European level into their decision-making structures. Are the party actors most closely involved in European Union (EU)-related affairs or issues gaining power within their parties? To what extent has European integration had a substantial impact on the internal workings of these five parties? Our research is guided by two main hypotheses. The first one proposes that the internal power of party elites will be enhanced by the increased access to resources and information of those who deal more directly with EU politics and the pre-eminence of executives and central governments in EU policy-making. The second hypothesis argues that EU specialists within the parties will also be beneficiaries in the intra-party balance of power, thanks to their policy specialization.[3]

Before we address these main issues we will briefly introduce the reader to the central features of the Spanish political system, paying special attention to the dimensions that are most relevant to our analysis.

Spain and Europe

Historical background

Spain joined the European Union (then European Community, EC) in January 1986. This was the final accomplishment of a long-desired goal of Spanish foreign policy that would put an end to a period of external political isolation (Maxwell and Spiegel 1994). Already at the end of the 1960s, when the country was attempting to modernize itself and to open up its economy, Francoist governments tried to link Spain to the process of European integration. At that time accession to the Common Market was set as a policy priority and a request for associate status was made in 1962 and 1964 (Powell 1995). The first Spanish applications were obviously rejected for political reasons. In spite of these initial rejections, Spain finally signed an association agreement in 1970.

During the transition to democracy the Spanish government renewed its application for EC membership in 1977 and the country finally gained membership of the Council of Europe in 1979.[4] After the Socialist victory in 1982, the foreign policy priorities of González's government were not radically different from that of the previous Centrist cabinets of the UCD (*Unión de Centro Democrático*). The government gave high priority to accession to the EC. The reasons behind this policy were both economic and, especially, political. Integration into the EC was seen as a factor that would foster the stabilization of the newborn democratic system and a very important asset for Spanish economic modernization. The negotiations for Spanish membership were long (1978–85) and difficult (with the Spanish government having a relatively weak position in the negotiation process), but eventually culminated with success in March 1985.

To some extent, one of the features of Spanish foreign policy during most of the present democratic period has been its consensual character. This applies especially to the policy towards European integration. The future and desirable Spanish membership of the EC was a shared goal of all relevant political parties during the 1970s and 1980s. All parties on the ideological spectrum, from communists to conservatives, evaluated EC membership as very positive for the consolidation of democracy in Spain, for its economic development, and as a way to heal certain historical wounds (Barbé 1999). As a consequence, EU-related issues have been hardly controversial in Spanish politics.

Institutional framework, party systems and party organization

The current political system was formed during the transition to democracy initiated in 1975.[5] This transition was characterized by negotiations between reformist political elites drawn from the dictatorship's ranks and the democratic opposition, as well as by the practice of a consensual process of constitution-making – a model of 'modern elite settlement' in Gunther's (1992) words. The transition was formally symbolized by the consensual elaboration and approval of a democratic constitution in 1978. This is a comparatively rigid constitution.

The Spanish parliament shows features of medium strength bicameralism with asymmetric chambers. The Spanish constitution favours parliamentary and governmental stability and, in particular, reinforces the role of the prime minister through several parliamentary procedures, including votes of confidence and non-confidence. Government stability is also fostered by the effects of the electoral system, formally proportional for the Congress, but with a strongly disproportional and almost majoritarian outcome.

Although the Spanish executive is selected by the legislative and is dependent on legislative confidence, executive–legislative relations are characterized by strong executive dominance (Heywood 1999).[6] The strengthening of the executive, and particularly of the prime minister, by the process of European integration has taken place in a framework in which executive dominance already exists (Heywood 1999; Closa and Heywood 2004). Given this, it is not surprising that the Spanish parliament did not play a very significant role in the process of

Spanish accession to the EC, or that it has had little control over the actions of successive governments (Molina del Pozo 1995). Besides that, the predominantly consensual nature of EU policy has meant that EU affairs are not often debated, thus downgrading the relevance of the parliament in giving domestic support to the position defended by the government in the EU (Closa and Heywood 2004: 74).

The main channel for the influence of parliament in EU matters is the Committee for EU Affairs – created in 1985 with the intention of controlling the daily initiatives of the government – and the General Committee for the *Comunidades Autónomas* (Autonomous Communities).[7] The Committee for EU affairs has not achieved its original goals, and its role has been reduced so that it is now the parliamentary recipient of information on EU affairs from the government. It is more a forum for uncontroversial debates rather than an organ of parliamentary control (Molina del Pozo 1995; Cienfuegos 1996 and 1997; Closa 1996b, Closa and Heywood 2004). The General Committee for the *Comunidades Autónomas* has created a new venue for participation of the regions in Spanish European policy but its role is limited given that this committee mainly receives government reports (Cienfuegos 1997).

One of the main features of the Spanish party system is the differentiation between a relatively consolidated party system in the national parliamentary arena and several (diverse) regional party systems. In the national arena the party system is a limited multi-party system with a low level of ideological polarization (Linz and Montero 1999). This multiparty system enables the relevant parliamentary representation of a relatively high number of small peripheral nationalist parties.[8] The Spanish party systems have been structured by two main cleavages: on the one hand, the traditional left–right socio-economic division and, on the other, the centre–periphery tension fostered by the presence and claims of nationalist and regionalist parties in the regional legislative assemblies and governments, and in the national parliament. In general, two nationwide political parties have attracted the majority of popular support. Since 1982 they have been the conservative PP and the social democratic PSOE. In addition to these two big government-oriented parties there is a third small nationwide and left-wing party: the IU. Ever since the period of UCD centrist governments, national office has been held by either the PP or the PSOE, which have always formed one-party cabinets, although not always with an absolute majority. In the 1993–96, 1996–2000, and 2004- terms there have been one-party minority cabinets.

Besides these three nation-wide parties, three regional parties have played a pivotal role in forming parliamentary majorities when absolute majorities were not available: the Catalan centre-right two-party coalition Convergence and Union (*Convergència i Unió*, CiU), in which the CDC is the biggest party; the centre-right Basque PNV; and the smaller Canary centre-right coalition Canary Coalition (*Coalición Canaria*, CC). The CiU, the CC and the PNV have also been in the governments of their respective regions for a long time. We thus include the pivotal CDC and PNV in our analysis, and exclude the CC only because of the minor size of the parties included in this coalition and because it has not obtained representation in the European Parliament (EP).

Spanish parties share a common model of party organization characterized by the typical structure of the mass party model but with very weak membership figures. Like other modern Western parties, the Spanish ones have access to substantial state funding, combine catch-all strategies with modern professionalized and marketing-guided campaign techniques, and have fragile roots in civil society. These features place Spanish parties close to the electoral-professional party type described by Panebianco (1988). All Spanish nationwide parties are internally differentiated at national, regional, provincial and local organizational levels. The non-nationwide peripheral nationalist parties are also structured – with some minor caveats – along national (that is regional), provincial and local lines. In all cases the congress is the pre-eminent and sovereign party body under which are a normally very large party council and/or national executive (on which the regional parties or organizations are represented), and the executive committee.[9]

The very cohesive Spanish parliamentary groups are formally and effectively under the leadership of the party in central office. The executive committee of the Spanish parties monitors and directs the parliamentary party but, simultaneously, there is – at least in the case of the two biggest parties, the PP and the PSOE – an important overlap between the party in central office and the national parliamentary group.[10] The party leader is, at the same time, the leader or chair of the parliamentary party, and the head of the government if that party wins the elections. In addition, the degree of factionalization is very low in all the parties and internal cohesion is generally very high.[11] This concentration of powers in the position of the party leader and the remarkable party internal discipline favour a presidentialization of Spanish party politics (van Biezen 1998 and 2000; Holliday 2002; Ramiro and Morales 2004).

Conflicts over European integration

Spanish membership of the EU is remarkable for the wide consensus it has found both among the public and the parties. Even among the traditionally EU-supportive South European countries, Spain stands out because, unlike Portugal or Greece, there was no significant rejection of membership among political and party elites at the time of accession. The EU has never become a cleavage in party politics or even an important political issue in Spain. In an uncharacteristic move for the Communist party family, the Spanish Communists supported EC membership since the beginning of the 1970s. Apart from this, the centrist UCD and CDS, the conservative AP/PP, the socialist PSOE, and the more relevant nationalist parties supported EC membership. In Spanish political discourse the EU and the very idea of Europe have traditionally been linked to democracy, and every major party has linked European integration to economic progress and to modernization of the country.[12]

The conservative AP (later PP) supported EC membership from the very beginning. This political position was viewed as helping to integrate the party into mainstream Spanish party politics, and contributed to blurring its radical conservative image at the same time as preventing criticisms based on the links of its leaders with the dictatorship. When Spain finally entered the EC, the AP was the main opposition party after the electoral disaster of the UCD in 1982. At this time the AP leader criticized the accession negotiations headed by the socialist government, the membership conditions imposed on Spain, and certain negative effects of these conditions for Spanish economic and political interests. That said, the conservatives never rejected EC membership, nor did they propose withdrawal from the Community. Rather, the European policy of the PP combines a pro-EU stance with the defence of the role of the nation state and of Spanish national interests (Closa and Heywood 2004: 47).

On the left, the PSOE had defended the integration of Spain into the EC since the early 1970s and the Marxist and anti-capitalist ideology of the party during the democratic transition did not affect its pro-EC position. Once in government it was González's cabinet that finally took Spain into the EC. During the 1980s and 1990s the González governments adopted a pro-integrationist stance and a federalist discourse (Closa 1996a). In the case of the Communist Party of Spain (PCE), the party maintained the orthodox Communist rejection of the EC as a capitalist instrument until the beginning of the 1970s. In this decade, the growing distance between the Spanish Communists and the Soviet Union through the new Eurocommunist strategy also fostered the acceptance of EC membership. After Spain joined the Community the PCE, and then the new coalition in which they participated (IU), approved Spanish membership. The PCE and IU frequently highlighted some negative effects that the process of European integration was having for the Spanish economy (and called for a renegotiation of membership conditions) and supported the most supranationalist arguments in the European political debate (in search of a more federal and internally democratic EU). However, as in the conservative case, the PCE and IU have never proposed that Spain leave the EU.

With regard to the main nationalist political parties, the centre-right Catalan CDC and the centre-right Basque PNV, they have been always clearly pro-European. The PNV was pro-European even before the democratic transition and maintained this position after accession. Both parties, while generally accepting the process of European integration, have highlighted the need to reinforce the participation of the regions and 'nations without a state' within European policymaking. The PNV has frequently highlighted the need to overcome some aspects of the membership agreements that constrain certain economic sectors that are especially relevant in the Basque Country, but these positions are far from a general critique of the integration process. For both Catalan and Basque nationalists the EU is a political organization that shows the declining role of the traditional nation state, and is thus functional for their nationalist discourse. Therefore, opposition to the EC among the Spanish parties was negligible and was initially limited to marginal parties of both extremes of the ideological spectrum and to certain left-wing nationalist parties. But neither the extreme right nor the extreme left parties have had any significant position within the Spanish party system.

During the 1990s Euroscepticism in Spanish party politics increased. However, in all of the most relevant cases this was just the expression of a soft Euroscepticism that did not reject Spanish membership or the process and idea of European integration itself. The current process of European integration was simply judged not to be developing in an adequate way and was deemed to 'run counter to the interests, policies or issues' (Taggart and Szczerbiak 2002: 8) that these parties supported. The IU (and the Communist PCE within it) and other left-wing nationalist parties that have become electorally important since the 1990s and 2000s (particularly the ERC and the BNG[13]) progressively adopted soft Eurosceptic stances (Llamazares *et al.* 2007 forthcoming). In the case of the IU this new party line had its most clear expression in the party's rejection of the Maastricht treaty. In relation to the position that IU MPs should adopt during the parliamentary session of ratification of this treaty an important internal division arose that entailed a rare (in Spanish terms) episode of parliamentary lack of discipline in the IU group. This internal party conflict today remains the most important division over EU policy issues and it is also the single Spanish case in which EU issues contributed to the factionalization of a party. Since 1992, the IU has maintained this soft Eurosceptic position and has demanded a more federalist, supranational, social, democratic and pro-welfare-state EU.[14] In this, the IU has been accompanied by other left-wing nationalist parties such as the BNG and the ERC, which, to the previous leftist claims, added the need for a greater recognition of the status of regions and 'nations without a state' within the EU (for example, the participation of the regions in policy-making and the recognition of the status of their minority languages).

The public debate in 2004 and 2005 on the ratification of the European constitution reflected once more the pro-EU stance of most of Spanish parties. Both the PP and the PSOE were in favour of the constitutional project. The Catalan nationalist party CDC and the Basque nationalist PNV had internal debates on this issue, and some party sections raised objections to the constitutional treaty due to the lack of recognition of the European 'nations without a state'. However, the party leadership bodies of both parties supported the constitution in their final decision. Only the IU and the smaller peripheral nationalist parties mentioned previously were against the constitutional project and campaigned for a No vote in the referendum of 2004. In any case, the result of the Spanish referendum on the EU constitution showed, even with the low turnout of 42 per cent, the pro-EU consensus among Spanish public opinion: 77 per cent of voters supported the constitution, while only 17 per cent rejected it.

The votes received by Eurosceptic parties in EP elections, normally fought around domestic issues, have been traditionally very small (see Table 6.1). Leaving aside the case of the IU, other minor left-wing peripheral nationalist parties, who also defend soft Eurosceptic positions, have seldom gained representation. At the attitudinal level, too, Spaniards have shown themselves to be very enthusiastic

Table 6.1 Elections to the European Parliament in Spain: votes, seats and turnout, 1987–2004

	1987		1989		1994		1999		2004	
	%	Seats	%	Seats	%	Seats	%	Seats	%	Seats
IU	5.2	3	6	4	13.4	9	5.7	4	4.1	2
PSOE	39	28	39.6	27	30.8	22	35.3	24	43.5	25
PNV	1.2	0	1.9	1	2.8	2	2.9	2	} 5.1	} 2
CDC	4.4	3	4.2	2	4.7	3	4.4	3		
PP	24.6	17	21.4	15	40.1	28	39.7	27	41.2	24
Others with seats	13.9	9	17.8	11	–	–	6.3	4	2.4	1
Others without seats	11.7	0	9.1	0	8.2	0	5.7	0	3.7	0
Turnout/total seats	68.9	60	54.6	60	59.1	64	63.0	64	45.1	54

Notes
In 2004 the IU ran in a coalition and only one of the two MEPs elected belonged to the IU. The CDC also ran in a coalition so the number of MEPs belonging to the party was: two in 1987, one in 1989, two in 1994, two in 1999 and one in 2004. The PNV ran in a coalition and the number of MEPs belonging to the party was as follows: one in 1989, one in 1994, one in 1999 and one in 2004. In 2004 the PNV and CDC were part of the same coalition.
*Others with seats' includes in 1987 MEPs from a centrist party (Centro Democrático y Social) and several nationalist parties (Herri Batasuna and Coalición por la Europa de los Pueblos); in 1989 this includes MEPs from a centrist party (Centro Democrático y Social), a tycoon party (Agrupación Ruiz Mateos) and from several nationalist parties (Partido Andalucista, Izquierda de los Pueblos, Herri Batasuna and Por la Europa de los Pueblos); and in 1999 and 2004 this includes MEPs from several nationalist parties (Coalición Europea, Bloque Nacionalista Galego and Euskal Herritarrok in 1999; and Europa de los Pueblos in 2004).

towards the EU, displaying a degree of support for European integration that is remarkably higher than the EU average. Diffuse support for the EU is consistently above the EU average (Closa and Heywood 2004: 37). However, the evaluation of membership benefits and of certain very distinctive EU policies (for example the Common Agricultural Policy or some policies related to the development of a common market) have never been very positive (Barreiro and Sánchez Cuenca 2001). In recent years, however, Spaniards have shown an increasingly questioning attitude towards the EU that takes into consideration the costs and benefits of EU membership (Closa and Heywood 2004: 40).

In the rest of the chapter we will examine the way in which the relevant Spanish parties have changed their organizations as a result of trying to adapt to the process of European integration and we will assess whether the party actors involved in the management of EU issues have gained power in the structures of their respective national parties. With this goal in mind, we first analyse the parties' structural adaptation.

Structural adaptation to European integration

Formal management and funding of EU-related activities

The presence in the Spanish government of a minister devoted specifically to EU matters has been rare and it only happened in some of the centrist UCD cabinets, soon after Spain had applied for EU membership. Apart from that brief experience, the management of EU matters has been mainly placed in the wider foreign affairs ministry, although the level of authority of the person responsible for European policies has been high and just under the level of the minister.

Parties have imitated this model in their internal structures: within the parties EU matters are dealt with under the heading of general foreign affairs. In all the parties under observation, a politician – the international secretary – is responsible for EU affairs, combining this domain with other world areas. However, the role of the international secretary in defining the parties' EU policy is shared with the party's MEPs and other EU specialists (for example, former ministers and party leaders). That said, since the mid-1980s, the international secretaries of the two bigger and governmental parties (PP and PSOE) have had little visibility when the party is in government, as the foreign minister acts as the real party spokesperson for EU matters.

Therefore, in spite of the growing importance of EU politics, there is no position devoted exclusively to EU issues in the structure of parties in central office, and the person who represents the party in the Europarty usually combines this role with other party positions, for example that of the international secretary.

Apart from the international secretaries, some other party positions are also concerned with EU issues. EU membership has resulted in the creation of parliamentary committees related to this policy area. Consequently the MP who acts as the party spokesperson in the parliamentary European affairs committee often takes the role of party spokesperson on EU matters. However, in the Spanish case this role is also frequently played by the party spokesperson in the parliamentary foreign affairs committee. In any case, these two roles of party spokesperson are to a great degree unofficial or informal.

Like the party spokespersons in other parliamentary committees, the party spokesperson in the European affairs committee is selected by the leadership of the parliamentary groups. In the context of Spanish party politics, this means that this decision is made under the surveillance and scrutiny of the party leadership in central office. Even if in certain parties the scrutiny of these appointments is not formal or embedded in party rules, it nevertheless takes place because of the great overlap (particularly strong in nationwide parties) between the party at central office and the parliamentary party. These appointments to the parliamentary committees are rarely controversial in Spanish politics – except for rare cases of factional struggle in which the party leadership would intervene. Thus, these EU specialist positions are not official EU spokesperson positions and, in any case, remain under the control of the party leadership.

In addition, the parties analysed have created some advisory groups that work on EU issues. However, it is interesting to note that even these specialized advisory groups are integrated into a wider advisory group devoted to foreign and international affairs and relations. Thus, very recently (in 2004) the PP formally created a Foreign Policy Council which included the international secretary, the EP delegation leader, the spokesperson in the parliamentary European affairs committee, the general secretary of the European People's Party (EPP) and some other MEPs, although it also included some other generic foreign affairs specialists. In the case of the PSOE, the party has a long-established International Relations and Cooperation Council within which there is a working group that concerns itself with a whole host of foreign affairs. From within this working group there emerged a less formal subgroup composed of top-level politicians who work on EU-related issues. Similar mechanisms are in place in the IU, the PNV and the CDC.[15]

The financing of Spanish parties heavily depends on state funding, and public subsidies are directly linked to the parties' electoral performance. Therefore, the financial and human resources that the parties devote to their different areas of activity can vary according to the amount of subsidies received and the party's electoral fortunes. Hence, when parties suffer significant electoral losses some drastic cuts follow. Spanish EU membership and EP politics have opened up an additional source of funding for Spanish parties. Very frequently they use EP funds for the organization of workshops or seminars (more or less closely) related to EU issues, for hiring personnel (in Spain and in the EP), and some parties (like the IU) also retain part of their MEPs' salaries. This pattern of funding usage has also implied that the main source of funds for EU-related party activity is not the national party organization, in spite of the extensive public subsidies received by the Spanish parties, but is instead the funding and resources that come from the EP.

The national party organization funds the international secretariat of the party and, as a general consequence, some of the resources of this secretariat are directed towards EU-related topics, activities and staff. Yet the situation is the same for party resources as it is for party officials with an EU brief: the party resources for EU issues are included within the wider office for international relations that concerns itself with party policies towards other world areas as well. Therefore, the amount of resources devoted to EU issues within the international secretariat is not very great. In any case, the resources of the international secretariats are modest and, although it is impossible to estimate the amount of money the parties devote to this field in their budgets, the personnel in charge of this area in the parties' headquarters is easily quantifiable: it ranges from around five persons in the larger parties (PSOE and PP) to only two or even one in the smaller organizations (PNV and IU). Among this staff in charge of the parties' international policy issues there is no one who exclusively takes on an EU liaison role or who is solely devoted to EU policies. According to the party officials the scarcity of the resources available to the international secretariats of the party in central office prevents the exclusive dedication of party staff to EU matters.

Leaving aside the variation in personnel due to the changes in the parties' budgets as a result of electoral performance, there is no clearly visible trend in the resources invested by parties in this field. In any case, party resources invested in this domain are judged very modest by the parties' own officials, and they seem not to have substantially changed in the past years. It should also be noted that the general party resources and the infrastructure of party headquarters have grown since the mid-1980s, and even if there has been a growth in the infrastructure and human resources in the international secretariats this has not been remarkable and does not indicate in any way that these secretariats are a high priority for the parties.

The situation is only slightly better as regards the national parliamentary groups. Even the biggest parties (PSOE and PP) do not recruit a person exclusively devoted to EU policies from among the staff of their national parliamentary groups. The PSOE and PP parliamentary groups have a single assistant engaged with the work of several parliamentary committees related to international affairs (defence, international affairs, cooperation, and EU affairs) and, on a part-time basis, this person assists MPs working on EU issues. The three smaller parties do not have such an assistant for international policy issues as they have very few parliamentary party staff.

Therefore, in all five parties the main source of resources for EU activities is clearly the EP. The party delegation in the EP, its infrastructure and its personnel are the predominant party structure for all EU-related party activity. The MEPs rely almost exclusively on the resources made available by the EP for their activity, and only in very rare cases do they ask for assistance from the party international secretariat in the party headquarters – for example, the possibility of using an office there. Finally, any liaising between the EP delegation and other party structures and offices is done through the MEPs' own resources and assistants.

Moreover, when the party is in government there is a certain use of governmental resources for EU-related party activity. Given that four of the parties under study have participated in national (PSOE and PP) or regional (PNV and CDC) governments this has been a quite general practice in almost all of our cases. This use of governmental resources has mainly taken the form of advice and exchange of information. Consultation of PSOE and PP MEPs with the foreign minister for tasks of policy analysis and positioning is certainly common when their party is in government. In contrast there is little consultation between MEPs and their parties' headquarters. In the cases of the PNV and the CiU – given their small organizational size, their comparatively lower number of MPs and MEPs, assistants and party staff – the use of regional government resources by the different types of party EU specialists is also very notable.

MEP candidate selection procedures

In all Spanish parties candidate selection processes are far from transparent, open or strictly formalized. When the time comes to deciding the electoral lists for the legislative national elections, the territorial organizations – their provincial or regional executives – usually propose lists of candidates that at a later stage are approved by a national committee in charge of designing the electoral lists or, alternatively, by the national executive.

This is the method commonly employed by the five parties under study, although there are also some party-specific peculiarities. For example, in the case of the PP, it is only the electoral lists committees at the different territorial levels (whose members are party politicians appointed by the executive committee) that intervene. In the case of the PSOE, there is (since 1997) a system of membership ballots to select the candidate for prime minister, but the remaining candidates are proposed by the territorial committees and approved by a federal electoral committee. In the case of the IU and the CDC the territorial organizations propose and the party council and national executive approve the final lists – although the process has become more complicated in the CDC since the formation of a party federation with the smaller Catalan Christian democratic party, the UDC, and the IU has in some instances used membership ballots. Only the PNV uses a more diverse approach. Here it is the executive committee that makes a proposal – after receiving suggestions from the territorial organizations – and it is the party council that approves the electoral lists. In sum, then, in Spanish parties the national leadership remains frequently in full control of candidate selection and it has substantial veto power over the lists proposed for provincial constituencies. In addition, candidate proposals do not come from the rank-and-file through membership ballots but from the territorial (provincial or regional) leadership directly or indirectly (through electoral list committees).

Is the selection of MEP candidates any different? Certainly we would expect to find some departures from the general approach described previously because of the institutional and electoral rules that affect EP elections. The main procedural variations come from differences in the electoral system: instead of the 52 electoral districts into which the country is divided for national elections, EP elections are run in a single nationwide electoral district; and instead of 350 MPs, only 64 MEPs (up until the 2004 EP elections) or 54 MEPs (since 2004) are elected.

Given this different institutional setting we would expect, on the one hand, a reduction in the influence of the lower-level territorial units of the party organization, due to the 'nationalization' of the electoral process. On the other hand, and especially for the smaller parties, given the reduction in the number of candidates finally elected, we would expect a greater intensity in the internal fights around the elaboration of the electoral lists, thus somewhat weakening the control of the central leadership over the entire process. However, none of these dynamics takes place.

In the case of the PSOE, the national executive committee formally proposes the EP electoral list to the national executive/party council, which then approves the proposal. In practical terms, the proposal is basically engineered by the organization secretary of the party (who controls the electoral lists committee). Given that within the Socialist party the EP delegation is under the authority of, and belongs to, the national joint parliamentary group (along with the MPs of the lower and upper national chambers), the party spokesperson in the lower chamber also plays an important role in the elaboration of the list. The EP delegation and its leader also retain a certain say (and submit a report to the party leadership) but they are not key actors in the elaboration of the list, and they simply offer an evaluation of the EP delegation's performance.

In sharp contrast to this secondary role, the influence of the regional organizations of the party is very high. In line with the growing federalization of Spanish nationwide parties – which have followed the parallel federalization of the Spanish political system – Socialist regional organizations have increased their influence in this process and they are capable of decisively affecting the proposal that the organization secretary prepares. As a result of this influence there is a distribution of candidates among the regional organizations and the larger regional parties have a number of reserved MEP positions to be filled by their members. Finally, the party national leader also intervenes, as in other processes of electoral list design, especially in regards to who should head the list.

The PP employs a very similar process for the elaboration of its list, and it has not changed significantly over time. There is an electoral committee that receives the proposals of the regional electoral committees but the former obviously also has certain stakes in the inclusion of specific candidates. As in the case of the Socialists, the power within these electoral committees is in the hands of the national organization secretary or general secretary (in the national electoral committee) and in the hands of the regional party leadership (in the regional electoral committees). The general secretary or party leader not only plays a relevant role in deciding who should head the list but also influences the possible inclusion of national party leaders in the European list – something that also happens in the Socialists.

In practical terms, the list is divided into two parts: candidates proposed by the regional parties and supported by the regional leaders, and candidates proposed and supported by the national leadership. After reaching a consensus between the proposals of the central and regional leaderships – in which the national leadership has the upper hand – the national electoral committee approves the electoral list. The influence of the EP delegation is clearly very much secondary in these procedures.

In the left-wing IU the process of list design takes place directly in the party council without any formal intervention from any electoral or lists committee. The party council decides on the final list based on a proposal of the executive committee with the candidates proposed, in turn, by the regional parties.

The candidate selection procedures of the peripheral nationalist PNV and CDC are not noticeably different from those of the other parties. In both cases the number of MEPs these two parties expect to gain is really low (one or two, or at the most three). According to the party leaders interviewed, this has favoured a more centralized candidate selection process. In both cases the selection of the head of the list – traditionally in the hands of the party leadership inner circle – is almost equivalent to the selection of the party's MEP. Therefore, in the PNV and the CDC, the party council approves the list of candidates proposed by the executive committee.

In summary, MEP candidate selection processes imply no involvement whatsoever of the rank-and-file. In four out of five of the parties analysed the final decision is made by the party council – whose composition is very similar to the traditional national executives – with some minor variations across parties in the proposal process. In all cases the central party leadership and the executive committee play a crucial role, and they dominate the selection committee that prepares the proposed list of candidates. In the cases of the nationwide parties (PP, PSOE and IU), accommodating the claims of the regional parties is also a relevant part of the MEP selection process (see Table 6.2). Therefore, there are no dramatic differences in the openness and inclusiveness of the selection procedures for national and EP elections, except for the fact that the EP selection process is even more elite-centred and guided by the party leadership and the party in central office than the national legislative one. The nationalization or centralization of the process is higher, the influence of the EP delegation and EU specialists is low, and the conflicts (except for personal rivalries) are less relevant. Besides that, there has not been any notable modification of these procedures over time.

Are the criteria for candidate selection different from the ones considered for the national elections? Not really. The Socialist Party takes into consideration the need for renewal of the delegation, but also the need for some expertise, to avoid a lack of activity in the future EP delegation resulting from the replacement of the more experienced MEPs. Besides this, the electoral list should respect two other quotas: the gender one and the regional one. The PSOE has not only introduced a gender quota but is also keen to achieve parity. At the same time, the delegation also needs to respect the desire for representation of the larger regional party federations. In this regard, the behaviour of the PP is similar, and takes into consideration expertise, the need to include a few national leaders on the list, and the regional quotas. In the IU, the most internally divided and factionalized Spanish party, and a party that only wins a low number of MEPs, the leadership must negotiate the elaboration of the list with the regional party leaderships to include national (or factional) leaders. In addition, some candidates at least need to have a certain degree of expertise, and the representation of the strongest regional parties should be guaranteed – something that is extremely difficult to achieve given the

Table 6.2 Candidate selection for European Parliament elections in Spain, 2004

	IU	PSOE	PNV	CDC	PP
Who chose the selection committee?	Party council	Congress	Party council	Congress	Executive committee[a]
Who could be nominated?	Anyone	Anyone	Anyone	Anyone	Anyone
Primary vote?	No	No	No	No	No
Was another body involved?	Regional parties	Regional parties	No	No	Regional electoral committees
Which body took final decision?	Party council	Party council	Party council	Party council	Electoral committee

Note
a Especially in the PSOE and the PP the national executive membership is very large and is a kind of mix between an executive committee and a national executive.

low number of MEPs eventually elected. The same combination of factors (except for the territorial one) works in the Basque and Catalan nationalist parties.

Acting nationally

The second hypothesis advanced in the theoretical framework presented in Chapter 1 argued that the influence of EU specialists in their parties is expected to grow. This increasing influence is expected to be evident not only in the specific party positions concerned with EU issues, but is also likely to be apparent in the day-to-day functioning of the national party organization. In this section we will examine this possible influence of EU specialists in the functioning of their national parties.

Elite selection

According to the research hypotheses there are several ways in which EU specialists might have become increasingly important in their national parties. One of them is elite selection. Given the scarce use within Spanish parties of participatory organizational devices, such as primaries or membership ballots, the party leading bodies have an especially influential position in this field. Therefore, one of the main ways in which actors may exert influence in elite selection is through membership of the party leading bodies. What is the presence of EU specialists in the leading bodies of the party organizations? Do EU specialists, or at least some of them (EP delegation leaders, MEPs), have *ex officio* positions in the leading bodies of their parties?

From the party statutes we should conclude that the influence of EU specialists in this field is not very remarkable. Only in the conservative PP does the EP delegation leader or spokesperson MEP have an *ex officio* position in the very large party executive committee. Besides this, all the conservative MEPs also have *ex officio* positions in the party council/national executive and in the party congress. None of the other Spanish parties give their MEPs a more significant formal position than the PP. However, we should stress that these formal leading bodies, all of them with remarkably large memberships, are not very relevant in terms of their internal leverage or power – that is exerted by the party leader's own inner circle within the executive committee. Next to the PP, the centre-right Catalan nationalist CDC also guarantees a more visible position to its MEPs. The CDC gives its MEPs (from one to three, depending on the elections) *ex officio* positions in the congress and party council, and a representative of the EP delegation is a member of the national executive. In the PSOE the MEP delegation leader is just an *ex officio* member of the highly populated party council. In the Basque nationalist PNV the MEP may be a member of the congress and of the party council (along with other MPs and local councillors), but this presence is formally incompatible with membership of other leading bodies. And finally, in the left-wing IU the MEPs or the EP delegation leader do not have any formally reserved positions in the leading party bodies (see Table 6.3).

This very restricted presence of MEPs or of EP delegation leaders in the most influential party bodies is sometimes increased in practice – aside from formal rules – but then the presence of EU specialists in such organs seems to be more dependent on their personal networking, internal prestige or influence than on their expertise or EU specialization. In a few instances the inclusion of certain MEPs in their respective party's national executive is directly related to their EU specialization, but in most cases of incorporation of EU specialists into top party organizations is related to internal party dynamics.

The lack of formal influence in elite selection and in party organs is also exacerbated by the fact that few elite interviewees thought that specialization in EU affairs was a useful way to speed up the career of an activist within the party hierarchy. However, the elites interviewed all argued that EU policy has an increasing importance and that it is already widely recognised as a relevant portfolio

Table 6.3 Ex officio positions of MEPs in Spanish party organs, 2005

	Executive committee	National executive[a]	Party council	Congress
IU	No	No	No	No
PSOE	No	EP delegation leader		No
PNV	No	May be part of a representation of MPs and LCs		May be part of a representation of MPs and LCs
CDC	No	EP delegation leader	All MEPs	All MEPs
PP	EP delegation leader	All MEPs		All MEPs

Note
a   In some Spanish parties the national executive and the party council form one single party organ.
LCs: local councillors.

– irrespective of the influence of EU specialists within party organs. At the same time it is increasingly common to find young members of the party elite with an EU or an EP brief. To a certain degree, the image of the EP as a retirement home for senior politicians – which could still apply in some cases – is also compatible with the image of the EP as an increasingly important training arena for junior party politicians. In this regard, the relevance of EU politics has been stressed in party discourses, although the factual and practical significance of EU specialists within party structures do not seem to be very high.

In this context of limited MEP power, the EP delegation leader is clearly the most influential position. How is this position selected and what role do MEPs and EU specialists play in this process?

In the case of the PP the MEPs play a very minor role because the leader of the delegation is – with very few exceptions – the head of the electoral list and, as mentioned previously, MEPs are not important actors in the selection of the head of the list. Therefore, the key actors in the selection of the delegation leader are, again, those who select the head of the list and, in the case of the PP, it is the top party leadership and the general secretary who have the greatest say in this process.

In the PSOE it is the executive committee which in practical terms appoints the delegation leader: the executive committee makes a proposal, on which the EP delegation then votes, but the proposal is expected to be passed without contestation. However, as in the case of the PP, the head of the list is also meant to be the delegation leader and is thus chosen (proposed in formal terms) beforehand by the same executive committee during the process of list elaboration.

We find the same selection process in the case of the IU: the head of the list proposed by the executive committee will become the delegation leader, although there is formally a vote among the MEPs. In the other two cases (PNV and CDC) this issue is less relevant because the PNV only has one MEP and the CDC normally has only two, but they follow the same logic as the other parties. Therefore, in Spanish parties the EP delegation leader is *de facto* chosen by the party leadership without MEPs having any determining say.

Finally, the most visible power EU specialists – and more specifically MEPs – retain is their role in the appointment of party staff. However, the influence of MEPs in this area is limited to the appointment of staff that work in the EP delegation and, even in this case, the MEPs formally share this responsibility with the party in central office and the organization secretariat.[16]

Formulating manifestos

Having examined the influence of EU specialists and, particularly, of MEPs in elite selection within the national party, we now move to analysing another relevant domain of decision-making within the national party: the formulation of party manifestos. Is the role of the MEPs and other EU specialists relevant in this field? Has the influence of EU specialists grown in the formulation of party manifestos?

All Spanish parties elaborate and approve their electoral manifestos following similar procedures. Platforms are elaborated by formal working groups or informal teams of specialists (MEPs, MPs, party staff, party secretaries, professionals, experts, etc.) appointed by the executive committees. These groups prepare drafts that are finally approved by the party councils (IU, PSOE, and CDC) or by the executive committees (PP and PNV). This is the common procedure both for national election manifestos and for EP election manifestos. However, there are very significant differences in the involvement of EU specialists in each of these electoral manifestos.

In spite of the growing influence of the EU on domestic politics, national manifestos – according to the interviewees themselves – devote little attention to EU matters; and the involvement of EU specialists in the drafting of national manifestos is fairly limited in all the parties considered. The participation of EU specialists in national manifesto formulation is mainly restricted to the international relations or EU sections. Their involvement in other parts is clearly much less relevant. However, the growing Europeanization of some policies areas has increased the chances of EU specialist participation in manifesto formulation. The involvement of EU specialists is greatest in the most Europeanized policy areas. Yet even here, this involvement assumes a rather subordinate position. It depends on the sensitivity of the persons leading the relevant working group, and EU specialists take a secondary role, with MPs or the party secretaries adopting the steering role in the drafting of those policy sections.[17]

In the case of EP election manifestos the involvement of EU specialists is very large, and some particularly important MEPs are usually major actors in the drafting committees. In the PP, EU specialists play a very important role in the committee in charge of the EP election manifesto – which usually includes the head of the delegation, although this is not mandatory – but this committee also incorporates some area specialists, who might strictly speaking not necessarily be EU specialists. This committee receives suggestions and ideas from other party officials (EU and non-EU specialists). The process is not very different in the Socialist party: the elaboration of the EP election manifesto is done by a group of specialists appointed by the executive committee. In this group EU specialists (MEPs, MPs involved in EU-related parliamentary committees, party staff, etc.) play a prominent role, but other party elites who hold portfolios in which EU policies have important implications are also involved (e.g. different policy area secretaries of the party and party spokespersons in diverse national parliamentary committees).

This same pattern is to be found in the cases of the smaller IU, PNV and CDC. The role of EU specialists (MEPs, MPs, staff) is central. In these cases manifesto formulation is also characterized by the involvement of a lower number of people. There can frequently be fewer than ten people engaged in the drafting. In the IU there have been EP elections for which the manifesto has been practically and exclusively elaborated by the MEPs, and in a clear overlap between the executive committee and the EP delegation many of the MEPs were at the same time party secretaries.

Another relevant aspect is that when the PP and the PSOE have been in government an important part of the materials, reports and information for the formulation of the manifesto has come from governmental departments; for example,
from the assistants to the ministers and the prime minister's foreign affairs office.
This has also happened in the case of the PNV and the CDC when they have been
in government in the Basque Country and in Catalonia respectively. In all cases,
this kind of government-guided manifesto formulation was reinforced by the fact
that governmental personnel linked to the party (ministerial staff, high-level civil
servants, public administration general directors, etc.) took part in the working
groups that elaborated the platforms. In the case of the PP, on some occasions the
foreign affairs ministry had the opportunity to supervise the final result of this
programmatic elaboration.

All these features result in the EP election manifesto formulation process being
a more restrictive process when compared to the formulation of national election
manifestos. The drafting of the programme involves a smaller number of party
officials and party structures, and a smaller number of working groups composed
of fewer people. Several interviewees from the PSOE and the IU defined the formulation of EP election manifestos as less participatory, more party elite-centred
and a mostly technocratic process. Although the importance of EU specialists in
the national manifesto elaboration has grown over time, their influence is subordinated to that of national party elites; and although their involvement in the
elaboration of the EP manifesto is crucial, they share this task with other party
politicians.

Acting supranationally

The changes in the parties' internal distribution of power due to the process of
European integration and to the possibly increasing influence of EU specialists
are expected to produce structural adaptation in the parties, as well as higher degrees of involvement of EU specialists in domestic party politics. We have already
examined these possible effects in the case of Spanish parties and we now turn our
attention to a third possible area of change in the internal balance of power.

The process of European integration is expected to result in an increase in the
power of party elites and EU specialists within their organizations due to their
participation in EU decision-making institutions. We can distinguish three main
potential consequences: (1) the internal power that MEPs may gain from their participation in EP decision-making processes; (2) the influence that national party
elites may derive from their participation in the Council of Ministers and the
European Council; and (3) the power that party officials involved in the Europarty
could gain within their national organization. We will analyse each of these three
aspects in the following paragraphs, and we will take into consideration the degree of autonomy/discretion and accountability of the different party actors in
order to define their position in the internal balance of power within their national
parties.

Parties and their MEPs

The relationship between the MEPs of all the parties analysed and their respective national parties is characterized by a high level of MEP autonomy. Besides this, the level of accountability of MEPs is remarkably low or even non-existent in practice. And, contrary to what we might expect, this situation has not drastically changed with the increasing importance of EU issues and the empowerment of the EP. The growing relevance of the EU and the EP has provided incentives for an increase in the exchange of opinions and information between the MEPs and other party and government officials, but this has not entailed a closer or more strict monitoring of the activities of MEPs. In fact, MEPs can decide whether they will consult and report more or less frequently to the national party, and in any case the communications are more frequently established by the MEPs than by the national party.[18] Some MEPs we interviewed mentioned that, although the exchanges with national party officials are more frequent nowadays, they still have the impression of acting independently and on the margins of the national party.[19]

Additionally, national parties do not strictly define the priorities for the delegations' actions in the EP. For this reason, all that MEPs are expected to do is to follow the party electoral manifesto, and to observe the priorities of the EP group to which they belong. The loyalty of MEPs to party lines is fostered by the party leadership's control over candidate nomination and the possibility of party leaders preventing sitting MEPs from being re-nominated. However, the goals defined by the national party for delegation action are very general. On the whole, then, the common behaviour of Spanish MEPs is to follow the party's general understanding of EU affairs, mainly based on its ideology and its views on how integration should proceed. Hence, MEPs benefit from wide discretion, unless they make any important mistake that provokes close scrutiny from the national party. In the IU, owing to the existence of party conflicts over EU politics during certain periods, the national leadership's surveillance of MEPs has been higher when factional division extended to the EP delegation.

In any case, in the different parties we analysed, the autonomy of MEPs mainly concerns their relations with the national party rather than relations within the EP delegation. In the bigger parties, the delegation meets frequently and defines its collective priorities, and MEPs have the opportunity to exchange opinions and views. In the same vein, even if mechanisms that could hold MEPs accountable to their parties are non-existent or are not put into practice, MEPs are more easily accountable within their own EP party delegation. Other mechanisms that the parties could use to control the behaviour of their MEPs – such as party working groups on EU issues that are devoted to policy formulation – are dominated by EU specialists anyway. Even if the party executive committee and the international secretary can use these groups to establish and enforce the party line on EU issues, they do not patronize them, and instead these groups are controlled in practical terms by the EU experts.

As confirmed by the elite interviews, there are several reasons for this remarkably wide autonomy and very low real accountability. One of the most important is that, although the relevance of EU politics is increasing and the party leadership clearly recognizes this, the practical importance that the party leading bodies accord to the daily EP decision-making processes is small. This is the general rule and the only exceptions are the very specific moments in which an issue with clear and potentially controversial domestic implications is dealt with in the EP. In this case the issue is discussed by the party executive committee or by the national executive, the MEPs start consultations and the party defines its overall position. But these are somewhat exceptional cases. Another reason that favours the high autonomy and low accountability of MEPs is the complexity of EU policies. The need for a certain expertise to manage EU issues enhances the autonomy of MEPs and of party officials in charge of these policies. Parties trust their MEPs and EU specialists because they are the ones who have the necessary expertise. In addition, as one interviewee declared, 'in practice it is not possible to make MEPs really accountable as this would require a huge amount of work and would entail a large involvement and interest by the executive committee'. One last factor that impinges upon this situation is that, with the exception of the IU, there have been no divisions over EU politics in the Spanish parties and in this context the perceived need for monitoring or for creating binding mechanisms is small.

However, there is an important nuance in this general picture. When the party is in national government the role of the MEPs is, to a certain extent, more limited or restricted, because the need for consultation with ministers increases and the action plan of the government should be considered as part of the political agenda for the party MEPs. As a Socialist interviewee stated, in these cases the MEPs are almost 'transmission belts' for the government.

Nevertheless, the autonomy of MEPs – which could alter the intra-party distribution of power in their favour – has not given them a more influential position in their national parties. They are autonomous and exert their expertise in a field that is not considered crucial by party elites. If we disregard the overlap between party executive positions and MEPs or EU specialist positions, frequent in the smaller parties, the influence of EU specialists and MEPs in the ordinary or day-to-day policy formulation of their parties seems to be weak. Although their public relevance has increased slightly over time (in line with the greater importance of the EU), they have not been empowered in any significant way within their national parties. In the PSOE the position of EU specialists seems to be weak, except for debates in the national parliament on EU issues, and on certain very specific areas, the most relevant of which is agriculture. There are several such debates in the national parliament per year, and these allow EU specialists to exert a certain degree of influence. This is the exception, however, and in general EU specialists remain relatively uninfluential. What is more, this situation is worsened when the party is in government, given that in these instances the influence of the 'party in government' (the ministers and their assistants) is decisive.

In the case of the PP the predominant role of government officials in policy formulation when the party is in office also applies. There are frequent contacts, talks and exchanges, certain periodic meetings of MPs and MEPs, and meetings between party officials responsible for certain areas (including the minister and

EU specialists), and all this certainly creates some opportunity for a certain degree of influence. Moreover, EU specialists join different workgroups created for programme and policy elaboration, and this facilitates this exchange. But their internal influence should not be regarded as great.

Parties and their ministers

The relation between parties and their ministers resembles, in some important ways, the relationship already described between parties and their MEPs. When involved in EU-level politics the autonomy of the prime minister and of government ministers vis-à-vis their national parties is very high, both for the PP and the PSOE. Their accountability towards their national party is very weak or even non-existent. In this field there has not been any relevant change in spite of the increasing importance of EU politics. In any case, the accountability takes place within the government itself, where ministers are held accountable by the prime minister, rather than in the national parties' leading bodies.

Besides the executive dominance, a permanent element of the Spanish political system since the early 1980s has been the clear primacy of the government in party–government relations.[20] It is for the government to design and define the policy priorities, and the party is just expected to support it and contribute to spreading the word and publicize governmental actions. This subordination of the party to the government is particularly strong in foreign relations and EU issues: the discretion of the government is total, and occasions on which it is held to account by the party are extremely rare. The prime minister has a very strong role in EU politics (and in foreign relations more generally), and this reinforces the whole dynamic of autonomy.[21] But in addition it is important to highlight that in the PSOE and the PP the prime minister has always also been the party leader. This fosters his political primacy and the disciplined subordination of already very cohesive parties.

In their involvement in EU politics, the prime minister and government ministers basically follow the policies defined by their advisory teams in the government (not in the national party), although they obviously also have the capacity to drive governmental action according to their personal agenda or political priorities. In this regard, ministers take advantage of the fairly unspecific nature of party platforms – or, to be more accurate, of their perception that these documents are general – so as to give themselves wide room for manoeuvre in EU politics. Although the accountability mechanisms are not in place, as we have already mentioned, when the party is in government the level of communication between the ministerial staff (including the minister and the general directors) and some party EU specialists is high, especially between the spokesperson MP for EU affairs, the leader of the EP delegation, and some other MEPs.

Parties and their Europarties

With regard to the Europarty our analysis will have to be restricted to the two bigger nationwide parties (PSOE and PP) because the experiences of the other three smaller organizations are limited and very recent. In any case, both PP and PSOE party officials interviewed considered the Europarty as an unimportant or clearly minor actor. This is particularly revealing because PP and PSOE representatives have occupied very relevant positions in the structure of the Party of European Socialists (PES) and the European People's Party (EPP), given the importance and size of their national parties. As in the two previous aspects analysed in this section, the autonomy of the party representatives in the Europarty meetings – the party leader or the international secretary, sometimes accompanied by some MEPs or the EP delegation leader – is high and their accountability is extremely low.

In the case of the PP one interviewee recalled that, in a particular Europarty session, the national party position was decided in a meeting of the Spanish representatives that took place just before the EPP meeting. In the case of the PSOE several interviewees did not even remember if there had been *ex ante* or *ex post* information on PES developments in the national party executive committee. In some cases there is, obviously, some reporting on PES matters but the interviewees did not remember any PES issue that required a specific debate in the executive committee. These situations clearly reflect the minor status of Europarty matters, and emphasize that involvement in their activities is unlikely to be considered an asset in the distribution of power within the national party.

Conclusion

The organizational and procedural changes in Spanish parties due to the process of European integration have been limited. As other research in the field of Europeanization suggests, the impact of the EU on the organization of domestic politics, in which political parties are a crucial element, is fairly low. Certainly, Spanish parties have not shown a remarkable degree of structural adaptation to the growing significance of EU politics. They have not created specific party secretariats devoted to these issues, there are no official spokespersons on EU issues (apart from the international secretary), and the policy working groups on EU topics generally remain informal or in a subordinate position within the party structure. In a certain sense, the organizational and procedural changes in party organization are more a reactive adaptation to a new institutional setting and its dynamics (including, for example, the creation of parliamentary committees) than a proactive strategy of change. In this vein, although there are certain modifications in the parties' functioning, these do not distort the internal balance of power.

Moreover, Spanish parties have not invested their own party resources in the implementation of these limited organizational modifications. Parties have not invested in the creation of party staff solely involved in EU issues either in the party headquarters or in their national parliamentary groups. In this context, the main source of resources for EU-related activity is the EP and the resources available to the MEPs. And, besides this, Spanish parties also take advantage of government resources when the party is in office, both for their parliamentary and political activity – for example, to obtain advice and information.

The limits of the procedural adaptations are evident when the selection of one of the most important EU specialist groups – MEPs – is analysed. The selection procedure is not dramatically different from the one followed for national elections, although, interestingly enough, the selection of MEPs is more elite-driven (closely controlled by national party elites although with significant interventions by the regional organizations) and the EP delegation is not a crucially important actor in the process.

Therefore, the structural adaptation of Spanish parties is limited, and the importance of EU specialists in the national party is equally low. Their presence in the party leading bodies is very limited: they do not have *ex officio* seats in the most important party organs, and they have minor opportunities to affect elite selection. MEPs do not play a significant role in the selection of the EP delegation leader because this position is filled by the head of the EP electoral list, who is in turn selected by the top party organs with crucial intervention from the national party leader. In manifesto formulation their participation is mainly restricted to the sections devoted to EU issues, and they have a very important role to play only in the elaboration of manifestos for EP elections. In the case of the two big nationwide parties the role not only of EU specialists but also of the party as a whole is non-existent in the definition of government EU policy when the party is in office. In this case it is the government that defines the policy priorities and the party acts as a transmission belt for that government platform and programme. Hence, the influence of EU specialists is generally low within the national party.

In addition, EU specialists gain little intra-party influence as a result of their involvement in EU-level institutions. Although they are highly autonomous and are not held to account by the national party, their activities are not considered crucially important by party elites. This obviously limits their possible power within the national party. MEPs enjoy a wide discretion in their work although when their party is in government their work is significantly subordinated to the government agenda. This is explained by the low importance that party elites give to the daily activities of MEPs, the specialization of their work in the EP, and the absence of divisions over EU policies (except for the case of the IU). As concerns prime ministers and ministers, they too enjoy wide autonomy, large discretion, and non-existent party accountability when acting in EU-level decision-making bodies. Organs of the governmental party rarely discuss the European policy of its government and, in any case, there is no contention about it and instead there is general support of the policies defined by the government. In the case of the Europarty, the party leadership and the international secretariat also exert wide discretion, but this activity is considered to be relatively unimportant anyway. In sum, this situation should lead us to conclude that the EU has become yet another arena in which certain party elites enjoy a lot of room for manoeuvre without the constraints sometimes imposed by their party membership and party leading bodies.

As regards our hypotheses, only the one that predicts that party elites are expected to gain power thanks to the process of European integration has found empirical support in the Spanish parties. However, even in this case, our conclusions should be put in the context of the pre-existent organizational traditions and models of Spanish parties and of wider developments in Western parties. These more general factors, independent of the EU developments, can also – at least to a certain extent – account for party elite and leadership empowerment and increasing autonomy. There are certainly some common patterns among the five Spanish parties studied, irrespective of their size or ideology, which could also support this impression. In general terms, there are no big differences among Spanish parties in the fields of structural and procedural adaptation due to the European integration.

In several of the areas analysed in this study there has been no significant change over time in the reaction of Spanish parties to European integration. Therefore, in spite of the increasing importance of the EU, the most important organizational aspects of the Spanish parties, especially those that imply a modification of the internal balance of power, are not different today from in the past when European integration was less advanced. However, this does not mean that change over time is not visible in some fields. Certainly the resources used in EU-related activities have grown (although they come from the EP) and, although the EU specialists' influence in the national parties is low, the perceived importance of EU issues in the national parties, the consideration of the EP and EU policy as a training field for junior politicians, and, as a logical consequence, the involvement of EU specialists in the formulation of the national electoral manifestos have also grown. This introduces doubts over future organizational evolutions. The EU, despite its increasing importance, is not considered a vital political arena for parties, which continue to focus on the national level. Only when this perception, which is generally widespread among Spanish party officials, changes, might we expect to see deeper organizational transformations.

European integration can be regarded fundamentally as a new arena into which Spanish party leaders can extend their internal power, which is already largely uncontested within their party organizations. The autonomy of the leadership and its low accountability – features that to some degree really characterize the style and dynamics of Spanish party politics – can also be found in the new political level created by European integration. Thus, if it has been argued that European integration has fuelled the 'presidentialization' of Spain's policy style, and has reinforced the role of the core executive and weakened the horizontal and vertical division of powers (Morata 1996; Heywood and Molina 2000; Molina 2001; Closa and Heywood 2004), a similar argument can be applied to the internal politics of Spanish parties. For Spanish political parties, European politics brings low levels of accountability and reinforces the power and role of party elites at the expense of party organs and party members.

Notes

1 We wish to thank Carolina Galvañ and Irene Palacios for their most valuable research assistance.
2 The social democratic Spanish Socialist Workers' Party (*Partido Socialista Obrero Español*, PSOE), the conservative Popular Party (*Partido Popular*, PP), the left-wing United Left (*Izquierda Unida*, IU), the Catalan centre-right nationalist Democratic

Convergence of Catalonia (*Convergència Democrática de Catalunya*, CDC) and the centre-right nationalist Basque Party (*Partido Nacionalista Vasco*, PNV).

3   The empirical material on which this chapter is based comes from party statutes and documents and from 19 interviews with party politicians and staff members in the five main Spanish parties. Interviewees included past and/or present party leaders, party chairs, members of the national parliamentary European affairs committee, European Parliament delegation leaders, other influential Members of the European Parliament, general secretaries of the European parliamentary delegation, other party staff in the European parliamentary delegation, and international secretaries. Interviews were conducted between spring 2003 and spring 2005.

4   During this period the action of the Spanish governments was not especially focused on foreign relations, although in 1981, in a very influential decision, Spain became a full member of NATO.

5   For a recent general overview of Spanish politics see Gunther *et al.* (2004).

6   The Spanish prime minister would belong to the 'first above unequals' type in Sartori's terms (Sartori 1994). According to King's (1994) classification of intra-cabinet prime ministerial power, Spain would be placed among the six countries that have a prime minister with the highest degree of influence within the cabinet.

7   The Spanish regions (Autonomous Communities) have legislative and executive authority in a large number of areas (education, health, environment, agriculture, etc.) and are responsible for the management of substantial budgets. In Moreno's (1994) terminology Spain has an imperfect federal system. Regional governments are increasingly calling for the right to participate in Spanish EU policy-making and to be represented in the EU institutions (especially the Council of Ministers). This is becoming an issue of growing political relevance in some regions.

8   To this multiparty nature of Spanish politics we should add the high degree of interest group pluralism, which contrasts with the more corporatist nature of other European countries (Lijphart 1999).

9   There are several party-specific variations to this structure. The main feature of this party structure is the practical fusion between what in other European parties are the national council and the national executive. In this vein, the executive committees are usually very large (for example in the PP), and the regional parties' representatives have *ex officio* seats not only on the national executive but also on the executive committee (for example, in PP, CDC and IU).

10 In the case of the nationalist parties this overlap takes place in their respective regional legislative assemblies. Only in the case of the Basque PNV are the positions of party leader and head of the (regional) government incompatible.

11 There have been certain periods of internal party turmoil in the PP, IU and PNV (apart from the normal internal party debates and differences). However, with the exception of IU and PNV, these conflicts have not led to the formation of party factions and have not generated divisive behaviour.

12 Except on very specific occasions foreign policy has not been a dimension of conflict in Spain (the main exceptions would be the conflict around NATO membership in the mid-1980s and the position of the Spanish government in the second Iraq war; in both cases it was the left that defined these issues as conflictual and campaigned on them).

13 The ERC (Republic Left of Catalonia, *Esquerra Republicana de Catalunya*) and the BNG (Galician Nationalist Block, *Bloque Nacionalista Galego*) are two increasingly significant left-wing nationalist parties.

14 In the Maastricht treaty (1992) and in issues related to EMU (1998) the IU was distrustful of what it saw as neo-liberal and non-democratic developments of the EU. The party's MPs and MEPs abstained on both issues. We consider this an expression of soft Euroscepticism.

15 For a while the IU had a European secretary, but this was not down to political priorities, and was instead attributable to internal power balances.

16 This is the formal procedure but obviously there are exceptions in which the decision rests basically in the hands of the MEPs. In the case of the PP, MEPs seem to be more autonomous in the hiring of their assistants. Apart from this, given that there is no party structure devoted exclusively to EU matters and that this issue falls under the remit of the more general international relations or international policy offices, the role played by EU specialists in the appointment of the small number of personnel working in these offices is minor.

17 The IU represents an exception to this general rule, since for a long time there has been an overlap between an important part of its EP delegation and the party executive committee that coordinated the formulation of manifestos. This overlap meant that those MEPs who were also party secretaries exerted a leading role in the formulation of certain sections of the manifesto that made reference to domestic issues.

18 As an interviewee declared, this partially depends on the knowledge and expertise of the MEP. MEPs with less expertise tend to consult the national party more frequently in order to be sure to adopt the correct stances. In such cases, the reduced autonomy of MEPs is a result of the MEPs' own actions.

19 It is worth mentioning that Spanish EU policy-making is characterized by a relative 'lack of coordination' (Closa and Heywood 2004: 65) within the Spanish administration, with the officials of the Spanish Permanent Representation having significant autonomy.

20 As prime minister, Felipe González (1982–96) imposed this model very early on, and in a forceful manner, in order to confront some moderate distrust of his government line within the Socialist party. The subordination of the party to the government in the Aznar and PP period (1996–2004) was probably even more intense.

21 For a similar view of the subordinate role of the party and the importance of the prime minister in the Socialist case, see Gillespie (1996).

References

Barbé, Esther (1999) *La política europea de España*, Barcelona: Ariel.

Barreiro, Belén and Ignacio Sánchez Cuenca (2001) 'La europeización de la opinión pública española', in Carlos Closa (ed.), *La europeización del sistema político español*, Madrid: Istmo, pp. 29–51.

van Biezen, Ingrid (1998) 'Building Party Organisations and the Relevance of Past Models: The Communist and Socialist Parties in Spain and Portugal', *West European Politics*, 21(2): 32–62.

van Biezen, Ingrid (2000) 'On the Internal Balance of Party Power: Party Organizations in New Democracies', *Party Politics*, 6(4): 395–417.

Cienfuegos, Manuel (1996) 'El control de las Cortes Generales sobre el gobierno en asuntos relativos a las Comunidades Europeas durante la década 1985–1995', *Revista de las Cortes Generales*, 38: 47–99.

Cienfuegos, Manuel (1997) 'La Comisión Mixta para la Unión Europea: Análisis y balance de una década de actividad en el seguimiento de los asuntos comunitarios', *Gaceta Jurídica de la CE*, D-27: 7–69.

Closa, Carlos (1996a) 'Spain: The Cortes and the EU – A Growing Together', in Philip Norton (ed.), *National Parliaments and the European Union*, London: Frank Cass, pp. 136–50.

Closa, Carlos (1996b) 'El nuevo papel de España en la Unión Europea', *Política y Sociedad*, 20: 111–24.

Closa, Carlos and Paul Heywood (2004) *Spain and the European Union*, Houndmills: Palgrave Macmillan.

Gillespie, Richard (1996) 'The Spanish Socialists', in John Gaffney (ed.), *Political Parties and the European Union*, London: Routledge, pp. 155–69.

Gunther, Richard (1992) 'Spain: The Very Model of Modern Elite Settlement', in John Higley and Richard Gunther (eds.), *Elites and Democratic Consolidation in Latin America and Southern Europe*, Cambridge: Cambridge University Press, pp. 38–80.

Gunther, Richard, José Ramón Montero and Joan Botella (2004) *Democracy in Modern Spain*, New Haven: Yale University Press.

Heywood, Paul (1999) 'Power Diffusion or Concentration? In Search of the Spanish Policy Process', in Paul Heywood (ed.), *Politics and Policy in Democratic Spain: No Longer Different?*, London: Frank Cass, pp. 103–23.

Heywood, Paul and Ignacio Molina (2000) 'A Quasi-Presidential Premiership: Administering the Executive Summit in Spain', in B. Guy Peters, R. A. W. Rhodes and Vincent Wright (eds.), *Administering the Summit*, Basingstoke: Palgrave, pp. 110–33.

Holliday, Ian (2002) 'Spain: Building a Parties State in a New Democracy', in Paul Webb, David Farrell and Ian Holliday (eds.), *Political Parties in Advanced Industrial Democracies*, Oxford: Oxford University Press, pp. 248–79.

King, Anthony (1994) ' "Chief Executives" in Western Europe', in Ian Budge and David McKay (eds.), *Developing Democracy: Comparative Research in Honour of J. F. P. Blondel*, London: Sage, pp. 150–63.

Lijphart, Arendt (1999) *Patterns of Democracy*, New Haven: Yale University Press.

Linz, Juan J. and José Ramón Montero (1999) *The Party Systems of Spain: Old Cleavages and New Challenges*, Madrid: Centro de Estudios Avanzados en Ciencias Sociales (Instituto Juan March de Estudios e Investigaciones), Estudio/Working Paper 1999/138.

Llamazares, Iván, Gómez-Reino, Margarita and Ramiro, Luis (2007 forthcoming) 'Euroscepticism and Political Parties in Spain', in Paul Taggart and Aleks Szczerbiak (eds.) *Opposing Europe?*, Oxford: Oxford University Press.

Maxwell, Kenneth and Steven Spiegel (1994) *The New Spain: From Isolation to Influence*, New York: Council on Foreign Relations.

Molina, Ignacio (2001) 'La adaptación a la Unión Europea del poder ejecutivo español', in Carlos Closa (ed.), *La europeización del sistema político español*, Madrid: Istmo, pp. 162–97.

Molina del Pozo, Carlos (1995) 'El control parlamentario nacional sobre los actos normativos emanados de las instituciones europeas', in Carlos Molina del Pozo (ed.), *España en la Europa comunitaria. Balance de diez años*, Madrid: Editorial del Centro de Estudios Ramón Areces, pp. 149–64.

Morata, Francesc (1996) 'Spain', in Dietrich Rometsch and Wolfgang Wessels (eds.), *The European Union and Member States: Towards Institutional Fusion?*, Manchester: Manchester University Press, pp. 134–54.

Moreno, Luis (1994) 'Ethnoterritorial Concurrence and Imperfect Federalism in Spain', in Bertus de Villiers (ed.), *Evaluating Federal Systems*, Dordrecht: Martinus Nijhoff, pp. 162–93.

Panebianco, Angelo (1988) *Political Parties: Organization and Power* Cambridge: Cambridge University Press.

Powell, Charles (1995) 'Spain's External Relations 1898–1975', in Richard Gillespie, Fernando Rodrigo and Jonathan Story (eds), *Democratic Spain: Reshaping External Relations in a Changing World*, London: Routledge, pp. 11–29.

Ramiro, Luis and Morales, Laura (2004) 'Latecomers but "Early-Adapters": The Adaptation and Response of Spanish Parties to Social Changes', in Kay Lawson and Thomas Poguntke (eds.), *How Political Parties Respond to Voters: Interest Aggregation Revisited*, London: Routledge, pp. 198–226.

Sartori, Giovanni (1994) 'Neither Presidentialism nor Parliamentarism', in Juan J. Linz and Arturo Valenzuela (eds.), *The Failure of Presidential Democracy*, Baltimore: Johns Hopkins University Press, pp. 106–18.

Taggart, Paul and Szczerbiak, Aleks (2002) 'The Party Politics of Euroscepticism in EU Member and Candidates States', paper presented at the ECPR Joint Sessions of Workshops, Turin, March 2002.

7   A long, slow march to Europe

The Europeanization of Swedish political parties[1]

Nicholas Aylott

This chapter turns to the Swedish political parties. I examine their organizational structures and processes, and explore how they have changed in light of European integration. Drawn from the discussion and hypotheses presented in Chapter 1 are three basic research questions. (1) How has the European Union (EU) impacted on parties' formal organizational structures? (Has the formal decision-making power of EU specialists increased? Have they increased their access to power resources, such as money and staff, over time?) (2) Has the power of EU specialists in internal party politics increased, as one of the hypotheses presented in Chapter 1 suggested? (Have their access to and consumption of power resources changed? Has their influence in formulating party programmes changed? Have they 'intruded' into policy areas traditionally regarded as domestic? Is EU specialization becoming more common?) (3) Has the power of party elites been enhanced, as the other hypothesis in Chapter 1 suggested? (How effective are intra-party mechanisms in holding elites accountable when they are engaged in EU-level forums? How effective are parliamentary mechanisms, such as European affairs committees? Who is involved in selecting candidates for election to the European Parliament and EU specialists?)

The parties surveyed are those with parliamentary representation after the election of 2002. They are, in a rough left-to-right order, the Left Party (in Swedish, *vänsterpartiet*, often abbreviated as v), the Social Democrats (*Sveriges social-demokratiska arbetareparti*, s), the Greens (*miljöpartiet de gröna*, mp), the Centre Party (*centerpartiet*, c), the Liberals (*folkpartiet liberalerna*, fp), the Christian Democrats (*kristdemokraterna*, kd) and the Moderates (*moderata samlingspartiet*, m).[2]

The three research questions inform the chapter, and I will return to them in the concluding section. The structure of the chapter, however, conforms to that found in the other country studies in this volume. First I offer some brief background about the Swedish party system, the parties and their organizations, plus the impact of EU membership. Then I review the structural adaptation that the parties have made in response to accession, with emphasis on the selection of candidates for European elections. Thereafter, the chapter is ordered according to the different arenas in which the parties are active. At national level, I examine how the parties manage internal processes in light of European integration, looking especially at manifesto formulation and the selection of party personnel. The following section, on parties acting supranationally, explores how the parties manage relations with the Europarties, with their MEPs and with their ministers when they participate in EU forums. Finally, there is a summarizing and concluding section.

Sweden and Europe

Historical background

Sweden is a relatively recent member of the EU. It joined at the beginning of 1995, along with Finland and Austria. All three countries had declared themselves neutral in the Cold War, and had interpreted their neutrality as debarring them from joining the then European Community (EC). Sweden's longest-serving prime minister, Tage Erlander, had ruled out EC membership in a famous speech to the Metal Workers' Union in 1961.

The end of the Cold War persuaded many Swedes that there was now no reason to avoid EC membership. Yet for others it was still far from obvious that Sweden should join. In many ways, neutral Sweden had more in common with its neighbours, Denmark and Norway, even though they were NATO members. All three Scandinavian countries are old nation states, with strong senses of national identity, much of which is associated with a certain 'model' of society. Mainly on the left of the political spectrum, but by no means only there (especially in Denmark), this model has often been seen as clashing with that found in the EU (e.g. Lawler 1997).

Put simply, many Scandinavians are Eurosceptics, and they have not been shy to express their sentiments in referendums on European integration. Sweden's vote on EU membership, in October 1994, was a close-run affair, but it approved the country's terms of accession by 52.3 per cent to 46.8 per cent. In 2003, however, Swedes voted against joining economic and monetary union (EMU), by 55.9 per cent to 42.0 per cent.

Political institutions, party system and party organization

Sweden is a unitary, parliamentary democracy. The parliament, Riksdagen, which since 1971 has been unicameral, is elected every four years through a system of proportional representation. The 349 MPs are chosen in multi-member constituencies, in which the parties present lists of their candidates. Parties holding government office, whether alone or in coalition, have only rarely controlled a majority of seats in parliament. Thus, the Swedish parliament is considered to be a relatively active or 'policy-influencing' parliament (Arter 1990). Its 16 standing committees play an important role in legislation and are the main forum for inter-party negotiation. The European affairs committee, however, is not counted as a standing committee. It is discussed in more detail later.

There are two features that are vital for understanding how the Swedish party system works. The first is that the parties represented in parliament are divided into two informal blocs. On the left, the 'socialist' bloc comprises the Social Democrats; the former Communists, known since 1990 as the Left Party; and arguably also the Greens, whose initial reluctance to be associated with either bloc has weakened since they were first elected to parliament in 1988. On the right, meanwhile, the 'bourgeois' bloc contains the Liberals, whose liberalism has usually been of a soft, 'social' variety, but who have moved somewhat to the right in recent years; the Centre Party, a rural-based movement that has historically been prepared to deal with the Social Democrats, but which has become less so since the 1990s; the Christian Democrats, whose moral-conservative platform first brought them into parliament in 1991; and the Moderates, who contain varying ideological shades of conservatism and neo-liberalism.

The second key element of the Swedish party system is that the Social Democrats dominate it. This broad, ideologically rather heterogeneous movement, which has historically enjoyed close ties to Sweden's powerful blue-collar trade unions, won an average vote of 44.2 per cent in parliamentary elections between 1945 and 2002, two and a half times that of the next biggest party, the Moderates. Moreover, the Social Democrats have dominated government office, and usually without needing a coalition partner; the party was in opposition for only a little over nine years between 1932 and 2006. From 1998 it governed with the formal support of the Left and the Greens. This 'contract' (Bergman and Aylott 2003) did not quite amount to a full coalition, but it provided a stable parliamentary base for the minority Social Democratic cabinet.

The parties have diverse origins, but their contemporary organizational similarity is quite striking. Despite losing nearly half their total paid-up members since 1991 (Petersson 2005: 11), they all conform to the basic 'mass-party' model. In each party, congress is the sovereign body; its members are elected by regional and local units. Congress meets at least every four years, and usually more often. It delegates day-to-day power to two organs: the national executive, which contains about 20–40 members, and which meets every month or so; and the executive committee, with just a handful of members, including the chair of the party organization – in other words, the party leader.[3] Between the national party organization and the municipal branches is the regional level of organization, run by its own congresses, which are composed of delegates elected by the municipal branches and basic party units. In all but the Left and the Greens, the regions are represented in another organ, the party council, which is officially the second most powerful body, but which is fairly insignificant in practice.

A party's leader is usually also an MP. Indeed, the leaderships of the extra-parliamentary organizations and parliamentary groups are well integrated (Hagevi 2000: 156). Two parties, the Social Democrats and the Left, stipulate in their statutes that the parties' MPs are formally subordinate to the party organization. But research confirms the impression that the parliamentary groups are important power centres in the parties, and have probably become more so (Isberg 1999: 135–51; Pierre and Widfeldt 1994). In general, and despite the internally democratic structures, leaders tend to be rather secure in their positions, although that naturally varies according to a party's standing at any given time. In modern times, only the Left has suffered from serious disunity (its most recent significant split was in 1977).

Conflicts over European integration

In the referendum in 1994 on Sweden's terms of accession, the leaderships of all four bourgeois parties and the Social Democrats all campaigned strongly for a Yes vote. But the party alignments that were visible in 1994 gave an important signal to how the EU would subsequently affect domestic politics.

The issue of EU membership split the socialist bloc. The Left and the Greens both supported a No vote, and after the referendum they continued to advocate that Sweden should leave the Union. They did so largely on the basis of democratic arguments. They insisted that transferring power to the EU takes it further away from the control of ordinary people and towards an oligarchy of bureaucrats and politicians, whose accountability to voters is weak. In addition, the two parties were critical of the Union's economic policies, including EMU, which they saw as much too favourable to market forces. Even more emphatically, they opposed the prospect of Sweden's participation in common European security or even defence policies. Although, by 2005, neither party's leadership was pushing very hard for exit from the EU, cautious attempts to remove that goal from their parties' programmes had been firmly rejected by the respective party congresses.

Their Eurosceptical positions complicated the Left and the Greens' relationships with the Social Democrats, who themselves have come a long way in their views of the EU. Although their governments had in the 1960s and 1970s shown interest in moving closer to the EC, there was a strong sense within the party that Sweden, with its successful economy, expanding welfare state and active neutrality, had little to learn or gain from union with the continental countries. That Swedish self-confidence was undermined during the economic crises of the 1980s; indeed, some argue that this, rather than the end of the Cold War, was the main reason for the party leadership's sudden decision in 1990 to support EU membership (e.g. Aylott 1999: 102–32). But during the 1990s the idea that Europe could be good for the left – through coordinating social protection to balance the effect of the market, for instance – became increasingly influential among Social Democrats. The party leader and prime minister since 1996, Göran Persson, became noticeably more enthusiastic about the EU as time wore on.

By 2005, no leading Social Democrat was against EU membership. Yet a degree of Euroscepticism remains in the party, even at elite level. Several cabinet ministers were against EMU in the 2003 referendum, which caused considerable difficulty for the party leadership's campaign for a Yes vote (Aylott 2005a). Moreover, the referendum result showed that the leadership's enthusiasm for the EU was out of step with many in the Social Democratic grass roots.

Over on the right, the bourgeois parties have also been divided over European integration. The Liberals and the Moderates were supportive from the beginning of the process. For them, the EU offered the promise of a more liberal, market-orientated economic policy, and maybe also a constraint on Social Democratic power in Sweden. They saw EMU as a way of promoting economic integration and thus prosperity.

The Centre Party, however, has oscillated in its attitudes. From around the 1960s, it shared much of the socialist bloc's criticism of European integration, especially that concerning democracy and security policy (Kite 1996). After some doubts, the party leadership was persuaded to support Sweden's EU membership in 1994, but nine years later it urged a No to EMU. Then, after the referendum in 2003, the Centre seemed to shift position once again, and began to sound surprisingly enthusiastic about the EU, even supporting a version of 'federalism' in the campaign for the 2004 election to the European Parliament (EP). A similar shift had already occurred in the Christian Democrats, whose leader of 30 years until 2003 led the party towards a pro-EU position and closer ties to continental Christian democracy. His enthusiasm was not always shared by his party's members and supporters, however.

Against this background of ideological alignment, the fact that division on European affairs has not been confined to the blocs, but has also occurred *within* some parties, will not be a surprise (Aylott 2007). Three parties – the Centre, the Christian Democrats and, above all, the Social Democrats – have contained significant and organized opposition to the party leaderships' pro-EU positions. This helps to explain why the Centre leadership decided to oppose EMU in 2003, and why the Social Democratic and Christian Democratic leaderships failed to persuade a majority of their supporters to vote Yes (see Table 7.1).

Clearly, there is a serious divide between political elites and the rest of Sweden on EU issues. In fact, it is arguable that the very device that reveals this divide – the referendum – has been used by the parties to minimize the implications for everyday politics. In effect, the EU has been quarantined in special zones, only to be discussed in special circumstances, such as in the context of a referendum. In particular, the two Swedish referendums on European integration have consti-

Table 7.1 MPs and party sympathizers in the Swedish referendum on EMU, 2003: percentages voting Yes to EMU

	MPs	Sympathizers	Difference
Left Party	0	7	7
Social Democrats	82	49	33
Greens	0	16	16
Centre Party	32	16	16
Liberals	100	74	26
Christian Democrats	88	47	41
Moderates	96	79	17

Source: Brothén (2004: 73). The figures for MPs come from a questionnaire survey by Swedish Television's *Rapport* programme, undertaken towards the end of the referendum campaign. For voters, the data come from a survey by the Department of Political Science, Göteborg University, and Statistics Sweden.

tuted a way for Social Democratic elites to keep the issue out of national election campaigns (Aylott 2002).

Apart from the two referendums, Sweden's three elections to the EP have been the main opportunity for Swedish voters to express their preferences about the EU, and they have been prepared to abandon their usual party sympathies. In 1995 and 1999 the two anti-EU parties, the Left and the Greens, took advantage. But in 2004 the beneficiary of popular Euroscepticism was not, strictly speaking, a party at all. The June List was no more than a collection of eight candidates with a platform of mild Euroscepticism. Sweden should stay in the EU, they argued, but not transfer any more power to Brussels. The List's entirely unexpected success – it attracted 14.5 per cent of the vote – was, even on a low turnout, remarkable. (See Table 7.2 for details of Sweden's elections to the EP.) However, in this chapter, the focus is on the seven established parties.

Structural adaptation and European integration

In this section, I address the structural adaptation that the parties have undertaken in response to European integration. Four aspects of this adaptation are discussed: formal management of EU-related activity; the funding of this activity; the selection of party actors who engage in this activity, with special emphasis on MEPs; and other groups that are relevant to the parties' engagement at European level.

Formal management of EU-related issues

Only some of the parties give specific responsibility for managing EU issues to *förtroendevalde* – people elected to a position, either in internal or public elections.

Table 7.2 Elections to the European Parliament in Sweden: votes, seats and turnout, 1995–2004

	1995		1999		2004	
	%	Seats	%	Seats	%	Seats
Left Party	12.9	3	15.8	3	12.8	2
Social Democrats	28.1	7	26.0	6	24.6	5
Greens	17.2	4	9.5	2	6.0	1
June List	–	–	–	–	14.5	3
Centre Party	7.2	2	6.0	1	6.3	1
Liberals	4.8	1	13.9	3	9.9	2
Christian Democrats	3.9	0	7.6	2	5.7	1
Moderates	23.2	5	20.7	5	18.3	4
Others	2.7	–	0.5	–	1.9	–
Turnout/total seats	41.6	22	38.8	22	37.9	19

Sources: Election Authority website <www.val.se> (accessed July 2004); Statistics Sweden and Department of Political Science, Göteborg University (1995).

Two members of the Left Party's national executive oversee EU issues, a system that replaced an earlier, slightly bigger sub-committee with the same functions. One of the Moderates' deputy leaders has ultimate responsibility for EU issues in the party. Otherwise, each party's senior MP on the parliamentary European affairs committee takes the unofficial role of party spokesperson in this field, although only a few engage with European questions in a publicly visible way.

Just two parties give the leaders of their European parliamentary delegations *ex officio* positions in their leading bodies. The Social Democrats' and the Moderates' delegation leaders enjoy seats on their parties' respective national executives and executive committees, but without voting rights.[4] No other EU specialists, elected or employed, have automatic positions on party executive organs.

When Sweden joined the EU, it was mostly the parties' international secretaries who dealt with European issues (Jerneck 1997: 149–54). But this pattern has changed. After the 1999 European election, for example, the Social Democrats reclassified EU-related issues as the responsibility of the organizational unit in its central office. Six 'EU officers' (*EU-ombudsmän*) remain, however. These are employed by the party's regional organizations, although not necessarily full-time in this particular role, and their job is to maintain links between the Social Democratic MEPs and the party regions. The Greens employ two functionaries in a similar capacity. By 2005, only the Left Party had a designated unit in its central office for handling EU issues, an 'EU Secretariat'. Apart from that unit, the party organizations contain no staff who are both based in Sweden and exclusively assigned to EU-level issues and connections.

If there has been a shift away from managing EU affairs through the parties' international offices, how can this be explained? To a large extent, the parties' own explanations can be taken at face value. In interviews, informants from nearly all the parties emphasize that this development is due not to neglect but to a conscious attempt to integrate the EU into the parties' normal activities, rather than isolating it. This is understandable. After all, it is difficult these days to separate neatly European issues from domestic ones. But an equally important reason is surely economic, to which I now turn.

Resources for EU-related activity

The precise sums devoted by the parties to EU-related activity are impossible to identify, as they fall in various categories, some of which may also cover non-EU-related activity. Some general observations about resources are, however, possible.

The main source of funds for EU-related party activity is not to be found in the party organizations, despite the relatively generous public subsidies that they enjoy in Sweden. At national level, it is the parties' parliamentary groups whose economic resources have risen fastest in recent years, allowing them to expand the secretarial and research assistance that they employ. All the parties' parliamentary groups employ specialist advisors to their members of the European affairs committee, although these functionaries often have responsibility for other specialist standing committees, too. By far the biggest source of funding for the parties' EU activity, though, comes from the Union itself – specifically, the EP.

Members of the European Parliament (MEPs) receive support for secretarial and research assistance. A party with a single MEP may have two or three assistants, most of whom (but not all) are stationed in Brussels. This subvention also pays for virtually all directly EU-related activity back in the national party organizations. The Left Party's EU Secretariat, for instance, is entirely funded by the party's MEPs, and its three functionaries are employed by them, even though these functionaries are based in Stockholm. True, some of the parties had already opened offices in Brussels before Sweden joined the EU. But ask informed people in a Swedish party – with the possible exception of the biggest, wealthiest party, the Social Democrats – about the consequences of a really disastrous European election, in which it lost all its MEPs, and the answer is clear. Not all of its EU-related activity would be ended. But the vast majority of it would. If the parties are devoting more human resources to European affairs, it is because Europe pays for them to do so.

The Social Democrats' exceptional status as by far the biggest party was reflected in the resources that they reportedly devoted to campaigning before the 2004 European election. At SKr 25m (about €2.7m), theirs was more than five times bigger than the Moderates' budget (*Dagens Nyheter* 26 May 2004). That was about half the sum that the Social Democrats were expected to spend on the national election in 2006 (*Dagens Nyheter* 4 December 2005), although this calculation excluded the other national campaign contributions that the party enjoys, especially from the unions.

In summary, then, it can be said that the human resources devoted by the parties to European affairs have increased, at least in their national parliamentary offices, although to a limited extent. It is in their European parliamentary offices that personnel have most clearly increased in number – and then only in the parties with substantial representations in the EP. The party organizations themselves have seen little change.

MEP candidate selection procedures

The ways in which parties choose their candidates in national elections is relatively clear, open and decentralized in Sweden (Bergman 2004: 215; Bille 2001). The main difference in elections to the EP is that the whole of Sweden constitutes a single electoral constituency, which requires the parties to choose their candidates at the national levels of their organizations. This, it could be argued, is to the advantage of the parties' elites, and to the disadvantage of their grass roots – especially when a leadership accords itself the freedom to invite a candidate from outside the party to run, as the Christian Democrats did in 1999 and the Liberals did in 2004. These candidates had no prior connections with the parties' grass roots.

Paradoxically, though, one other institutional difference makes candidate selection harder for the party leaderships to control. Since 1998, national parliamentary elections in Sweden have incorporated a new feature: an element of optional personal-preference voting. If at least 8 per cent of a party's voters in a constituency indicate a preference for a particular candidate, that candidate is propelled to the top of the party's list, superseding the order of candidates that the party earlier decided. In European elections in Sweden, the same system has been employed, but with a lower threshold of 5 per cent (as in municipal and county elections). Thus, a candidate who rallies personal support among the party's sympathizers has a fair chance of being promoted to one of the top, 'electable' places on its list. This complicates the candidate selection process – as became clear in the 2004 European election.

Before that election, all the parties, through different mechanisms, allowed their members to nominate individuals as election candidates. In most of the parties, nominees were then subject to an advisory internal primary ballot. In 2004 this included the Christian Democrats, who had not held such a vote before previous European elections. Only the Social Democrats and the Left have not held primaries. Of the parties that did hold an advisory primary in 2004, all but one allowed all their members to vote for their favoured nominees, although again the precise voting system varied. The exception here was the Moderates. They had held a membership primary before the 1999 European election, but in 2003 they baulked at the cost (estimated at SKr 1m, about a quarter of their election budget) and limited the final franchise to a group of just 436 activists, including congress delegates. As for the identity of the final candidate-selecting body, the Left and the Greens gave the job to the party's sovereign body, congress;[5] the others gave the decision to their respective party councils.

Overall, even if its culture precludes the adoption of candidates from outside the party, the Social Democrats' candidate selection process was still the most elite-steered (for a summary of the cross-party comparison, see Table 7.3). In effect, the party leadership constructed the party list, without reference to a primary or even a congress-appointed election committee. Admittedly, in most of the primaries that the other parties held, turnout was very poor, often around 10 per cent. Still, these primaries did most to shape the lists that the parties eventually presented to the electorate. If the leaderships did want to amend the candidate order that the primaries had produced, it was usually a contentious process, which attracted media attention and protests from the disfavoured candidates – as the Christian Democrats and the Moderates discovered when the winner of the primary in 2004 did not ultimately top the list. By contrast, when the Social Democrats' party secretary, who sits in the executive committee, proposed that party's list, it had already been implicitly endorsed by the party leadership. Any subsequent challenge to the list by the party council would thus have been interpreted as a challenge to the leadership's authority, and party regions would have been reluctant to make such a challenge.

Why did the Social Democrats adopt this relatively centralized system? There are probably several reasons. Achieving balanced lists is even more important to them than it is to other parties, thanks to the panoply of groups within the labour movement – regions, women, youth, immigrants and, especially, trade unions – that want to see 'their' people on the party list.

Table 7.3 Candidate selection for European Parliament elections in Sweden, 2004

	Left	Social Democrats	Greens	Centre	Liberals	Christian Democrats	Moderates
Who chose the election committee?	Congress	National executive[a]	Congress	Congress	Congress	Party council	National executive[a]
Who could be nominated?	Any member	Any member	Any member	Any member	Anyone	Any member	Any member
Primary vote?	No	No	Yes	Yes	Yes	Yes	Yes
Who could vote in the primary?	–	–	Members	Members	Members	Members	Restricted
Was another body involved?	National executive	No	No	No	No	National executive	No
Which body took final decision?	Congress	Party council	Congress	Party council	Party council	Party council	Party council

Note
a In practice, the national executive – or, more accurately, the party secretary – took on the role of the election committee.

But a further reason for centralized candidate selection for a European election concerns the Social Democrats' division over the EU. In Sweden's first election to the EP, in 1995, the party went so far as to present ten lists to voters – half comprising supporters of integration, half comprising more sceptical candidates. The outcome was that several anti-EU Social Democrats were elected, and they used their mandates as a Eurosceptical platform within the party (Aylott 1999: 156). (The Greens, the Centre and the Liberals in 1995, and the Liberals in 1999, also presented more than one list.) In 2004, by contrast, maintaining control over candidate selection helped to keep Eurosceptics off the list, or at least a long way down it. The only declared Eurosceptic on the Social Democrats' list was placed so far down that voters had to turn over the ballot paper to find her name. But whether or not there was a conscious attempt to keep Social Democratic Eurosceptics away from the EP, which the leadership denied, that was not the outcome of the election – due to the effect of the preference-vote mechanism. The lone Social Democratic Eurosceptic succeeded in winning one of the party's seats (Aylott and Blomgren 2004).

Once the election is over, how is the position of European parliamentary dele-gation leader decided? Interestingly, some informants, even MEPs, have difficulty answering the question precisely. This is because, in Sweden's short time in the Union, the process has rarely required much deliberation. Some parties have only had one MEP after a European election, which removes the need for a choice. The first name on a party's election list – who, of course, will almost certainly have the party leadership's confidence – will have a strong claim to be delegation leader, although, in two cases (one in the Liberals, one in the Moderates), a more experienced but lower-placed candidate has taken the job.

Indeed, it is mainly in the two parties that can consistently expect to win more than a couple of MEPs, the Social Democrats and the Moderates, that the choice of delegation leader has been remotely contentious. After the 2004 election, there were rumours (e.g. *Dagens Nyheter* 21 June 2004) that the party leadership might not approve as delegation leader the top name on the Social Democrats' list; but it did. The Moderates' top candidate, meanwhile, also got the job, after discussions with the party leadership, despite his attracting fewer preference votes than the second-placed candidate.

Overall, the mechanisms of candidate selection for European elections can be compared over time, across the parties and against each party's procedures in national parliamentary elections. The practice of holding an advisory primary has spread to the Christian Democrats, but partially retreated in the Moderates, and left the Social Democrats and the Left unaffected. In 2004, for the first time, each party presented a single national list. Successful candidates have been recruited from outside party structures, but not in any great numbers. The existence of a sin-gle national electoral constituency in European elections has undoubtedly given the partly leaderships a much greater, albeit varying, influence in the process than they enjoy in national elections. And yet, also as in national elections, the scope for preference voting has caused some disruption to party lists – especially in the

Social Democrats.[6] The implications of these trends for our research questions and hypotheses will be discussed in the concluding section.

Additional EU-related bodies

Some of the parties have certain other groups that are concerned in some way with EU affairs.[7] The Social Democrats have an 'EU Reference Group', which comprises about 20 people, among them representatives of the party's regional units, its women's and Christian sections, and its youth and student wings, all appointed by the national executive. A former foreign minister was for some years chair of this group. Its role has generally been to reflect on longer-term, strategic issues, such as the party's approach to the European Convention in 2002–3; but it plays a part in formulating the Social Democratic manifesto for EU elections. In 2004 the Liberals started an internet-based 'Europe Network', coordinated by one of their MPs, the deputy chair of the European affairs committee in parliament. They also have an International Committee, which oversees, inter alia, relations with other European parties. Otherwise, some parties have more or less formal institutions designed to integrate their MEPs and their assistants with national organizations. These are examined in a later section.

Finally, a brief word is in order here about another category of EU specialists who are politicians rather than functionaries, namely, those who sit in parliament's European affairs committee (EU-nämnd). This body was instituted when Sweden joined the EU. Although its form – it consists of 17 MPs plus reserve members, with the parties represented in proportion to their strengths in parliament – is similar to those of the standing committees, its formal status is consultative; it has no legislative function. The parties' parliamentary groups select the members of the committee, who often, but not always, have a prior interest in European affairs. Its members include some senior, well-known parliamentarians from across the spectrum, indicating its relatively prestigious status (although this is offset by the unattractiveness of its meeting times, on Fridays). The governing party supplies its chair.

Acting nationally

Recall that one of our main hypotheses is that EU specialists are gaining influence within national parties. The likeliest area in which this increased influence would be apparent is, of course, when the party deals with EU-related issues. However, it may also be the case that EU specialists are shaping the parties' internal processes in a more general way. In this section, as well as considering the general influence of EU specialists, I pay particular attention to two internal processes: manifesto formulation and selection of party personnel. These are often rather complex, but I will look to uncover the role that EU specialists play in them and, to some extent, to discern whether their input has changed in scope.

Formulating manifestos

Swedish parties' procedures for writing their manifestos for national parliamentary elections are, like their organizational structures, fairly similar. The national executive is the steering organ. It appoints a group with the task of writing a draft, in collaboration with both the party leadership and the parliamentary group. The draft is usually then referred to the party regions for their reactions and comments, and these will influence the final version of the manifesto, which is amended or approved by congress, the party council or the national executive.

Certain EU specialists, both politicians and functionaries, are closely involved in drafting the EU-related sections of party programmes and manifestos. There have, though, been instances – in the Left and the Liberals, for example – in which EU specialists have had a broader drafting role, covering policy areas that are not directly EU-related.

When it comes to formulating manifestos for elections to the EP, the similarities between the parties' processes are again striking. In all the parties, EU specialists have a much greater role than they have in formulating manifestos for national elections. Because of the party organizations' relatively weaker interest in European election manifestos, but also because of the specialists' own knowledge and expertise, quite small groups of actors have considerable scope to form the parties' positions in EU affairs. This could be seen as a type of internal power shift to the advantage of the EU specialists. Yet European election manifestos are vague documents, without concrete objectives. Their content is not something that arouses controversy, even within the more divided Swedish parties.

Of course, policy is not shaped only in the formulation of party programmes and manifestos. Policy documents are produced frequently, and party positions often have to be decided as issues arise. This requires communication between the party leadership and its elected representatives, including MEPs. In interviews, MEPs in most parties, particularly the bigger ones, complained about a sense of isolation from their parties. Yet some also suggested that the situation had improved, especially regarding informal, everyday contacts between them and their party colleagues back home, particularly MPs. Much of this communication is conducted by assistants via telephone and e-mail. The Social Democrats have a sophisticated system of electronic newsletters, which flow daily from Stockholm to the party's MEPs and weekly in the other direction. The party's MEPs have access to the national parliamentary group's information database, and both groups share a common 'early warning system' for breaking political issues.

Selection of personnel

Numerous figures within the parties are not elected internally at congress, but are instead appointed. The people directly responsible for making the appointment are the party secretary, if the job is in the party organization; the party secretary and the chair of the parliamentary group, if it is in the party's parliamentary office; or the party secretary and MEPs (individually or collectively), if it is in the

European parliamentary office. Clearly, then, the party secretary is in a crucial position for influencing the selection of party staff. No one with an EU-specialist background as been secretary in a Swedish party. But what about the national executive, the organ that appoints the party secretary? After all, to be elected by congress to the national executive, a person obviously needs support within the party's grass roots, plus a willingness to work to keep that support. Achieving that is in itself an indicator of influence.

By 2005 six MEPs were ordinary members of the parties' respective national executives (that is, not appointed *ex officio*, but elected by congress and with full voting rights). The Social Democrats and the Christian Democrats lacked a current MEP in their national executive, although the Social Democrats had one former MEP. The Left also had on its national executive an employee of the European parliamentary group to which its MEPs belong.

Without more comparative reference points, it is hard to say whether these figures indicate high or low influence for EU specialists. More qualitatively, when asked whether specialization in EU affairs could be a useful way to accelerate an ambitious activist or politician's progress up the party hierarchy, very few interviewees answered positively. Purely domestic issues are still much more important to voters, and thus also to most politicians. Yet there are some signs of change and, intriguingly, of variation between the parties. By 2005, the European parliamentary delegation leaders for the Liberals and the Left – the former a member of her party's executive committee, the latter previously a member of his – were the two politicians to have become genuinely national figures on the platform of their being MEPs. The Moderate MP in charge of European issues, a former MEP, was one of the party's deputy leaders and a member of the executive committee; she was also a vice-president of the Europarty to which the Moderates are affiliated.

As for the personnel chosen to work as party functionaries, there are few obvious signs of EU specialists advancing beyond the positions of international secretaries and advisors to the parties' parliamentary groups in Stockholm and Brussels. One exception uncovered during research for this study was the head of the Liberal leader's office, who was recruited at least partly on the grounds of his experience in the party's European parliamentary office. The aim was partly to integrate the Liberals' MEPs into the party's work, rather than leaving them – in the informant's words – as 'satellites'. Another example was the Social Democrats' appointment of their international secretary as 'leader' of the party's 2004 European election campaign.

Overall, then, the advancement of non-elected EU specialists beyond their natural positions as international secretaries and parliamentary advisors has not progressed very far, even if some signs of such a development can be detected. A similar observation can be made about those who appoint such personnel, that is, the members of the national executives. MPs on the European affairs committee, meanwhile, are sometimes political heavyweights – although such a quality, and thus any change its presence on the committee, is hard to measure.

Acting supranationally

In this section, I address the autonomy and accountability of the parties' representatives in EU-level arenas. I focus on the degree of instruction from the party leadership that such representatives have; the extent to which the leadership can ensure that any instructions are followed; the degree to which such representatives can act autonomously; and, finally, whether this autonomy actually translates into intra-party power. I tackle these questions by looking at different EU-level arenas: the Europarties, the EP, the Council of Ministers and the European Council.

Parties and Europarties

The Swedish parties all have long histories of international engagement (Jerneck 1997). They have also forged ties with Europarties (see Table 7.4). Furthermore, since Sweden joined the EU, the parties' MEPs have sat in various European parliamentary groups with like-minded deputies from other member states. There has been very little controversy in the Swedish parties about which parliamentary groups and Europarties to align with.

The Europarties have undoubtedly solidified their organizations in recent years (e.g. Sandström 2003). The relevant question for us is the extent to which this solidification has influenced the internal power relations of national parties. Comparison between the Swedish parties is complicated by the different organizational structures in the Europarties. But three observations can be made.

First, primary responsibility for managing relations with Europarties is held

Table 7.4 Swedish parties' affiliations to European parliamentary groups and Europarties, 2005

	European parliamentary group	*Europarty*
Left Party	GUE/NGL	NELF, Nordic Green Left Alliance[a]
Social Democrats	Socialists	PES
Greens	Greens–EFA	European Green Party
June List	Independence/Democracy	–
Centre Party	ALDE	ELDR
Liberals	ALDE	ELDR
Christian Democrats	EPP–ED	EPP
Moderates	EPP–ED	EPP

Source: www.parties-and-elections.de

Notes
European parliamentary groups: ALDE – Alliance of Liberals and Democrats for Europe; EPP/ED – European People's Party/European Democrats; Greens/EFA – Greens/European Free Alliance; GUE/NGL – European United European Left/Nordic Green Left.
Europarties: ELDR – European Liberal, Democrat and Reform Party; EPP – European People's Party; NELF – New European Left Forum; PES – Party of European Socialists.
a   Neither NELF nor the Nordic Green Left Alliance, which coexist, can be classified as a Europarty. The latter instead constitutes 'cooperation between independent and sovereign parties' (www.vansterpartiet.se).

by functionaries in some parties and by politicians in others. Jerneck (1997: 132) observed that such ties had become 'institutionalized' since Sweden joined the EU. Nevertheless, to the outside observer, clear demarcation of responsibility is sometimes rather elusive. According to informants, the Social Democrats', the Liberals' and the Moderates' international secretaries still have substantial liaison and coordinating responsibilities. The Social Democrats' international secretary, for instance, is a member of the Party of European Socialists' 'Coordination Team'. In the Left, the Centre and the Christian Democrats, the party secretary takes a more pronounced role.

Still, in most of the parties, politicians do have important positions. A Social Democratic minister usually sits in the Presidency of the Party of European Socialists. A Liberal MP sits in the Council of the European Liberal, Democrat and Reform Party. The Greens' practice is to have one MP and one member of the national executive represented in the European Greens' Council, although in 2005 others filled those roles, including the party's MEP. For the Christian Democrats and the Moderates, senior parliamentarians sit in the Political Bureau of the European People's Party. In 2005 the Moderate MP in charge of European issues was also a vice-president of European People's Party.

A second, tentative observation, drawn from interviews, is that reporting requirements for representatives in the Europarties are relatively firm in the Left, the Greens and the Social Democrats (and informants regarded these obligations as entirely normal) and looser in the Centre and the Moderates. Indeed, the Moderates' representatives – particularly those associated with the circle that led the party from the mid-1980s until 2003, several of whom had backgrounds in the European Democrat Union, an association of conservative parties – were for some time seemingly left to manage relations largely at their own discretion.[8]

The third observation is that these contact positions are of limited significance as power resources for the individuals who hold them. One Moderate informant emphasized their value as facilitators of cross-EU network-building. When a government minister reports to parliament on a Council of Ministers meeting, it was argued, an experienced, well-connected opposition MP can try to verify the account by contacting old associates in other EU governments (see also Gidlund 1992: 163–4; Heidar and Svåsand 1997: 265; Jerneck 1997: 146; Johansson 2003: 27). Some observers became interested in the way that the Social Democrats appeared to have used their contacts in the Party of European Socialists to push a domestic policy priority, the fight against unemployment, which was subsequently included in the Treaty of Amsterdam (Jerneck 1997: 158; Johansson 1999a: 91–2). Clearly, international contacts can be useful, and those who are responsible for relations with Europarties are usually personally interested in the task and thus find it enjoyable. However, interviews for the current project offered little evidence that individuals work hard to acquire these contact positions as a means of enhancing their influence within the party, or that holding them can be an asset in internal party manoeuvring. A highly placed informant in one party admitted that he did not take his formal contacts with the relevant Europarty very seriously.

Overall, then, the parties appear to vary in the interest that they have in contacts with Europarties. In some, perhaps most, there is insufficient interest in the party organization to enforce the accountability mechanisms that do exist. This in turn suggests that the autonomy that EU specialists and – in so far as they are involved in this arena – party elites enjoy in conducting relations with Europarties does not translate into much intra-party influence.

Parties and their MEPs

There are good reasons to suspect that parties' representatives in the EP are considerably more autonomous than their counterparts at national level. Quite apart from the physical distance, there is much less overlap with the party leaderships. But does this greater autonomy, if it exists, bring commensurate influence to MEPs in their parties?

All parties invite their MEPs to meetings of their national parliamentary groups, although in practice few attend. As mentioned earlier, the leaders of the Social Democrats and the Moderates' groups in the EP are made *ex officio* members of the parties' executive organs. Otherwise, some parties have more institutionalized mechanisms for integrating their MEPs into the life of the national organization. For instance, the Left Party's main mechanism is known as the 'big meetings', which involve its MEPs, its EU Secretariat, its MPs on the European affairs committee, the parliamentary group's specialist advisor, and the two members of the national executive with responsibility for EU issues. These meetings occur biannually, and they discuss longer-term, strategic issues. Weekly telephone meetings keep the Left's MEPs in touch with the EU Secretariat. Between those forms of contact, the party's MPs and MEPs have occasional joint discussions.

Other parties go further. The Moderates' 'EU Group' consists of the party's MEPs; representatives of the national parliamentary group, including those who sit on the European affairs committee; representatives of the party leadership; and functionaries stationed at both national and EU levels. The group's intention was originally to meet every month (Blomgren 2003: 158–9). It did so considerably less often from about 2003, but appeared to revive after the 2004 European election. The Christian Democrats' 'EU Forum' (EU-samråd), an equivalent body, also met frequently. The Centre had a comparable group, which included regional representatives and other relevant party figures; but after 2001 it became moribund. The Liberals and the Greens lack such bodies; informants suggest that, with so few MEPs, their integration does not need to be institutionalized. Integrating organs are also absent in the Social Democrats, although the party does require that the statutes of its European parliamentary delegation be confirmed by the national executive. The Social Democrats' MEPs, like their MPs, are also declared to be responsible to the party congress, and must report to congress about their activity (Social Democrats 2005: §§12–13). The Left requires the same type of report. Other parties require their MEPs to report to the national executive, around twice a year.

One further aspect of staff recruitment is worth highlighting in this sub-section. Precisely who employs MEP-funded functionaries is sometimes a mildly contentious question. Social Democratic MEPs form an association that hires these assistants collectively. In practice, an individual MEP nominates an assistant and then clears it with the rest of the parliamentary group. In all the other parties, it is now the national party organizations that formally employ the assistants. In several cases, however, with the Left and the Moderates prominent among them, MEPs have fought successful battles since 1995 to prevent their party organizations from foisting assistants on them. Now MEPs all have, in effect, not only an informal right of veto over appointments, but also the right of initiative, with their preferred candidates then approved by the party secretary in Stockholm. Moreover, while assistants will usually have some sort of background in or association with the party, only the Left insists that they be party members. In the other parties, particularly the smaller ones, a trend towards employing assistants with special education or experience in a relevant field, probably relevant to an MEP's membership of European parliamentary committees, can be observed.

Finally, there is one other mechanism through which parties seek to bind their candidates. The Swedish parties, like most others in the EU, insist before elections to the European Parliament that their candidates agree that MEPs' assistance funds should be devoted to their parties' EU-related activity (Blomgren 2003: 176–8). Thus, the party organizations ensure their control of the resources that are derived from membership of the European Parliament. In some parties, including the Social Democrats, this pledge also explicitly mentions adherence to the party programme and manifesto. But this binding mechanism does not seem to play much of a role in practice. Most MEPs see such policy coordination as natural and obvious; no examples of a party issuing formal instructions to its MEPs on how to vote in the EP were uncovered during interviews. Those MEPs who have deviated from the party line – that is, the Eurosceptics elected via the Social Democrats', the Centre's and the Christian Democrats' lists – have not been formally penalized by their parties.[9]

So the evidence does seem to bear out the complaints of some MEP informants that they are isolated from their parties. Certainly, these informants did not equate their relative autonomy with any significant, consistent influence in shaping party policy. This is perhaps not so surprising. With so few MEPs between them, the Swedish European parliamentary delegations are unlikely to have a decisive impact on policy formulation at EU level, which reduces the incentive for their parties to take much interest in them. Moreover, in one fundamental way, party leaderships actually have *more* control over an MEP than they do over a national MP – at least if that MEP wants to retain his or her seat after the next election. Because MEP candidates are chosen at the parties' national levels, the leadership has a stronger say in whether a sitting parliamentarian is reselected or deselected than it would have in a national election, when the party's regional levels decide the lists for their constituencies.

Parties and their ministers

The position of minister for European affairs was abolished in 1996.[10] Early in 2005 the Social Democratic government announced that the deputy prime minister would henceforth oversee the coordination of EU policy across the government. The nature and significance of this role was not immediately obvious, however.

According to the rules of Swedish parliamentarism, ministers are responsible – both collectively and individually – to parliament, which implies a scrutinizing role for parliamentarians. Those MPs who are most informed about EU issues are likely to be found either in one of parliament's 16 standing committees, which mostly shadow particular ministries, or in the European affairs committee.

Opinion is mixed on how effective the European affairs committee is in holding ministers accountable for their engagement at EU level. It can require ministers to outline the government's position before they engage in the Council of Ministers or the European Council, and such briefings, which are also attended by ministerial advisors, have become standard practice. According to some observers, the committee has influenced the government's stance on particular topics (Larsson 1999: 333); occasionally, a significant government retreat has been achieved (Hegeland 2002: 35). Indeed, EU membership has given parliament some insight into policy areas that were previously consigned to foreign policy, in which parliamentary scrutiny was much weaker than in domestic policy (Hegeland and Mattson 2000: 91; Hegeland 2002: 38). Nevertheless, there are practical constraints on what the committee can achieve.

For a start, there is the appreciation that, as in foreign policy, the Swedish position in multilateral negotiations can be weakened if a minister is mandated too tightly (Hegeland and Mattson 2000: 88). This constraint is perhaps most visible before important meetings of the European Council; even Eurosceptical parties are reluctant to be seen to damage national interests by limiting the government's room to bargain.[11] Then there is the question of information – or rather the government's control of it (Lindgren 2000: 218–19; Hegeland 2002: 39). Informants complained that, by the time an issue is brought before the European affairs committee, it can have been subject to perhaps years of negotiations between national representatives in the EU, and thus be almost a *fait accompli*. All the Swedish parties are dissatisfied with how the committee works in this respect, and the Centre and the Greens wanted to abolish it.[12] Indeed, a survey found that Swedish MPs were markedly less impressed with their European affairs committee's ability to influence EU policy than their Finnish counterparts were with theirs. Swedish MPs had an even lower opinion of their parliament's standing committees' scope to influence EU policy (Jungar and Ahlbäck Öberg 2002: 58–73).

In fact, that survey's findings are not very surprising. Whereas Finland tends to have broad majority coalition governments, the Social Democrats' extraordinary domination of national government in Sweden means that most Swedish MPs, who are not Social Democrats, were likely to feel excluded from policy-making. The same survey showed that Social Democratic MPs were much less concerned about the government's dominance of EU issues, and much more supportive of the European affairs committee's role and potential to influence policy, than other MPs were (Jungar and Ahlbäck Öberg 2002: 70). If parliament and its committees are perceived by MPs as ineffective means to control ministers' activity in EU arenas, that is likely to reflect (a) the partisan character of Swedish parliamentary politics and (b) the exceptionally strong position of the Social Democrats.[13]

Indeed, the Swedish system of parliamentary scrutiny of European policy was designed to encourage MPs to exercise influence through their parliamentary groups (Jungar and Ahlbäck Öberg 2002: 77). To some extent, this does occur. Ministers and under-secretaries of state (*statssekreterare*) brief their own party's parliamentary group in order to secure support for the government's line, and European policy is not excepted. The question is whether non-EU-specialist MPs are sufficiently well-informed about or interested in European issues to demand accountability effectively in this way. It is not clear than they are.

What about ministers' accountability to the wider party organization? In some countries, ministers, like ordinary MPs, would have to work to retain their party's confidence if they wanted to be re-nominated to run under its banner at the following election. In Sweden, that is only sometimes the case, thanks to the prime minister's right to appoint anyone, not just MPs, to ministerial positions. Of the 21 cabinet ministers in mid-2005, just seven had given up seats in parliament to begin ministerial careers[14] – a proportion that has been steadily falling over several decades (Medelberg 2004). Clearly, the party has little or no sway over ministers in whom it never vested confidence in the first place, and who may even be only loosely connected to it. As it happens, of the nine cabinet portfolios with a strong EU policy component (excluding the prime minister's), whose incumbents could be expected to take part frequently in Council of Ministers meetings, six were held in 2005 by ministers with no parliamentary experience.[15]

In autumn 2004 the government announced that responsibility for coordinating EU policy across the government was being moved from the foreign ministry to the prime minister's office (Larue 2006: 82). The office comprises four units, of which the most important is the prime minister's secretariat. The secretariat itself is divided into four sections, including the EU department. The prime minister's secretariat is directed by – in addition to the prime minister – the deputy prime minister and three under-secretaries of state. In some ways, concentrating the coordination of EU policy in the prime minister's office has increased the 'partyness' of that policy. This is partly because the under-secretaries in charge of it are political appointees, unlike the neutral civil servants who mostly ran it in the foreign ministry. For instance, the crucial position of chief negotiator in intergovernmental conferences has usually been filled by an under-secretary, often the same one on several occasions (Johansson 2003: 31), who has at least some affiliation to the governing party. Furthermore, the prime minister – of course, unequivocally a party figure – is firmly responsible for EU policy, if not in charge of its day-to-day execution. However, as with the Social Democratic parliamentary group, it is unlikely that many in the party organization have sufficient knowledge or interest to put this ministerial engagement with the EU under serious scrutiny.

If this points to considerable ministerial autonomy from the party, there may be limits to that autonomy when it comes to the most important EU issues. EU policy is certainly not completely immune from party pressure. The story of the ill-starred attempt to take Sweden into EMU – the concession of a referendum on the issue, the appointment of five euro-sceptic ministers after the election victory of 2002, the failure to rally activists and supporters behind a Yes vote (Aylott 2005a), the appointment of a Eurosceptic as party secretary a year later – illustrated the enduring influence of the party on European policy. On the other hand, the Social Democratic government seemed determined to ratify the European constitutional treaty without a referendum, despite disquiet in sections of the party, until the process was halted by the French and Dutch referendums in mid-2005.[16]

Conclusion

In this chapter, I have shown how the main Swedish parties have adapted their organizations to the exigencies of EU membership. In this concluding section, I assess our three research questions and consider the two hypotheses presented in Chapter 1. Is it the case in Sweden that, as expected, the process of adaptation has strengthened the intra-party positions of both party elites and EU specialists? And can any variation be discerned between the parties that might be systematic?

The national context of the Swedish parties' response to European integration is clearly relevant to any broader comparison. While various aspects of governance have been affected by EU membership (Johansson 1999b; Ersson 2000), the sub-heading to one study of Swedish administrative adaptation – 'The State Joins the European Union' – exemplifies the argument that '[s]tate and society at large are out of touch on the issue of how best to deal with the inevitable slide forward in the territorial and temporal redefinitions of European policy-making' (Ekengren and Sundelius 1998: 146). Swedes are nearly all polyglot, and many are well travelled. But the country's political class, or at least most of it, has felt much more comfortable in a supranational union than much of the rest of the electorate has, despite the fact that all four national newspapers are broadly pro-EU.

This popular Euroscepticism is strongest on the left. The reasons for that are not mysterious. Over much of the twentieth century, Swedish nationalism became channelled into the project of constructing a comprehensive welfare state, which later became augmented by a righteous self-image of neutral Sweden's role in the world (Stråth 1992: 201). Bolstered by decades of economic success, Social Democratic governments were mainly responsible for cultivating this 'welfare nationalism' (Aylott 1999: 34–65; Elvander 1994). Despite harder times since the 1970s and a profound societal diversification, many Swedes retain a basic faith in the governing capacity of their nation state. Since Sweden joined the EU in 1995, Euroscepticism has certainly become less intense, even among the two parties, the Left and Greens, who still advocate withdrawal from the Union. But, as the referendum on EMU illustrated, it is still widespread.

Against this background, how have the parties adapted to European integration, and what affect has change had on their intra-party power structures?

Regarding (1) the formal structure of the parties, not that much has changed since Sweden's accession to the Union. EU specialists – MEPs, MPs on the European affairs committee, party functionaries with EU-related jobs – have not become greatly empowered in a strictly formal sense. In fact, the only formal change that clearly favours EU specialists is in the allocation of material and human resources within the party. Although EU specialists within the party organization itself are quite scarce, advisors with expert knowledge have become more numerous – modestly but noticeably – in the national and, especially, the European parliamentary offices. The Social Democrats' MEPs, for example, have a substantial office, plus their EU officers back in Sweden. This is thanks to the munificence of the European Parliament. The party organizations, however, have ensured that they have a good deal of control over how these resources are utilized. Overall, change has not been dramatic.

What about (2) EU specialists' position in internal process – that is, in the dynamics of intra-party politics? In some ways, the most obvious of the parties' EU specialists, the MEPs, enjoy more autonomy than do national MPs, due to the lack of personal overlap with the party leadership, the physical distance from the national capital and, moreover, the relative paucity of national media interest in the European Parliament. In other ways, MEPs may be *more* beholden to the party leadership, at least if they want to be re-selected, given that, for European elections, party lists are constructed at national level. There are two possible impediments to the leadership's ability to steer candidate selection. The first, internal advisory primaries, has spread to all the parties bar the Left and the Social Democrats. Yet even these parties were vulnerable to the second impediment, the preference-vote facility. Indeed, it may be no coincidence that in 2004 it was on the Social Democrats, whose list was most shaped by their party leadership, that voters inflicted the greatest disruption to their list order.

Once they have been elected, the parties have different ways of integrating the MEPs into their activities. Some have more or less formal groups for that purpose. In at least two parties, however, the Centre and the Moderates, these groups ran out of steam, at least for a while. Meanwhile, the leaderships of the two biggest parties, the Social Democrats and the Moderates, seem to be taking an increased interest in who becomes leader of their European parliamentary delegations. On the other hand, MEPs from several parties have established greater independence in appointing their assistants. Moreover, the 'partyness' of these EU specialists has weakened in some bourgeois parties, as MEPs have increasingly recruited assistants who have no previous connection to their parties.

There is, then, a mixed picture in terms of MEPs' autonomy. Their relative freedom once elected is offset by their need to keep the party leadership happy in order to keep its support during candidate selection before the next European election, particularly in the parties without primaries. Are there implications for the *influence* of the MEPs in their parties?

As far as policy and manifesto formulation is concerned, there is not much evidence that the influence of EU specialists extends beyond the formulation of European election manifestos and into the formulation of national party programmes and manifestos. Yet there have been exceptions. The Left Party and the Liberals have each had an MEP who became an important party figure; a former MEP became a leading figure in the Moderates. With a mildly heroic interpretative leap, therefore, it could be inferred that EU specialists have risen highest in the most EU-enthusiastic parties, the Liberals and the Moderates, and also – less predictably – in the two most Eurosceptical parties, the Left and the Greens. Indeed, informants in the Left talk of a conscious effort to encourage MEPs to stand for executive positions, despite the party's ideological stance.[17]

The parties in which EU specialists have been least evident, meanwhile, have two things in common: they have been divided over Europe, rather than having a solid view, either for or against; and they have organizational histories that most conform to the mass-party model. The most interesting case in this context is the Social Democrats. Historically, it was almost an ideal-typical mass party, and yet it has also dominated power at national, regional and local levels. It could be that the party's division over Europe springs from a clash between its pragmatic, office-seeking elements and its more ideological, policy-seeking traditions. It could also be that the divisive potential of the EU has discouraged aspiring Social Democratic politicians from profiling themselves as EU specialists. In parties with a less ambivalent view of the EU, by contrast, EU specialization might be seen as more of an asset – even if it is used to inform a critical perspective on the Union. At this stage, however, all these propositions are speculative.

The final research question concerned (3) the power of party elites when they act at EU level. Regarding the management of contacts with Europarties, there is some variation between parties. For instance, the Christian Democrats and the Moderates give this role to experienced, internationally well-connected politicians. But although there is evidence that such positions can help in building international networks of contacts, which can on occasion be useful to an individual and perhaps also to the party, there is not much to suggest that these advantages are so great that contact roles have become especially sought-after in internal party politics.

In Sweden, members of party elites often double as cabinet ministers when the party is in office, and cabinet ministers are often involved in EU decision-making in the Council of Ministers and the European Council. This aspect of elites' intra-party empowerment due to European integration is only relevant to one party, as by 2005 Sweden had only had Social Democratic governments since it joined the Union.

It is clear that leading Social Democratic ministers have indeed become more independent of their party, thanks to the logic of EU policy-making. Despite its relative strength in cross-national comparison, the parliamentary European affairs committee is not a very effective mechanism through which MPs – certainly opposition MPs, but perhaps also Social Democratic ones – can exercise control over ministers who engage in the Council of Ministers. Yet the committee was never really designed to fulfil such a role. Rather, that was seen primarily as a job for the parliamentary groups – and it is here that the information asymmetry mentioned in Chapter 1 is relevant, with non-specialist MPs probably lacking the knowledge and interest to scrutinize properly 'their' ministers' activity in the EU. Much the same could be said about ministers' accountability to their party organization. That weak accountability is exacerbated by other trends, such as the increasing readiness of Social Democratic prime ministers to recruit to the cabinet from outside parliament. Such ministers need have no base in the party, which makes them, in practice, accountable only to the prime minister. This aspect of 'presidentialization' (Aylott 2005b) may well have causes other than European integration, however.

In sum, European integration has certainly affected Swedish parties, but not dramatically. The supranational level has been integrated quite smoothly into their activities, with the customary procedures of delegation and reporting extended upwards and to a new parliamentary arena. In such a relatively organized country, with such institutionalized parties, this was perhaps to be expected. Thus, the hypothesis about the empowerment of EU specialists is only very weakly supported. While the functionaries and politicians in this category have come to enjoy moderately greater autonomy than their closest equivalents at national level do (and even this is often debatable), neither group has become very influential in their parties by dint of such specialization. The other hypothesis, about party elites, finds stronger support, from some well-known consequences of the EU's style of policy-making through multilateral bargaining. But, importantly, this verification applies only to a governing party.

EU membership has – so far, at least – meant business pretty much as usual for Swedish parties. As Heidar and Svåsand (1997: 269–70) concluded in their survey of 'internationalization' in Scandinavian parties, the national level is still where the serious action takes place. Assuming that European integration continues and possibly deepens, EU specialists may become more influential and elites may see their power further enhanced, as our hypotheses predicted. In Sweden, however, this is likely to be a slow process.

Notes

1 Earlier versions of this chapter were presented at the Nordic Political Science Association conference in Reykjavik and the ECPR general conference in Budapest, and at research seminars at Södertörn University College and Luleå University of Technology, all in 2005. Many thanks to the participants in those events, plus Torbjörn Bergman, Magnus Blomgren, Hans Hegeland and Thomas Larue, for their helpful comments, which informed my interpretation of the data in various ways. Thanks, too, to Svante Ersson for help with some data and to Bella Lawson for excellent research assistance. Any errors, including in translations from Swedish-language sources, are the responsibility of the author.

2 The empirical material on which this chapter is based is drawn largely from semi-structured interviews with 32 informants at high levels of the parties' organizations (party secretaries, international officers, campaign directors for elections to the European Parliament, internally elected members of the national executive), their national parliamentary groups (including members of the parliamentary European affairs committee), their European parliamentary delegations (including several heads of delegations) and specialist advisors in the parties' parliamentary offices at both national and European levels. These interviews were conducted over two and a half years from autumn 2003. Unless otherwise stated, the situation described refers to that obtaining at the end of 2005.

3 The Greens differ much less than they used to from this model of organization, but they still have two 'spokespersons', a man and a woman, rather than a single leader.

4 Interestingly, there is no mention of this representation in either party's statutes, al-

though the Moderates' statutes mention the national executive's right to co-opt individuals to its meetings (Moderates 2004: §8.2).

5 In the Left's case, this was because a congress fell at a convenient time in the candidate selection process.

6 As a writer for the Social Democrats' newsletter complained after the 2004 European election, 'For the first time, the party completely lost control over who got into parliament' (*Aktuellt i Politiken* 21 June 2004).

7 In the early 1990s, as EU membership was ascending up the political agenda, the three most Eurosceptical parties – the Left, the Greens and the Centre – each instituted an 'EU Council', with the brief of monitoring and interpreting developments in Europe (Gidlund 1992:164–70).

8 Interestingly, this observed variation in the institutionalization of contacts with Europarties chimes with earlier research. In the early 1990s Gidlund (1992: 165–8) noted that whereas the Left's 'International Group' was clearly responsible to its executive organs, and its (temporary) 'EC Committee' had been set up by a congress decision, the Moderates were consciously trying to avoid creating special structures for their international engagement.

9 Swedish MEPs tend to vote with their national parties rather than their European parliamentary groups in case of conflict between the two, and do so to a greater extent than Dutch and Irish MEPs do (Blomgren 2003: 271).

10 It was not possible in this chapter to refer in any detail to the election of September 2006, after which a coalition of the Centre Party, the Liberals, the Christian Democrats and the Moderates took office. However, it is worth mentioning that this new government included a minister for EU affairs, based in the prime minister's office.

11 An example of this reluctance to bind the government could be seen before the intergovernmental conference in 2003–4 on the proposed European constitution. The combined parliamentary committees on foreign affairs and constitutional affairs declared that, although they were generally in favour of the draft produced by the European Convention, they were against the proposal for a president of the European Council. This objection reflected majority opinion in parliament. But the committee also recognized that it was 'important that the government has room for manoeuvre in the negotiations'. 'Countries that threaten to use their veto risk being marginalized in the negotiations,' argued a Liberal MP. The Moderate vice-chair of the joint committee stated that 'Our task as parliament is to clarify Sweden's positions, not to polemicize' (see *Dagens Nyheter* 13 November 2003). The Social Democratic government duly ignored parliament's opposition to a European Council president.

12 In late 2005 a special committee of MPs (Riksdagskommittén), chaired by the speaker, proposed changes to many of parliament's procedures, including its handling of EU-related issues. The committee suggested that parliament should take up at an earlier stage policy ideas originating at European level; give more scope to the standing committees to decide the EU-related issues about which the government should furnish parliament with information; and permit members of standing committees to take part in meetings of the European affairs committee. Subject to confirmation by the new parliament after the election of September 2006, these reforms were to be implemented at the beginning of 2007.

13 The 'contracts' signed in 1998 and 2002 between the Social Democrats, the Greens and the Left, which underpinned the parties' parliamentary cooperation, excluded European policy from that cooperation.

14 Two more had earlier parliamentary experience (one representing another party). Another two had earlier been parliamentary substitutes. In Sweden, an MP who joins the government must pass on his or her seat to a substitute.

15 A seventh – the minister for coordination of EU issues – had only brief parliamentary experience as a substitute. Figures on ministers' backgrounds are calculated on

the basis of information taken from the biographies on the chancery website (www. regeringen.se).

16 An exception to the Social Democratic government's strict control of Swedish European policy occurred with the Convention that prepared the constitutional treaty (Johansson 2003), as opposition parties could nominate members of the Convention. Interestingly, the Left Party was dismayed to see its nominee emerge as a warm supporter of the treaty.

17 Gidlund (1992: 168) noted a comparable enthusiasm in the Left for European issues as long ago as the early 1990s – soon after the party had officially 'annulled' its transnational contacts, which hitherto had nearly all been with dictatorial communist parties (Jerneck 1997: 135). For a slightly different view on Euroscepticism and the 'internationalization' of party organization, see Heidar and Svåsand (1997: 259).

References

Arter, David (1990) 'The Swedish Riksdag: The Case of a Strong Policy-Influencing Assembly', *West European Politics*, 13: 120–42.

Aylott, Nicholas (1999) *Swedish Social Democracy and European Integration: The People's Home on the Market*, Aldershot: Ashgate.

Aylott, Nicholas (2002) 'Let's Discuss This Later: Party Responses to Euro-Division in Scandinavia', *Party Politics*, 8(4): 441–61.

Aylott, Nicholas (2005a) 'Lessons Learned, Lessons Forgotten: The Swedish Referendum on EMU of September 2003', *Government and Opposition*, 40(4): 540–64.

Aylott, Nicholas (2005b) '"President Persson" – How Did Sweden Get Him?', in Thomas Poguntke and Paul Webb (eds), *The Presidentialization of Politics: A Comparative Study of Modern Democracies*, Oxford: Oxford University Press, pp. 176–98.

Aylott, Nicholas (2007 forthcoming) 'Softer but Strong: Euroscepticism and Party Politics in Sweden', in Paul Taggart and Aleks Szczerbiak (eds), *Opposing Europe? The Comparative Party Politics of Euroscepticism, Volume 1: Case Studies and Country Surveys*, Oxford: Oxford University Press.

Aylott, Nicholas and Magnus Blomgren (2004) *The European Parliament Election in Sweden, June 13 2004*, Sussex: European Parties Elections & Referendums Network, 2004 European Parliament Election Briefing Paper 7.

Bergman, Torbjörn (2004) 'Sweden: Democratic Reforms and Partisan Decline in an Emerging Separation-of-Powers System', *Scandinavian Political Studies*, 27(2): 203–25.

Bergman, Torbjörn and Nicholas Aylott (2003) 'Parlamentarism per kontrakt – blir den svenska innovationen långlivad?', in *Riksdagens årsbok 2003/03*, Stockholm: Riksdagen, pp. 4–7.

Bille, Lars (2001) 'Democratizing a Democratic Procedure: Myth or Reality? Candidate Selection in Western European Parties, 1960–1990', *Party Politics*, 7(3): 363–380.

Blomgren, Magnus (2003) *Cross-Pressure and Political Representation in Europe: A Comparative Study of MEPs and the Intra-Party Arena*, Umeå: Department of Political Science, Umeå University.

Brothén, Martin (2004) 'Bristande förankring', in Henrik Oscarsson and Sören Holmberg (eds), *Kampen om euron*, Gothenburg: Department of Political Science, Göteborg University, pp. 62–80.

Ekengren, Magnus and Bengt Sundelius (1998) 'Sweden: The State Joins the European Union', in Kenneth Hanf and Ben Soetendorp (eds), *Adapting to European Integration: Small States and the European Union*, London: Longman, pp. 131–48.

Elvander, Nils (1994) 'Självbelåten välfärdnationalism styr nej-sidan', *Svenska Dagbladet* 6 November.

Ersson, Svante (2000) 'Konsekvenser av medlemskapet? Sverige och EU under 1990-talet', paper presented at Swedish Political Science Association conference, Örebro, 8–10 October.

Gidlund, Gullan (1992) *Partiernas Europa*, Stockholm: Natur och Kultur.

Hagevi, Magnus (2000) 'Parliamentary Party Groups in the Swedish Riksdag', in Knut Heidar and Ruud Koole (eds), *Parliamentary Groups in Parliamentary Democracies: Political Parties Behind Closed Doors*, London: Routledge, pp. 145–60.

Hegeland, Hans (2002) 'Nationella parlament i Europeiska unionen – potentiella vinnare?', in SOU 2002:81, *Riksdagens roll i EU*, Stockholm: Prime Minister's Office and EU 2004 Committee, pp. 7–46.

Hegeland, Hans and Ingvar Mattson (2000) 'Another Link in the Chain: The Effects of EU Membership on Delegation and Accountability in Sweden', in Torbjörn Bergman and Erik Damgaard (eds), *Delegation and Accountability in European Integration: The Nordic Parliamentary Democracies and the European Union*, pp. 81–104, London: Frank Cass.

Heidar, Knut and Lars Svåsand (1997) 'Politiske partier og den internasjonale arena', in Knut Heidar and Lars Svåsand (eds), *Partier utan grenser?*, Oslo: Tano Aschehoug, pp. 258–70.

Isberg, Magnus (1999) *Riskdagsledamöten i sin partigrupp: 52 riksdagsveteraners erfarenheter av partigruppens arbetssätt och inflytande*, Stockholm: Gidlunds.

Jerneck, Magnus (1997) 'De svenska partiernas utlandsförbindelser – från internationalisering till europeisering?', in Knut Heidar and Lars Svåsand (eds), *Partier utan grenser?*, Oslo: Tano Aschehoug, pp. 129–66.

Johansson, Karl Magnus (1999a) 'Tracing the Employment Title in the Amsterdam Treaty: Uncovering Transnational Coalitions', *Journal of European Public Policy*, 6(1): 85–101.

Johansson, Karl Magnus (ed.) (1999b) *Sverige i EU*, Stockholm: SNS Förlag.

Johansson, Karl Magnus (2003) *Föreberredelser inför regeringskonferenser. Framtidskonventet i sitt sammanhang*, Stockholm: Swedish Institute for European Policy Studies, SIEPS report 3.

Jungar, Ann-Cathrine and Shirin Ahlbäck Öberg (2002) 'Parlament i bakvatten?', in SOU 2002:81, *Riksdagens roll i EU*, Stockholm: Prime Minister's Office and EU 2004 Committee, pp. 47–82.

Kite, Cynthia (1996) *Scandinavia Faces EU: Debates and Decisions on Membership 1961–94*, Umeå: Department of Political Science, Umeå University.

Larsson, Torbjörn (1999) 'Konflikten som försvann. Hur har det svenska EU-medlemskapet påverkat maktdelningen mellan regering och riksdag?', in SOU 1999:76, *Maktutdelning*, Stockholm: Ministry of Justice, pp. 319–48.

Larue, Thomas (2006) *Agents in Brussels: Democracy and Delegation in the European Union*, Umeå: Department of Political Science, Umeå University.

Lawler, Peter (1997) 'Scandinavian Exceptionalism and European Union', *Journal of Common Market Studies*, 35(4): 565–94.

Lindgren, Karl-Oskar (2000) 'EU-medlemskapets inverkan på den svenska parlamentarismen', *Statsvetenskaplig Tidskrift*, 103: 193–220.

Medelberg, Ola (2004) 'Statsrådens kompetens: En granskning av efterkrigstidens svenska ministrar', unpublished undergraduate dissertation (*C-uppsats*), Uppsala: Department of Government, Uppsala University.

Moderates (2004) 'Stadgar för moderaterna', Stockholm: Moderates.

Petersson, Olof (2005) 'De politiska partiernas medlemsutveckling', report to SNS Democracy Council, Stockholm: Center for Business and Policy Studies.

Pierre, Jon and Anders Widfeldt (1994) 'Party Organizations in Sweden: Colossuses with Feet of Clay or Flexible Pillars of Government?', in Richard S. Katz and Peter Mair (eds), *How Parties Organize: Change and Adaptation in Party Organizations in Western Democracies*, London: Sage, pp. 332–56.

Sandström, Camilla (2003) *Liberal partisamarbete i Europa. ELDR – en ny typ av parti?*, Umeå: Department of Political Science, Umeå University.

Social Democrats (2005) 'Stadgar 2005: Stadgar för Sveriges Socialdemokratiska Arbetareparti', Stockholm: Social Democrats.

Statistics Sweden and Department of Political Science, Göteborg University (1995) *Valet till Europa parlamentet 95*, Stockholm: Statistics Sweden.

Stråth, Bo (1992) *Folkhemmet mot Europa: Ett historisk perspektiv på 90-talet*, Stockholm: Tiden.

8 Some things change, a lot stays the same

Comparing the country studies

Nicholas Aylott, Laura Morales and Luis Ramiro

In the preceding chapters, we have seen how national political parties in six member states have adapted, or not adapted, to the institutions and processes of the European Union (EU). Some parties have changed organizationally to quite a significant degree, while others have barely changed at all. We have seen detailed accounts of the ways in which such change has, or has not, occurred, and of some of the consequences for intra-party power relations. We have also seen that variation is observable within national party systems. But we need now to lift our gaze from the national level and see whether this variation follows identifiable, cross-national patterns. Are, say, socialist parties more inclined to adapt to European integration? Are Eurosceptical parties, or those divided over the EU, less inclined to do so? Does being in government promote or impede change? Indeed, are any cross-national patterns visible at all?

Comparing our cases

The aim in this chapter, then, is to see whether the country in which a party is based is the primary explanation for the extent of change in that party or other factors – ideological identity, for example, or the party's particular role in the national party system – are as important or more so. These 'explanations' or 'factors' can be described as intervening variables. The dependent variables, the varying outcomes that we wish to explain, are – as will be familiar by now – the degree to which party elites and the individuals whom we call EU specialists have been empowered vis-à-vis the rest of the party. The prime cause of this change, the independent variable, is European integration itself. The intervening variables mediate the effect of the independent variable on the dependent variable in particular cases (specific national parties).

We need at the outset to declare our caution in drawing firm conclusions from this analysis. Certain types of data are readily quantifiable and relatively concrete, which naturally aids comparison among a medium-sized or large number of cases. Such data are often used in the study of political parties, although their validity is sometimes debatable. Membership figures, for example, are easily comparable, but, because the party is the source of the data, they often have question marks placed against their accuracy. In our country studies, as their authors repeatedly remark, quantitative data on things like personnel and resources devoted to EU affairs were hard to come by. Instead, we have relied largely on qualitative data – detailed, contextualized description of institutional features, formal rules and the practice of intra-party decision-making. We certainly see no inherent problem with this type of data and their use in comparative analysis. In many ways, they offer greater validity than many types of quantitative data do (Munck 2004: 115–16; George and Bennett 2005: 19–20). Still, potential drawbacks with our data must be taken seriously.

While a party's formal rules, its 'official story', may 'reflect the resolution of real conflicts and struggles', it 'cannot be regarded as a wholly adequate reflection of what constitutes the "real" story of the party' (Katz and Mair 1992: 7). Though the rules are the obvious starting point, this 'real story' must be completed by the researcher, and it may not be easy to get a rounded view of it. There may also be reliability problems involved. We rely not only on the description contained in our country studies, but also on the authors' own analysis and interpretations – and researchers are inevitably influenced by the boundaries of their context. Differences between national parties might seem striking within that political system, but when they are seen from a wider, transnational perspective, they may be compressed into insignificance.

Throughout the course of the project that gave rise to this book, however, the project members strove to minimize these potential validity and reliability problems through constantly and collectively reassessing and redefining concepts, indicators and questions, and through discussing and comparing the empirical material that had been gathered. Numerous earlier drafts of the country studies were presented at conferences and project workshops. We believe that, as far as possible, the project members are talking the same language.

A third potential difficulty is of a more practical nature. As Ragin (2003) points out, there are good reasons why predominantly qualitative data are employed in 'case-oriented' research, in which only a small number of cases is addressed. Qualitative data are suited to addressing complexity, both in the constitution of the case itself (what is it a case of? what is the relevant population?) and, perhaps especially, in identifying causation (George and Bennett 2005: 21–2; Ragin 1987: 19–33). It could be that a certain independent or intervening variable has no effect on the outcome, except in combination with another variable. Equally, that variable or combination of variables might be only one of several possible paths to the same outcome. Case studies are good at identifying such subtleties in the cases that they address, and tackling more cases might increase the scope to generalize conclusions across the whole population. The trouble is, the more cases that are compared in this way, the greater the complexity becomes, so that it is increasingly hard to keep track of all the possible and actual constellations of conditions and outcomes. With 30 cases (relevant national parties) in six countries, that is clearly a potential difficulty in our study.

One possible solution to the last of these methodological problems is the fuzzy-set comparison pioneered by Ragin (2000). Qualitative data are simplified and, to some extent, quantified, and the conditions or combinations of conditions that are necessary or sufficient to induce a certain outcome are computed. The method is ideal for a medium-sized number of cases, which is what we have. However, we decided against using fuzzy sets here. Converting largely qualitative data into fuzzy-set membership scores is a demanding task at the best of times, and we were aware that, with our data, there was too much room for error to creep in during conversion. Instead, we adopted a simpler approach. We constructed a number of bivariate tables in which the cases were arranged.

Our analysis approaches our basic hypotheses through concentrating on several distinct indicators, which capture key aspects of our dependent variables. On the power of EU specialists, these are: (1) whether members of the European Parliament (MEPs) sit in their party's executive organs automatically, by dint of their representative positions, or whether they do so by convention; (2) the degree to which EU specialists are integrated into their party's everyday life; and (3) the extent of EU specialists' influence in drafting national election manifestos. Other indicators of EU specialists' empowerment, such as the role given to national politicians with an EU brief, or the numbers of and influence enjoyed by party functionaries with specialist knowledge of the EU, are not included in the following tables, largely because of the difficulty of comparison between parties with varying political and economic circumstances. These indicators are, however, referred to in the concluding section.

On the power of party elites, the indicators are: (1) the party leadership's influence in the selection of candidates for elections to the European Parliament; (2) the degree of active policy coordination with the party's MEPs that is initiated by the leadership; and (3) the control exercised by a governing party over its ministers when they are active in EU decision-making forums. Furthermore, we also opted to present two tables that reflect our impression of the overall extent of (4) EU specialists' accountability to their party and (5) their influence in their party.

The intervening variables that we consider are central to the project's hypotheses. They are: (1) the status of the party as 'governmental' – in other words, how much time it has spent in recent years in government office in its country; (2) the state of opinion within the party on European integration; (3) the party's association with a party family, in the sense of its having an ideological affinity with certain parties in other countries; (4) the time that the country within which a party operates has been an EU member; (5) the size of the party's delegation to the European Parliament; and (6) national-level institutional features and party organization traditions. Some of these variables structure the tables, but most are just discussed in the text.

As will become clear below, the likely effect of these intervening variables on our cases is frequently far from obvious in advance. In more than a few instances, we can formulate quite different but equally plausible expectations about the way in which the intervening variable will influence the indicators on the dependent variable. We do not see this as a problem. Rather, it reflects the exploratory and inductive character of our comparison. It is important to note that this is an initial dip into the rich empirical waters of our subject matter.

The rest of the chapter develops as follows. In the next section, we address the power of EU specialists, along the lines outlined above. In the following section, we turn our attention to party elites, again as outlined above. In the final section, we draw some general conclusions about the extent and consequences of party adaptation to European integration.

EU specialists' intra-party power

Chapter 1 in this volume spelt out our expectations with regard to the shifting balance of power in favour of what we have termed EU specialists. This subset of party politicians and functionaries is characterized by their expertise and involvement in EU politics, and, thanks to the process of European integration, it is precisely this specialized knowledge that facilitates their increasing empowerment – at least, that is, according to our hypothesis. However, as we have seen in the country chapters, it is frequently not appropriate to bundle different types of experts into the same category. By doing so, we risk blurring any relevant finding. For this reason, we mainly focus in this section on MEPs, as these are arguably the primary sub-group of EU specialists within the parties.

Integration of European parliamentary delegation leaders into party leadership organs

For party actors to be influential, they usually need to be present within party leadership organs. Thus, one first assessment of EU specialists' internal power simply entails evaluating their presence in the national leadership bodies of their parties, which could – at least potentially – mean a significant ability to influence the highest decision-making processes (for example, elaboration of internal rules, selection of party leaders and candidates, decisions on party strategies and so on). In this light, having European parliamentary delegation leaders (or other MEPs) sitting *ex officio* in high-ranking leadership organs thanks to their representative position would indicate that MEPs are considered significant actors, and thus that they need to be integrated into internal party dynamics. Moreover, national party leaders, being aware of the significance of EU specialists, may want to monitor formally what MEPs do. So, whether because of the recognition of their importance, or because of the perceived need by party leaders to monitor their behaviour, or both, we would expect to find European parliamentary delegation leaders in these organs.

What about relevant intervening variables? In this comparison, we emphasize two in particular. First, there is the time dimension. It may be that parties in long-standing EU member countries will have adapted their internal organization in this formal respect to a greater extent. Alternatively, because of their countries' long involvement with incremental European integration, these parties may have adapted *less* than parties in newer member states. For example, the intra-party procedures that were established to select and accommodate MEPs at a relatively early stage of the EU's existence, when the Parliament was politically insignificant, may have persisted despite a changing political environment – for instance, direct elections to the Parliament (1979), the Single European Act (1985), the Maastricht treaty (1992) and the Treaty of Amsterdam (1997), plus the launch of the euro (1999). For parties in countries that joined at a more advanced stage of the Union's development, accession will have occurred in rather different institutional circumstances, and may have delivered more of an organizational shock. After all, and as party scholars are aware, 'external stimuli' are often the precursor of party change (Harmel and Janda 1994: 267–8).

A second, especially relevant intervening variable is the divisiveness of the EU issue in the party. It could be that the party leadership offers places in executive organs to MEPs in order to assure the compliance and accountability of the European parliamentary delegation.

In Table 8.1, the parties are arranged according to two variables. On the vertical axis, the parties are placed according to their country, in a descending order that corresponds to the duration of each state's EU membership. On the horizontal axis, we gauge whether or not they award the heads of their European parliamentary delegations automatic places in the executive organs, plus whether these individuals tend to find themselves on these organs anyway. Looking at the evidence in the table, we see, first of all, that most parties do not grant *ex officio*

Table 8.1 Formal incorporation of MEPs into party executive organs

	Does the EP delegation leader usually sit on the national executive or executive committee?[a]		
	No	*By convention or in practice*	Ex officio
FR	PCF, Verts	PS, UDF, UMP	
DE	Left, GRÜ	SPD	CDU, CSU, FDP
GB		Cons	Lab, LibDem[b]
ES	IU	PSOE, CDC, PNV	PP
AT		SPÖ	FPÖ, GRÖ, ÖVP
SE	v, kd	mp, c, fp	s, m

Notes
a Very frequently *ex officio* membership of the higher-rank organ (executive committee) also entails membership of the lower-rank national executive. See Poguntke (1998).
b Not delegation leader but an elected representative of MEPs.

In this and following tables, countries are ordered according to accession 'waves'.
Country and party abbreviations:
FR: France (EU founder member); PCF: French Communist Party; PS: Socialist Party; UDF: Union for French Democracy; UMP: Union for a Popular Movement.
DE: Germany (EU founder member); Left: Left Party; SPD: Social Democrats; GRÜ: Alliance 90/The Greens; CDU: Christian Democratic Union; CSU: Christian Social Union.
GB: Great Britain (EU member since 1973); Lab: Labour Party; LibDems: Liberal Democrats; Cons: Conservative Party.
ES: Spain (EU member since 1986); IU: United Left; PSOE: Spanish Socialist Workers' Party; CDC: Democratic Convergence of Catalonia; PNV: Basque Nationalist Party; PP: Popular Party.
AT: Austria (EU member since 1995); SPÖ: Social Democratic Party of Austria; GRÖ: Greens; ÖVP: Austrian People's Party; FPÖ: Freedom Party.
SE: Sweden (EU member since 1995); v: Left Party; s: Social Democrats; mp: Greens; c: Centre Party; fp: Liberals; kd: Christian Democrats; m: Moderates.

seats to their European delegation leaders. Thus, these results would not support (as yet) the suggestion that MEPs are gaining substantial internal power or significance, nor that party leaderships perceive an increasing need to monitor MEPs' activities. On the other hand, up to three parties in each of the six states in our sample have grown accustomed to having a representative of their MEPs on their executive organs, even if that representative is not there automatically by dint of his or her seat in the European Parliament. That in itself may be an indicator of influence. The selectorate for these executive positions may be impressed by the credentials derived from being a leading MEP, even if the party's statutes are not. This is an intriguing finding.

As for our intervening variables, the divisiveness of the EU issue within the party does not seem to increase the likelihood of *ex officio* representation. In fact, those parties that grant delegation leaders access to their executive organs are more frequently *not* divided internally around EU issues, although there are exceptions. Nor can duration of EU membership be seen to have much impact. All but two of the 18 cells in the table contain cases, showing a fairly even distribution of parties across all three vertical categories within each country.

Are other intervening variables influencing these results? Party family may play some part. Only two of the eight parties that allocate *ex officio* seats are from the social democratic family, only one is from the green family and none is from the radical-left family. Of the eight parties that do *not* automatically allocate such seats, and in which there is also no practice of electing a leading MEP to executive organs, all but two parties *are* from one of those three families. This is not so surprising. Left-of-centre parties are probably likelier to emphasize legitimacy through internal election to decision-making bodies than are parties further to the right, which may be more comfortable with their executive members acquiring legitimacy in other ways. Otherwise, though, the evidence does not suggest that governmental status or the size of a party's MEP delegation has any relevance.

Integration of EU specialists

The incorporation of MEPs into party executive organs through *ex officio* seats is not the only way in which EU specialists can be integrated into the national party organization, nor is it the only type of formal adaptation that would indicate that EU specialists have internal importance and influence. Certainly, there are other organizational mechanisms that, although they do not entail the same internal power as formal presence in executive organs, could also signal that EU specialists enjoy a reasonable degree of internal power. These organizational mechanisms are the working groups or coordination groups that may serve to integrate EU specialists.

Our expectations in this aspect run parallel to those concerning *ex officio* seats. The creation of certain mechanisms for the integration of MEPs, for example, implies that the party leadership acknowledges their relevance, and it could also signal willingness by the leadership to monitor more effectively their activity by integrating them into the party organizational structure. Thus, our expectations with regard to the effect of the length of EU membership, and the effect of internal divisions around EU issues, are similar to those applied to the previous table: that long EU membership will either promote or hinder organizational adaptation; and that greater divisiveness will correlate with the existence of these organizational structures.

In addition, it is worth considering the possibility that the degree of 'parliamentary' intervention in EU-related policy through the national parliamentary European affairs committees can be an important factor here. In those countries in which this parliamentary committee has a greater role in policy design and implementation, these working groups may be more likely to exist as part of normal political management within the parties. This would mean we should find certain national uniformity in the data.

Table 8.2 reveals a nuanced picture. At least in terms of policy activity, it would seem that most parties have incorporated their EU specialists by means of working groups, party committees and the like. Therefore, although analysis of the existence of *ex officio* seats for MEPs portrays an image of limited internal empowerment and relevance of EU specialists, there are signs that national parties are creating organizational structures that serve to integrate EU specialists, thus acknowledging to a certain extent their importance within the parties. Still, this trend is fairly restricted.

Once again, we find little evidence of any clear intervening variable affecting the results. Divisiveness of EU issues does not seem to be relevant here. Nor do national-level factors, such as length of EU membership and parliamentary scrutiny styles; indeed, the countries in our sample with what are usually seen as more powerful parliamentary European affairs committees – Sweden and Austria (Raunio 2005) – do not show the expected results. Party-family affiliation does not appear to play a relevant role in the degree of integration of EU specialists. Nor does it seem to make much difference whether the party is frequently in government, or whether it has a large or small European parliamentary delegation. The extent to which MEPs are structurally integrated into party life through workgroups or committees could depend rather more on party-specific factors.

Table 8.2 Relative degree of integration of EU specialists, especially MEPs, into party

	EU specialists integrated into party		
	Not integrated	*Moderately integrated*	*Significantly integrated*
FR	PCF, PS	Verts, UMP	UDF
DE		Left, SPD, GRÜ, FDP, CDU, CSU	
GB		LibDem, Lab, Cons	
ES		PP, PSOE, IU, CDC, PNV	
AT	FPÖ		SPÖ, GRÖ, ÖVP
SE		v, mp, fp, c, kd, s	m

Note
Country and party abbreviations: see Table 8.1.

Extent of EU specialists' influence in drafting national election manifestos

A final signal of EU specialists' significance would be their involvement in the tasks of manifesto formulation. Our general hypotheses would lead us to expect an increasing role for EU specialists in the drafting process, and for national elections as well as elections to the European Parliament, due to the increasing relevance of their expertise and the growing salience of EU policy for national policies. In this case, it would be also reasonable to expect that the length of the country's EU membership has an effect on the role of EU specialists, although, again, exactly what effect – will change be greater in long-standing member states or in those parties subject to the shock of late membership? – is open to discussion. In addition, we might expect EU specialists to have acquired a stronger manifesto-drafting role in parties with a united, positive view towards European integration.

As the data shown in Table 8.3 demonstrate, in the majority of parties, the role of EU specialists in the drafting of national elections manifestos is modest and mostly confined to sections specifically addressing European integration or EU institutions. There is no clear trace of a time effect that could link the length of EU membership with a greater or more marginal role of EU specialists in manifesto drafting. Attitudes within the party towards the EU do not seem to be relevant; the column that indicates the cases in which EU specialists are most involved in drafting national manifestos includes both pro- and anti-EU parties. Party family seems not to be relevant, and governing propensity does not seem to matter much – although it is interesting to note that nearly all the parties that attribute to EU specialists a significant role in drafting national manifestos are smaller, 'progressive' parties, in which MEPs might be prominent personalities just because of the smaller size of both European parliamentary delegations and of the party elites in general.

Table 8.3 Relative degree of influence of EU specialists in drafting of national election manifestos

| | *EU specialists' influence in drafting national election manifestos* | | |
	Little	*Modest[a]*	*Significant*
FR	PCF	PS, UMP	Verts, UDF
DE		Left, SPD, GRÜ, FDP, CDU, CSU	
GB		Lab, LibDems, Cons	
ES		PSOE, CDC, PNV, PP	IU
AT	FPÖ	SPÖ, GRÖ, ÖVP	
SE		s, mp, c, kd, m	v, fp

Notes
a Mainly reduced to EU sections (not general 'national policies', even if they are affected by EU decision-making).
Country and party abbreviations: see Table 8.1.

European integration and party elites

In this section, we turn to our other hypothesis, on party elites. For our purposes, we define elite as the 'inner leadership' of the party – usually, but not always exclusively, the members of its executive committee – and the party's members of the national cabinet, if it has any. To what extent is it possible to capture the effect of European integration on their intra-party standings?

Candidate selection for elections to the European Parliament

It might be assumed that the more divided the party, the more the leadership will have to accommodate the demands of its opponents for representation in the construction of the party's list or lists for elections to the European Parliament. Such division over Europe could be 'vertical' in character, in which a party elite takes one position (probably pro-integration), while activists and members take another (probably more sceptical); or it could be 'horizontal', in which two or more tendencies or factions (Hine 1982), which include elements of both the elite and the grass roots, take different positions on the EU (perhaps as part of a wider ideological conflict). In either type of division, the dominant coalition or faction might feel obliged to concede places on the list to rival factions or to discontented grass roots. Perhaps more likely, though, it might seek to control the construction of the list more fully, in order to preclude the presence of rival factions or grassroots dissidents among the party's representatives in the European Parliament – positions that, as has been amply shown in the preceding country studies, are a source of significant material resources for the individuals who hold them (and even for some small parties as a whole).

A further, somewhat more tentative expectation can also be considered. It might be that the longer a country has been an EU member state, the less constrained its parties' leaderships will be in candidate selection. This expectation is based on the idea that time dampens Euroscepticism at all levels of the party and the electorate: the longer a country has spent in the EU, the more accepting it becomes of the Union's structure and processes. Alternatively, of course, the longer the duration of EU membership, the more Euroscepticism might grow, as the increasing powers of the EU encroach on sensitive national issues.

The first observation to be made about Table 8.4 is that there is little mileage in the second, time-related expectation. Length of EU membership does not seem to affect the degree of party leadership control in candidate selection for European elections. But what about the first, stronger expectation, about an inverse relationship between leadership control and internal party division?

The results do not show much support for that expectation. If anything, a review of each of the cases presented in Table 8.4 suggests that the counter-expectation outlined above – that the more EU-related division there is within a party, the likelier its leadership is to have control over candidate selection for European elections – has the firmer empirical footing. Certainly, while measuring reliably the level of EU-related division in a party is not entirely straightforward,[1] a rough

Table 8.4 Degree of national party leadership influence in candidate selection for elections to the European Parliament

	Relative influence of national party leadership		
	Low	*Moderate*	*High*
FR	Verts		PCF, PS, UDF, UMP
DE	SPD, GRÜ, CDU, CSU	Left, FDP	
GB	LibDems, Cons	Lab	
ES			IU, PSOE, CDC, PNV, PP
AT	GRÖ	SPÖ	FPÖ, ÖVP
SE	mp, c, fp	v, kd, m	s

Note
Country and party abbreviations: see Table 8.1.

estimate is that about half the parties that have relatively high leadership influence have experienced some type of internal dissent over particular EU-related issues. This might indicate that, when the party is divided, control of the process is indeed considered an important strategic resource by the dominant coalition.

Other intervening variables show some signs of being relevant. Most tentatively, we might infer that leaderships of parties often in government have a greater propensity to steer candidate selection. With the exception of the two biggest German parties, all the parties in which the influence of the leadership is considered low are parties with limited experience of holding government office in recent years. Interestingly, the effect of party family is also visible. According to this measure, the tendency of green parties to profess their commitment to internal party democracy and non-hierarchical structures does not appear to be merely rhetorical: all four green parties among our cases display low levels of leadership influence, irrespective of their national context. Again, the size of the delegation may have some relevance. The parties in which leadership influence is high have a slight tendency to have fairly large European parliamentary delegations, which might give their MEPs a somewhat greater influence over the Parliament's legislative output – which, in turn, should make them more interesting to the national party. But again, this is a tentative observation.

If any reasonably clear inference can be drawn from Table 8.4, it is that national tradition is the best explanation of variation in leadership influence over candidate selection. All the Spanish parties, for instance, whether divided on Europe or not (and all but one are not), feature a relatively high level of leadership influence. There are certainly exceptions to national patterns. The Left Party in Germany and the Social Democrats in Sweden have higher leadership influence than might be expected both with reference to other parties in their countries and, looking back to the relevant preceding chapters, from general party practice in national elections. Overall, though, the importance of national tradition and practice does seem hard to deny.

Political coordination with MEPs

The relationship between a party's organization and its elected representatives is not always entirely straightforward. At national level, the problem is usually – although by no means always – mitigated through personal overlap: the party organization's leadership and the parliamentary group's leadership often comprise much the same people, which thus naturally aligns their preferences and strategies. When it comes to a national party's relations with its members of the European Parliament, however, this overlap is, as we have seen in the country studies, somewhere between very weak and non-existent. This might mean that the party organization's leadership has felt compelled to acquire tools with which to align the behaviour of the party's elected representatives in the European Parliament with the leadership's preferences. In other words, we might expect that national party leaderships are ready to maintain active political coordination with their MEPs, and even occasionally issue explicit voting instructions to them. Such instructions might be given when issues with discernible policy or electoral consequences at national level are being discussed – a scenario that, given the advance of European integration and the expansion of EU competence, is occurring with increasing frequency.

Is, then, such political coordination with MEPs actively pursued? And if we see differences between parties, what can explain the variation? We might expect at least two intervening variables to be relevant here. One is whether a party is in government. If a party is in national office, and assuming that, to use Katz and Mair's (2002) terms, the leadership of the party in public office (its ministers) is largely synonymous with the leadership of the party in central office (its organizational leaders),[2] then this joint leadership will not want the positions that it takes at national level and then defends in the Council of Ministers to be contradicted by the party's own MEPs. Governing parties, then, should actively coordinate with their MEPs more often than opposition parties do. Second, parties that are divided over European integration should behave in a similar way. The leaderships of these parties should want to keep their MEPs' behaviour under control, to limit the latter's scope to reflect the views of EU dissidents within the party.

Table 8.5 arranges the parties according to two variables. One, represented horizontally, is the extent to which a party's MEPs are actively involved in political coordination with the party leadership. The nature of this coordination is captured in three categories: considerable, limited and none. The vertical variable contains three categories that reflect the extent to which, since the middle of the 1990s, parties have been in government, either alone or in coalition: 'often', defined as at least half of the period 1995–2005; 'sometimes', defined as less than half the same period; and 'no', if they have not been in office. Note that this is an arbitrarily assigned time period, which aims to reflect office-holding in the decade or so prior to the collection of the data.[3]

The first thing to be observed from Table 8.5 is that most parties in our sample maintain either only limited coordination with their MEPs or none at all. Only one, the Austrian People's Party, falls into the 'often-governing' category; the German Christian democratic parties are (perhaps slightly misleadingly) in the

Table 8.5 Relative degree of active political coordination between MEPs and national parties

In government	Coordination		
	Considerable	Limited	None
Often	ÖVP	PS, UMP, SPD, GRÜ, Lab, PP, SPÖ	s
Sometimes	UDF, CDU, CSU	FDP, Cons, PSOE, FPÖ	PCF, Verts
No	Left, IU		LibDems, CDC, PNV, GRÖ, v, mp, c, fp, kd, m

Notes
A party is classified as often in national government when it has been formally in office for at least half the period running from the beginning of 1995 to the end of 2005 (being in government for only a part of a calendar year is counted as half a year). A party is counted as sometimes in office if it has been in office for less than half the same period. Parties which have not been in office at all during this period are counted as non-governmental.
Party abbreviations: see Table 8.1.

'sometimes-governing' group; and the Spanish United Left and German Left Party have never been in national office. That militates against our expectation that governing parties would be keener to maintain active coordination. On the other hand, there is a concentration of parties that maintain 'limited' coordination in the often- and sometimes-governing categories, even if the non-instruction-issuing and often-governing Swedish Social Democrats are noteworthy exceptions here. Governing parties do, then, seem to be somewhat more interested in how their MEPs vote in the European Parliament. This is an important and interesting, though far from unequivocal, finding. The expectation that divided parties would behave in a similar way does not appear to have empirical support, however.

We also see the possible relevance of two other variables. Party family seems to play a certain role. The German Greens are the only member of the green party family that actively coordinates with its MEPs, albeit to a limited extent. Otherwise, and again conforming to their libertarian reputation, green parties seem prepared to give their MEPs wide freedom. That said, the four European parliamentary delegations that experience what we judged to be 'considerable' levels of coordination span the political spectrum, from the Christian democratic centre-right to the radical left. The size of the delegation, moreover, is seemingly of some relevance. The European parliamentary delegations that experience least coordination with the national party mostly represent smaller parties. This may be because their potential for influencing legislative outcomes in the European Parliament is judged in their respective national capitals to be slight.

National patterns are visible, but not in a way that would suggest that duration of EU membership has much relevance. All Austrian parties but the Greens engage in at least limited active coordination. No Swedish party seeks actively to coordinate. Perhaps surprisingly, nor do any French parties, bar the Socialists. This might well have a lot to do with prevailing institutional conditions at national level, such as the extent to which MEPs are dependent on the party organization's control of their re-nomination as candidates, and the level – constituency or national – at which this process is conducted, both formally and *de facto*. As we saw above, the French party leaderships energetically involve themselves in screening potential European election candidates, which might make further, active policy coordination after the election unnecessary; the party's MEPs can be relied on to follow the leadership's preferences. Yet the Austrian People's Party, the German Left Party and the Spanish United Left combine centrally steered candidate selection with considerable levels of coordination. In sum, national and specific party traditions seem at least as important as any cross-national variable.

Party control of ministers acting at EU level

As we saw in Chapter 1, our basic premise that European integration has empowered party elites is rooted in numerous analyses of decision-making in the EU. This system is said to contain an 'executive bias'. Therefore, and also in light of the growing intrusion of EU competence into hitherto national areas of policy-making, we expected that the leaders of parties in government, who can often (if by no means always) be assumed to double as cabinet ministers, will have attained greater freedom from *ex post* and *ex ante* party controls, thanks to the EU.

However, it is also likely that country-specific variables will play a significant part in explaining the outcomes. One such variable concerns the national parliamentary European affairs committees. As the country chapters made clear, these are among the most important forums in which parties can try to exercise control over their ministers' actions at EU level, and they vary in their scope to control the executive. Indeed, the relative power balance between legislature and executive more generally will probably have a similar effect: the more powerful the legislature, the more energetic the national parties may be in controlling their ministers. Similar national uniformity is also likely to be encouraged by other systemic norms. Parties in which leadership roles (such as being head of the party organization and head of its parliamentary group) are concentrated in a single individual may be less inclined to ministerial control than those whose power structure is bicephalic (leadership roles are spread between different individuals).

Furthermore, party division over the EU might also be relevant here. It is not implausible to suggest that divided governing parties might place their ministers under tighter control than those in which a consensus on the EU exists. On the other hand, elites in divided parties might actively seek to exploit their ministerial positions to enhance their autonomy from their troublesome party colleagues.

We have, then, a number of expectations about party control of ministers acting at EU level. Are they confirmed by the data?

Some inferences from Table 8.6 are fairly clear. The first is that our basic supposition about the 'executive bias' introduced by EU decision-making also being relevant to intra-party power relations looks to be supported by the data. No parties subject their ministers to what our chapter authors judge to be significant

Table 8.6 Relative degree of national party control over ministers' actions in EU bodies (governing parties)

| | Party control over ministers | | |
	None	Ex ante	Ex post
FR	PS, UDF, UMP		
DE	SPD, GRÜ, FDP, CDU, CSU		
GB	Lab, Cons		
ES	PSOE, PP		
AT	SPÖ, ÖVP, FPÖ		
SE		s	

Note
Party abbreviations: see Table 8.1.

ex post controls (that is, compelling them to explain their voting and negotiating positions after the event). Some governing parties, such as those in Britain and Sweden, might have their ministers brief committees of their parliamentary groups, and British ministers might face questioning about Council meetings in the parliamentary European affairs committee; but neither procedure is seen as a serious control mechanism.

Perhaps even more strikingly, just one party – the Swedish Social Democrats – is thought to exercise any *ex ante* controls (mandating ministers before EU-level meetings). It is no surprise to see this relatively assertive party operating in a parliament in which this committee is relatively strong.[4]

Clearly, parties operate within the institutional constraints that exist in their respective national systems. Equally, however, they are often key actors in the original design of those constraints, especially in more recent years, as interest in European affairs committees has grown and new member states have had the chance to design scrutiny mechanisms from scratch.[5] In this sense, national tradition is obviously relevant here, but so is the duration of a country's EU membership – that is, the more recent the membership, the greater the chances of relatively developed control of ministerial activity at EU level. EU-related internal division, on the other hand, does not seem to be relevant. Nor does party family and the size of the European parliamentary delegation.

It is worth emphasizing that ministerial empowerment has many causes, quite apart from European integration, as Webb and Poguntke (2005: 347–52) discuss in their study of 'presidentialization' in modern parliamentary democracies. But the incremental transfer of policy competence from national level to the EU has clearly favoured national governments over national parliaments, and that has had consequences for parties, too. In light of the evidence presented above, and thanks to the specific answers that our informants offered to specific questions about the effect of EU membership, we can reasonably infer that the EU's style of decision-making has, as expected, enhanced ministers' autonomy vis-à-vis their parties.

Summarizing change

What sort of picture do the preceding tables and discussion paint as regards change in party organization and intra-party power relations as a result of European integration? When it comes to one of our basic hypotheses, about the empowerment of party elites, we are aware that disentangling the effect of our particular causal variable is not straightforward. Elites have become relatively more powerful within their parties, to the cost of the lower levels of the organization, such as the members and mid-level activists. But this is hardly news. Numerous scholars have been drawing this conclusion for decades (see Harmel 2002: 122–5). Our difficulty is in distinguishing the part in this process played by European integration, as opposed to all sorts of other causes – public subsidies, media technology, increasing state-administrative complexity, to name just a few. We return to the question of elite empowerment in the concluding section.

When it comes to our other hypothesis, about the influence of EU specialists, variation across cases and over time is somewhat easier to attribute to the cause that interests us, namely, European integration. After all, it is unlikely that EU specialists' empowerment, if it has occurred, could be for any other reason. The following paragraphs look more closely at this hypothesis.

Accountability and influence of EU specialists

Table 8.7 focuses on the degree of accountability that EU specialists enjoy vis-à-vis the party leadership in their activity at EU level. Our expectation was that this would have diminished, as the growing relevance of EU specialists' knowledge about the EU's institutions and processes has given them an increasingly valuable power resource, which in turn has afforded them a more privileged position in intra-party affairs. In this context, the EU specialists that we have most in mind are elected ones – that is, MEPs. After all, functionaries are directly accountable to the leadership of the party organization. They have no other principal; if they become unduly autonomous, they can simply be sacked.

We have countervailing expectations, however. One is that this process of EU specialists' growing autonomy and influence will have been more limited in often-governing parties, which will want to maximize policy coordination in different arenas, than in non-governing parties. In addition, the same trend might be less pronounced in parties that are divided over Europe. Following the reasoning presented earlier, we expect that, when the issue is sensitive in the party, the leadership should want to keep its EU specialists on a tighter leash. As so often, though, there is an equally plausible alternative expectation. Leaderships of divided parties might let their MEPs do much as they like, hoping that they thus refrain from stirring up intra-party controversy at home.

Table 8.7 estimates the relative accountability of parties' MEPs across our cases, plus the extent to which this has changed. Readers familiar with the country chapters will not be surprised to see that accountability is perceived as low in the vast majority of our cases. MEPs' feelings of isolation from their national organizations are noted time and again. Only in a few cases – the Austrian parties,

Table 8.7 Relative change in accountability of EU specialists, especially MEPs, to their parties

Current accountability	Change in accountability over time		
	Increase	*No change*	*Decrease*
High		ÖVP	
Moderate		Left, IU, SPÖ, GRÖ, v	s, m
Low		PCF, PS, Verts, UDF, UMP, SPD, GRÜ, FDP, CDU, CSU, PP, Lab, LibDem, Cons, PSOE, CDC, PNV, mp, fp	FPÖ, c

Note
Party abbreviations: see Table 8.1.

the German, Spanish and Swedish radical-left parties and the two biggest Swedish parties – is accountability judged to be at a somewhat higher level. As for change, which gets to the essence of our hypothesis about EU specialists, the evidence in support of our expectation is – to put it as positively as possible – very limited. Only in the Austrian Freedom Party and in three Swedish parties (the Centre, the Social Democrats and the Moderates) have EU specialists acquired greater freedom from their respective party leaderships; and even here, the change has been pretty slight.

Meanwhile, of the two intervening variables mentioned above, national incumbency seems not to have any relevance. The second one, internal division over Europe, has been present in three of the four parties in which accountability has diminished. But when the numbers are so small, no causal inference can really be made. Nor do the additional intervening variables considered here – party family, duration of EU membership, size of the European parliamentary delegation, and national practice – have any obvious effect.

In sum, as regards the accountability of EU specialists, not much has changed in our parties. Our hypothesis about their increasing autonomy seems, at least, to lack empirical support. On the other hand, neither have most party leaderships succeeded in reducing their MEPs' autonomy and thus subjecting them to greater accountability. This might have been because MEPs were already so autonomous that they have not felt the need to acquire an even freer hand. Equally, it might be that party leaderships have, quite simply, not felt the need to care much more about what their elected representatives in the European Parliament are up to. If a single national party's MEPs have only limited scope to shape European legislation, why should that party's leadership take much interest?

If little variation and even less change is visible in the accountability of EU specialists, what about their general influence in their national parties? Lack of accountability might be a contributing factor in their empowerment, as our basic hypothesis about EU specialists implies. To reiterate, we expected that EU specialists would be more influential than they were previously. Autonomy in faraway Brussels combined with the European Parliament's growing power might mean that MEPs, for instance, have real influence in setting the policy agenda – at European level, at national level and within their own parties. Yet there is no necessary connection between lack of accountability and influence. Indeed, party actors might be given lots of autonomy and left unaccountable by the party organization precisely because they have little influence in the party.

It might even be the case that, despite their gaining a growing role in EU legislation, MEPs might be largely left to their own devices because of a simple lack of knowledge and attention on the part of their parties. In other words, perhaps the location of power is in the eye of the beholder. Certainly, informants among MEPs frequently complained that their national parties underrate the influence that their MEPs really have. Is a more objective estimate of EU specialists' intraparty influence possible?

Table 8.8 places our cases according to two simple indicators: on the vertical axis, the degree of influence that (elected) EU specialists enjoy in the national party; and, on the horizontal axis, the change that can be perceived in that influence. The idea here is to distinguish between, for example, parties in which influence might be high, but has always been so, and parties in which it has become high only recently.

The table reveals some variation on the static measure. In only a handful of parties – the main Austrian parties and two fairly small French parties, the Greens and the UDF – is EU specialists' influence judged to be relatively high (and the relative nature of this judgment cannot be over-emphasized). But in quite a few cases it is judged to be moderate; this is slightly more than the number in which is it is thought to be low. No patterns – such as a difference between governing and non-governing parties, the state of intra-party opinion on the EU, party family, the duration of EU membership, the size of European parliamentary delegations, or the national tradition – are visible.

There may be a little more coherence to the variation in change over time. Party family may be relevant here. The two parties in which EU specialists have

Table 8.8 Relative change in influence of EU specialists, especially MEPs, in their parties

Current influence	Change in degree of influence over time			
	Significant increase	*Some increase*	*No change*	*Decrease*
High		UDF, ÖVP	Verts	
Moderate	Lab	PS, SPD, CDU, CSU, PP, SPÖ, GRÖ, v, s, mp, fp	GRÜ, PSOE, CDC, PNV	
Low			PCF, UMP, FDP, LibDem, Cons, IU, FPÖ, c, kd	

Note
Party abbreviations: see Table 8.1.

seen their stock rise most appreciably – the British Labour Party and the Austrian Social Democrats – are both in the social democratic family. Several more social democratic parties have experienced some increase, along with parties from across the spectrum, half of which are either sometimes or often in government, and among which four of our six countries are represented. No pattern as regards intra-party opinion, duration of EU membership, size of European delegations, or national tradition is apparent. Overall, a small majority of our cases have not experienced any significant change – which is an appropriate note on which to sum up this chapter's summary of the national studies that preceded it in this volume.

Conclusion

It would be wrong to conclude that our two basic hypotheses, concerning the empowerment of EU specialists and party elites due to the effects of European integration, have been entirely disconfirmed. Change has clearly taken place, and a few interesting patterns can be observed.

As far as EU specialists are concerned, some national parties have tried to ensure that their MEPs are involved in intra-party decision-making bodies. A large minority of the cases in our sample have an MEP, usually the delegation leader, on the party's executive organs, in an *ex officio* capacity, by informal convention or according to current practice. There seems little systematic variation in this pattern, however. Much the same can be said of the extent to which parties otherwise seek to integrate their MEPs in general into their activity.

Although this has not been illustrated in the preceding tables, our country studies show that national-level EU specialists have not, as a rule, seen a perceptible increase in their intra-party standing. For politicians, the prestige and influence associated with being a party spokesperson on EU affairs is generally low. Although responsibility for managing relations with the relevant Europarty has been subject to very light controls by the party organization, and while the symbolic value of such responsibility is significant in some parties (such as the French Socialists), nowhere does it amount to a serious power resource for the individuals concerned. (In more than a few parties among our other cases, such links are not taken terribly seriously. The Europarties have no formal power to force the affiliated national parties to do anything.)

Functionaries employed by the party have, meanwhile, increased in number, albeit much less so in party organizations than in parliamentary groups at national and European levels. But such EU specialists are often junior figures, with little influence in the party beyond the management of definitively European issues.

In sum, some structural adaptation has occurred in some parties' administration of national issues and in the representation on executive organs that is accorded to MEPs. But this does not appear to be an indication that great value is attached to the specialist knowledge possessed by these or other types of EU specialists, value that would bring with it real political influence.

Regarding the intra-party power of party elites, our hypothesis about the effect of European integration finds rather firmer empirical support. The problem of isolating the effect of European integration has been mentioned earlier. To some extent, and as we discussed above, the specificity of our questions to informants, and the detailed answers that they elicited, can help us to pin down this type of causal relationship. This, after all, is exactly what qualitative techniques are good at, and they do allow us to make 'contingent generalizations' (George and Bennett 2005: 112–14). One such generalization is that involvement in European-level decision-making processes, particularly in the Council of Ministers and the European Council, has indeed increased the autonomy of party leaderships in driving party policy. For reasons discussed in Chapter 1, just as it is hard for national parliaments to mandate ministers *ex ante* and to hold them to account *ex post* when they engage in decision-making at EU level, so it is hard for their parties to do the same.

As we saw in Table 8.6, almost no parties hold their ministers to account for their actions at EU level in a meaningful way – which adds a further slant to the ongoing debate about the Union's democratic deficit. So we can assert that elites in governing parties have been more favoured by European integration than have elites in non-governing parties. This distinction is most relevant in a country like Sweden (despite its relatively strong European affairs committee), where one party, the Social Democrats, is usually in office alone, and all the other parties – even the Social Democrats' allies – are in opposition, with no cabinet seats. But, of course, parties have always had problems holding their ministers to account when the party is in government. European integration has thus aggravated a situation that already existed.

When it comes to the party leadership's relations with the party's MEPs, both pre-election (when aspiring candidates are screened) and post-election (when policy coordination can be attempted), signs of significant change are somewhat harder to find. The main variable influencing the degree to which the party leadership involves itself in candidate selection before elections to the European Parliament is, quite simply, how the process has traditionally been managed for national elections. Much the same can be said of political coordination between parties and MEPs. The customary balance of power between a party's organization and its national parliamentarians is usually replicated with its MEPs, even if often-governing parties do seem marginally keener to keep their representatives in the European Parliament aligned with national party policy.

Overall, our conclusion is that change induced by European integration has been limited and patchy. Not too much has really changed for national political parties, at least in terms of EU specialists' presence and influence. The power of party elites, on the other hand, does seem to have been enhanced – even if only really in often-governing parties, and even if the effect of the EU is to accelerate an already ongoing process. In the final chapter of this volume, the reasons for the varying performances of our hypotheses are investigated more closely.

Notes

1   Though it can be done: see, for instance, Marks and Steenbergen (2004) and Ray (1999).
2   Exceptions might be parties in federal countries, where leaders of parties' regional sections are often incorporated into their national executives.

3 Of course, this classification is crude. For instance, the Austrian Social Democrats and the Spanish Socialists would be seen by many observers as frequently governing, but are only sometimes governing according to the indicators used here. However, some counter-intuitive results are probably unavoidable, irrespective of the way the classification is constructed.

4 In his summary of earlier research on European affairs committees in the 15 pre-2004 member states, Raunio (2005: 335) ranked Austria and Sweden as occupying the third highest category on a seven-point scale of committee strength (only Denmark and Finland were ranked higher, in the second highest category); Germany was in the fourth highest, mid-range category; Britain and France were in the fifth highest; and Spain was in the sixth highest. (There were no cases in the highest or lowest categories on the scale.) Why there is such variation in the committees' strength is a question that Raunio (2005: 336–8) subsequently explored. He concluded that a generally strong legislature vis-à-vis the executive was the only necessary condition for relatively effective parliamentary scrutiny of the executive's actions at EU level, and that a combination of a powerful parliament and a relatively Eurosceptical electorate were jointly sufficient conditions.

5 Deliberate emulation is also visible in the design of European affairs committees in the ten states that joined the Union in 2004 (Jungar 2006; Raunio 2005: 337).

References

George, Alexander L. and Andrew Bennett (2005) *Case Studies and Theory Development in the Social Sciences*, Cambridge, MA: MIT Press.

Harmel, Robert (2002) 'Party Organizational Change: Competing Explanations', in Kurt Richard Luther and Ferdinand Müller-Rommel (eds), *Political Parties in the New a Changing Europe: Political and Analytical Challenges*, Oxford: Oxford University Press, pp. 119–42.

Harmel, Robert and Kenneth Janda (1994) 'An Integrated Theory of Party Goals and Party Change', *Journal of Theoretical Politics*, 6(3): 259–87.

Hine, David (1982) 'Factionalism in West European Parties: A Framework for Analysis', *West European Politics*, 5(1): 36–53.

Jungar, Ann-Cathrine (2006) 'The Rules of Attraction: Policy Transfer in the Design of Parliamentary EU Scrutiny in the Ten New EU Member States', paper presented to the conference of the Swedish Network for European Studies in Political Science, Umeå, 16–17 March.

Katz, Richard. S. and Peter Mair (1992) 'Introduction: The Cross-National Study of Party Organizations' in Richard S. Katz and Peter Mair (eds), (1992), *Party Organization: A Data Handbook*, London: Sage, pp. 1–20.

Katz, Richard S. and Peter Mair (2002) 'The Ascendancy of the Party in Public Office: Party Organizational Change in Twentieth-Century Democracies', in Richard Gunther, José Ramón Montero and Juan J. Linz (eds), *Political Parties: Old Concepts and New Challenges*, Oxford: Oxford University Press, pp. 113–35.

Marks, Gary and Marco R. Steenbergen (eds) (2004) *European Integration and Political Conflict*, Cambridge: Cambridge University Press.

Munck, Gerardo L. (2004) 'Tools for Qualitative Research', in Henry E. Brady and David Collier (eds), *Rethinking Social Inquiry: Diverse Tools, Shared Standards*, Lanham, MD: Rowman & Littlefield, pp. 105–21.

Poguntke, Thomas (1998) 'Party Organizations', in Jan W. van Deth (ed.) *Comparative Politics: The Problem of Equivalence*, London: Routledge, pp. 156–79.

Ragin, Charles C. (1987) *The Comparative Method: Moving Beyond Qualitative and Quantitative Strategies*, Berkeley, CA: University of California Press.

Ragin, Charles C. (2000) *Fuzzy-Set Social Science*, Chicago, IL: University of Chicago Press.

Ragin, Charles C. (2003) 'Making Comparative Analysis Count', COMPASSS working paper 2003-10 <www.compasss.org>.

Raunio, Tapio (2005) 'Holding Governments Accountable in European Affairs: Explaining Cross-National Variation', *Journal of Legislative Studies*, 11(3/4): 319–42.

Ray, Leonard (1999) 'Measuring Party Orientations Towards European Integration: Result for an Expert Survey', *European Journal of Political Research*, 36(2): 283–309.

Webb, Paul and Thomas Poguntke (2005) 'The Presidentialization of Contemporary Democratic Politics: Evidence, Causes, and Consequences', in Thomas Poguntke and Paul Webb (eds), *The Presidentialization of Politics: A Comparative Study of Modern Democracies*, Oxford: Oxford University Press, pp. 336–56.

9 Europeanization and national party organization

Limited but appropriate adaptation?[1]

Robert Ladrech

The European Union (EU), whether or not it has become a politicized and contentious issue in the domestic politics of its member states, is undeniably interwoven in the policy and decision-making processes of domestic governance. Institutional adaptation by national governments to this structural development is an area of scholarly enquiry that is often labelled 'top-down' Europeanization (see Chapter 1). Policy adaptation and changes in interest group strategies and organization are further examples of Europeanization. It is therefore reasonable to assume that national political parties may have also exhibited internal organizational change as elements of their domestic environment have altered (Ladrech 2002). Let us remember that national government decision-making is conducted by party-political personnel, and in many cases the same individuals (national government ministers) are participants in the EU inter-institutional decision-making process. The assumption that parties *as organizations* may also experience some form of organizational modification and/or change in their internal balance of power is entirely appropriate. Furthermore, as Peter Mair has stressed, 'far too little systematic attention has been paid to analysing the indirect impact of Europeanization on parties and party systems, especially at the domestic level where it is likely to be more important' (Mair 2006).

The two hypotheses leading this project have been based on the assumption that *parties as organizations* adapt to significant changes in their environment. We expect to see the result of this adaptation reflected in altered balances of power within national party organizations. If party elites are indeed gaining power as a result of increased European integration, if the number of EU specialists has grown, and if the political influence of these people has also increased, then we may conclude that political parties are not exempt from the penetration of EU 'top-down' influences, suggesting that Europeanization is not only confined to understanding changes in national governmental institutions, policies, and private and semi-public actors.

This would have a potentially profound significance for the legitimacy of what we refer to as *party government*. If our hypotheses are confirmed, this would mean that the diffusion of EU influence in domestic political systems, already detailed in the adaptation of institutions and policies, extends into the *operation* of key representative actors – parties – whose interest aggregation and linkage functions render them critical to the legitimation of government. In other words, the Europeanization of national party organization along the lines we have set out in Chapter 1 would mean that the appreciation of EU policy-making and the logic of the EU's institutional rules and procedures have become internalized in the routine operation of party policy development and, by extension, interest representation, through the increased power of EU specialists and party elites. If political power enhancement for party elites and EU specialists depends on, even partially, the resources and systemic logic of European governance, it is unlikely that these actors would countenance a diminution of EU competences.

This is not to say that the neo-functionalist notion of a transfer of loyalties to the European level is occurring, simply that the framing of EU considerations in policy development (in particular) balances purely domestic considerations. In a sense, the supranational constraints on national government policy manoeuvre and scope for discretion (Mair 2000) are extended into national *party* government itself. One effect of this could be, according to Bartolini, for 'main national parties [to] silence those EU constitutive issues of membership, competence and institutional design that are more likely to agitate national voters and anti-EU *lumpenelites*' (2005: 385). It is this depoliticization (Mair 2000, 2006) that has implications for party government legitimacy.

The results of our study, documented in the six country chapters and addressed in a comparative manner in Chapter 8, do indeed point to change in national party organization. The first hypothesis regarding party elites, namely that they will gain power as a result of increased European integration, is confirmed, but mainly insofar as it is related to incumbency of national government. The second hypothesis was that EU specialist positions would have been created and, further, that they would have gained power as a result of increased European integration. Our evidence in support of this hypothesis is limited in the main to our documentation of the creation of a modest number of EU specialist positions during the time period of our study and the incorporation of some of these actors into leading party bodies. We can therefore say that there has been a limited Europeanization of national party organization. How do we explain this result? Does it suggest that parties are somehow insulated from the influence of the EU, whereas other aspects and structures of their political environment are not? Could it be that there is something intrinsic in national party organization that *prevents* adaptation in this context? Perhaps the central insights of the concept of Europeanization do not apply to political parties? This chapter attempts to answer these questions of why we have a limited degree of organizational adaptation by national parties. Before turning to potential explanations, a brief summary of our findings is presented.

Summary of findings

Party organizational change

Has the increased scope of EU policy competence penetrated domestic political systems to the extent that national parties have begun to re-orient themselves, especially in organizational terms? We have found a limited degree of organizational change in national parties that could be attributed to the influence of the EU. These changes have been both formal and informal. Formal changes involve creating statutory links between national delegations in the EU and national parties' governing bodies. In some cases the leaders of the parties' delegation to the European Parliament (EP) are *ex officio* or *de facto* members of national executive bodies. Statutory changes also include voting rights of Members of the European Parliament (MEPs) at national party congresses. In many cases a position has been created, mainly funded by the EP delegation, to liaise between the delegation and the party. Additional formal intra-party organizational change has involved further specialization within a party's international secretariat, that is, a post whose remit is focused on EU affairs. In most of our parties, the individual concerned is a staff member. In France, there is also the higher rank position of national secretary for Europe, which combines the functions of spokesperson and advisor to the party leadership. To summarize, the formal changes we have seen have been modest, in that they primarily involve statutory changes to link a party's EP delegation to the national party organization – central office and congresses; creation of posts to strengthen the liaison between EU-level actors and the national party; and in limited cases, the creation of a post filled by an elected politician whose party organization function is Europe spokesperson/advisor.

The formal party organization posts primarily associated with the party in central office are complemented by parliamentary and governmental positions filled by party actors. The most obvious are those associated with membership of the national parliament's European affairs committee. As most MPs have more than one committee assignment, these are essentially part-time EU specialists, although in many cases the chair of such a committee is also the national parliament's representative to COSAC,[2] and may also liaise with the entire national EP delegation on a regular basis, and so has a much more extensive responsibility than the other members of the committee. Country variations include regularized meetings of such committee chairs with members of the national executive, as in Austria (Chapter 2 above). Regarding the national executive, some countries have a minister for Europe, usually at a junior ministerial level, whether placed in a foreign ministry, as in France, or the prime minister's office, for example in Sweden. Germany does not have such a position. The responsibility of this post is essentially to ensure coordination between various ministries regarding the European element of legislation. This position has fluctuated in terms of its political significance, and has even been occupied by non-party individuals.

In addition to these formal positions, there are informal ways in which EU specialists are linked to parties – mostly to the party occupying national executive government. Apart from the British Labour Party's formal MEP link system which provides for a relationship between MEPs responsible for a policy area and their policy expert counterparts in a government ministry, individual MEPs may have, through personal networks, deep knowledge of certain issues, or informal links with the national party, whether in government or in opposition. They are called upon to advise on particular issues that migrate from the European level to the national arena. Some parties, particularly in Germany, have also created working groups which bring together EU specialists and party personnel, but on a rather infrequent basis (three or four times a year).

To summarize, institutional adaptation by national governments and parliaments has created relatively few EU specialist positions for party actors to occupy. European affairs committees have very limited power vis-à-vis the national executive, having mostly an advisory and scrutiny function. Ministers for Europe, where they exist, occupy junior positions assisting in the coordination of EU legislation between different government ministries. Neither of these bodies or positions is viewed as particularly politically prestigious. The intra-party positions are mostly aimed at providing better or stronger links with MEPs and other EU actors and surveillance of EU issues that may intrude into the domestic arena.

Policy formulation and candidate selection

We hypothesized that EU specialists and national party elites may use their expertise and involvement in EU affairs as a resource in intra-party power struggles over policy formulation and elite recruitment. Indeed, technical expertise, whether held by selected MEPs or party staff, is a contributing factor to the development of programmatic documents as well as election manifestos. However, this is understood as more a resource available to the upper echelons of the party that finally agree on the documents in question than a quotient of power that accrues to the individual expert in intra-party debates. In addition, many parties belonging to the social democratic, Christian democratic and Green Europarties have adopted for EP elections the manifesto of their respective Europarty, taking the drafting process out of national party responsibility (though not surveillance of that Europarty process and of its approval). Supporting party documents are often retrospective in nature, drawing attention to the achievements of the party's EP delegation (by association with the achievements of its respective EP party group in eventual EU legislation). As far as party programmes are concerned, discussion of EU affairs is necessarily general, as these documents are intended to last for a number of years.

Candidate selection procedures were also evaluated, seeking to determine to what extent, if any, national party elites have seriously influenced this process in regard to positions involved with the EU, i.e. EP delegation leaders and MEPs. The general finding is that no fundamental changes have occurred. The exceptions have been in Britain with changes in the mid- and late 1990s regarding Labour Party MEP candidate selection (which were precipitated by a change in the electoral system for the 1999 EP elections, but which were then more or less reversed in time for the 2004 elections), and France with a formal change from national to regional lists for EP elections in 2004. In the former case, this was a conscious attempt by the party leadership to select candidates who were more 'on message' to New Labour's approach to Europe. In the French case, the creation of regions simply obliged all parties to adapt, adding more complexity to the usual elite control of the process (and for the Greens, more complexity in the coordination of grassroots nominations).

To summarize, the documentation that parties produce for public consumption in the context of competitive elections – manifestos – presents opportunities for EU specialists to participate, but their contribution does not necessarily enhance their intra-party power. The value placed on EU expertise does not translate into a political resource. Though the EP has certainly grown in power in the EU inter-institutional legislative relationship, attempts by party elites to influence more firmly the procedures used to select delegation leaders or MEPs are not a widespread phenomenon.

The power of party elites vis-à-vis party organization

Party elites in those parties that regularly occupy government have gained power at the expense of the parliamentary party and the extra-parliamentary party in all countries under the study. The fundamental reason for this phenomenon is that the national government executive itself has become more powerful vis-à-vis other domestic actors by virtue of government ministers' participation in EU bodies – Council of Ministers, European Council summits – of which *ex ante* and even *ex post* control by parliaments and national parties are weak (Raunio 2002). To be more precise, it is incumbency of the national government executive, in conjunction with the institutional changes in the EU, that empowers party elites. The party elites of a party in opposition at the national level do not, therefore, derive a significant increase in power within their party organization because of the increased influence of the EU. This is not to say that there may not be some residual form of power or influence for opposition party elites that comes from personal networks that have been established in government, more familiarity of the EU inter-governmental bargaining experience, and continued Europarty involvement. The nature of EU intergovernmental bargaining is an added element in the autonomy of party elites/government ministers, allowing them to argue that efforts to constrain their negotiating flexibility in such forums, either by national parliaments or their party, would produce sub-optimal results (Kassim 2005). In some cases, such as Sweden, the European affairs committee is briefed about the government's position prior to such bargaining sessions, but of course negotiation dynamics can alter positions.

Party elites belonging to one of the main Europarties in particular, the Party of European Socialists (PES) and European People's Party (EPP), whether in government or in opposition in their domestic setting, may at times find these organizations useful for networking and, on occasion, for developing a common position that may then influence an intergovernmental bargaining process (Johansson 2002). Although they are fairly marginal in the greater scheme of EU policy and decision-making, Europarties do have a function for national parties, though their precise relevance may vary according to the national case and party family (Hanley 2006).

Party elites and power in parties

Two areas of change have been noted: first, that party elites in government in-crease their power vis-à-vis the rest of the party organization; second, that there has been a modest or limited degree of expansion in the number of EU special-ist positions (beyond the existence of MEPs) in either the parliamentary or the extra-parliamentary party organization. However, these EU specialists, though acknowledged for their expertise, have not witnessed any substantial accrual of power, and certainly nothing approaching a significant shift of the internal balance of power within the party. The documented increase in power attributed to the EU is directed to the already most powerful segment of the party, its elite. Further-more, this increase in power is mostly confined to elites in national government, and lastly this enhancement dissipates significantly once the party returns to op-position.

Power is therefore linked to the site at which authoritative decisions concern-ing policy are taken. Two issues arise from this observation. The first concerns incumbency. What is it about incumbency of national government (and hence participation in the Council of Ministers and the European Council) that trig-gers the increase in power for only one segment of the national party? Somewhat related is the second issue, which is why there is no transfer of this power to EU specialists, especially MEPs, who are also directly involved in the EU decision-making process.

National government incumbency and the EU

Our operating definition of power is discussed at some length in Chapter 1. Essen-tially we conceptualize power in terms of resources and autonomy. We can say the national party elites in government are indeed empowered by the *resources* avail-able to them: access to information and expertise found within government min-istries by experts charged with the EU dimension of different policy sectors; the permanent representation in Brussels; and if necessary, their MEPs. Party elites in government are therefore not dependent upon their party for resources. In opposi-tion, resources in terms of expert advice and information derive from key MEPs and EU specialists in the parliamentary and central office. We will return below to the *uses* of resources, which clearly distinguishes government and opposition parties in terms of their need for such resources.

Incumbency also affects the *autonomy* of party elites vis-à-vis their parties. Autonomy in our use of the term refers to the ability to act without constraints enforced/imposed by the parliamentary and extra-parliamentary party. There are several reasons why the autonomy of party elites has increased. First, as party election manifestos and programmes are fairly general with regards to EU poli-cies, government ministers are not tied to specific party policy positions. Second, the intergovernmental nature of decision-making at the European level, in particu-lar where national governments participate directly, i.e. the Council of Ministers and European Council summits, have necessitated a high degree of latitude for the government from national parliaments and, by extension, their national parties. We found that *ex ante* and even *ex post* reporting of positions is fairly weak. Thus, low accountability translates into high autonomy. Variations between our countries were slight. The expansion of qualified majority voting (QMV) in the Council of Ministers since the Single European Act in the late 1980s has strengthened national ministers' argument that flexibility in negotiations is necessary in order not to be outvoted and thus to protect national interests (Kassim 2005).

Third, the very nature of EU policy coordination in national government makes it difficult to isolate and thereby hold accountable a particular minister. It also makes surveillance by a national party difficult. There are several reasons for this. One is simply the fact that a minister for Europe, who could potentially be a focal point of a country's EU policy, is not present in every member state, and ministers for Europe differ quite markedly in their actual responsibility. As we have seen, ministers for Europe sometimes fulfil a liaison function between an executive ministerial coordination committee and the cabinet, while others are simply spokespersons for the government. All, however, are relatively junior positions. In addition, coalition government also means that policy coordination is often a matter of compromise and coordination among two or more sets of party elites, and finally there is the ever-present dynamic of inter-ministerial jealousy over policy jurisdiction (Kassim 2000). Thus, national coordination of EU policy is an opaque process making it difficult for an outsider to keep abreast of developments without a high degree of effort, whether or not the government is a coalition.

Fourth, and following from the previous point, the nature of the EU policy-making process can be used as a smokescreen for national government elites' policy intentions (Cole and Drake 2000). Under cover of Brussels, national government elites may advance policy initiatives that may be too politically risky if confined solely to the domestic arena (Radaelli 1997; Dyson and Featherstone 1999). The EU is then a powerful resource in driving change, and later 'blaming it on Brussels' (Smith 2000) in response to political opposition.

A critical factor explaining why incumbency increases elites' power when in government, and why it does not 'stick' upon return to opposition, is the difference in roles between government and opposition. Moravcsik (1994) and others have argued that European integration strengthens the national executive because its participation in EU decision-making is beyond the reach of domestic actors and institutions such as national parliaments. In other words, intergovernmental decision-making by national executives in the EU gives them greater autonomy. So it is the *institution* of the national government executive that is empowered in this way, and the party in office – national party elites – benefits from its occupancy. This explains why elites in opposition do not retain any substantial benefits from their prior experience in executive office. Their personal knowledge of the interaction of national and European decision-making remains, but this is not a factor that can be turned into a substantial advantage in intra-party power dynamics. When we consider the value of EU specialists (including MEPs) as a resource to party elites *in opposition*, their only contribution is information – on legislative amendments in the European Parliament, for example, or expert advice on high profile issues such as the EU constitutional treaty – but this information and advice do not enable party elites to directly influence the EU legislative process, or even challenge the incumbent national government in a meaningful manner (although opposition MEPs can help shape legislation in the EP).

EU specialists and power in parties

MEPs, we find, are not enhanced in terms of power in intra-party dynamics, even though they have a high degree of autonomy from their national parties and have significant inside information and resources regarding the EU legislative process. We find that, since the Single European Act came into effect, since the political mobilization around the Maastricht treaty in 1991, and since the EU Constitutional treaty in 2005, MEPs' autonomy is more precisely defined as a symptom of detachment deriving from national party ignorance and lack of interest. Statutory changes linking EP delegations to the extra-parliamentary party are more a formality than a sign of increased relevance. The same is true for those parties in which the delegation leader is an *ex officio* or *de facto* member of the party's national executive committee. Though one may have expected that with the growth in the power of the EP during the 1990s national party elites would take their MEPs more seriously, for example in their EP committee assignments (Whitaker 2005), we find this is not generally the case. There are, of course, exceptions, as when an MEP drafts a report on an issue of significant national importance, but this alignment of EP action and national resonance such that it highlights the action of an MEP is intermittent (see below). This brings our discussion more specifically to why MEPs and other EU specialists have not experienced an increase in power.

Our reasoning behind the expectation that EU specialists will have gained power rests on their high degree of autonomy and a growing demand from national parties for their expertise. From the discussion above, we have determined that the autonomy enjoyed by MEPs does not translate into power in terms of influencing intra-party contests for elite positions. Their ability to play critical roles in the EP, for example, as a rapporteur on a legislative committee, also has little resonance in their party. Though we find that selected EU specialists, at times perhaps a MEP, are valued for their expertise on specific issues, for example EU constitutional developments, this does little to enhance their political position in the party. This suggests that the autonomy experienced by MEPs vis-à-vis their national parties is conditioned by a certain factors. Already noted is the fact that the bulk of MEPs' respective national parties pay fairly little attention to their activities. This is an obvious reason for their lack of power in national politics. Added to this is the fact that their influence as individuals in the EP is quite low, as it is the collective action of national delegations, party groups and, on certain institutional issues, the EP as a whole that matters in the EU inter-institutional relationship. In other words, neither individual MEPs nor a national party's delegation to the EP will normally have any veto power in EP decision-making. Coupled with the lack of attention to what MEPs do in the EP, their MEPs' autonomy is definitely not a factor that enhances power in domestic intra-party politics.

Other EU specialists, national politicians with an EU brief, such as ministers for Europe, and party staff, are also largely unchanged in terms of their political positions in their respective parties. Ministers for Europe – who have low political salience in national executives – are not involved with actual decision-making, nor is there an EU council for such national actors. They are therefore not categorized along with national party elites in government, as in almost all cases the incumbent of this office is not a member of the party elite. As for staff EU specialists, e.g. individuals in a party's international secretariat charged with Europe (or, in the case of France, a national secretary for Europe), we find that at moments when an EU issue slips into domestic salience these individuals' expertise is sought. However this is an *ad hoc* measure that essentially defines that post-holder as a resource for the party leadership, especially when the party is in opposition. Parties in government, by contrast, will turn to official government spokespersons, who themselves may be briefed by specialists within the executive. These particular EU specialists, despite having information on the EU policy-making process, especially in the case of French national secretaries, many of whom have been concurrently MEPs, are not 'free agents', as their task is essentially liaison and briefing updates for the political leadership of the party. Although they may have expertise, they have relatively little autonomy.

The discussion so far has addressed the fact that EU specialists' expertise has not translated into power in their national parties. Here the 'demand' aspect of our hypothesis is relevant for understanding this finding. We argued in Chapter 1 that, as the scope of the EU grows, there is a greater demand within national parties for expertise in European affairs. The increased demand translates into higher value for EU expertise. We hypothesized that not only would this make EU specialist positions more integral to the needs of the party, but also the positions themselves would become more prestigious. But we have found that this is not really the case. It is clear from interviews in all countries that an EU specialist position, elected or appointed, is not seen as a route to a leadership position in one's party.

Again, the government/opposition status of a party is a significant explanatory factor. Parties in government depend on the expertise available in the national government executive, which is far more extensive than that which exists in the extra-parliamentary party or the parliamentary European affairs committee. Therefore, demand is low to non-existent. With regard to a party in opposition, again, the party representatives on a European affairs committee have a certain amount of expertise in legislative issues, but they are unable to translate this into personal influence because the committee itself is not a decisive arena for an opposition party's positioning vis-à-vis European policies. Committee assignments to a parliamentary European affairs committee were not considered prestigious. As for EU specialists in the extra-parliamentary party organization, they cannot possibly have any extensive knowledge of normal EU legislative agenda items, especially in the policy development phase, and are limited to advice on those issues that migrate from the European to the domestic agenda. As with MEPs, *ad hoc* use of their advice does not transfer into personal power. What becomes clear is that parties do not actually value EU expertise very highly in the pursuit of their main objectives. Understanding this fundamental point allows us to better evaluate how European integration has impacted national party organization, the subject to which we now turn.

National party goals and the European Union

Another way of posing the question of whether or not the growing influence of the EU in domestic politics and institutions has impacted on national party organization is to ask if the basic goals and functions of parties have been significantly affected. Has the undoubted growth of the EU over the past 20 years made it more difficult for parties to pursue the objectives of 'office seeking', 'vote maximization' and 'policy shaping' (Müller and Strøm 1999)? If so, then we should expect some degree of organizational adaptation. After all, the Europeanization of government institutions and policies, the blurring of the boundaries between supranational and national levels, the detachment of national executives from parliamentary oversight, etc. certainly make national governance more complex, a phenomenon that the multi-level governance approach has highlighted (Hooghe and Marks 2001). Turning to the party organization literature, Panebianco has drawn attention to the fact that 'the more complex the environment the less predictable it is' (1988: 205). Further, this increase in environmental complexity creates pressures that 'increase organizational complexity and, consequently, tension within the organization'. The initial reaction to this situation is towards internal specialization, 'i.e. to the multiplication of specialized roles in dealing with different aspects of the environment, in the hope of dominating it' (1988: 205). Our expectation of an increase in number and influence of EU specialists may be said to follow this logic, in that the function of EU specialists is to provide expertise with which to control the new uncertainties created by the EU. More authoritative personnel in a party, however, may represent a potential threat to the internal management of the party, as the personnel are dispersed. So we must ask ourselves, what are the incentives for the party leadership to countenance the creation of more numerous and influential personnel in the party organization? In other words, if party goals are indeed adversely affected by the Europeanization of the domestic political system to the extent that creating EU specialists is an appropriate response, then this must be balanced by the party leadership's estimation of the cost to the internal balance of power in the party. In this section, we explore the impact of the EU on the attainment of party goals (Ladrech 2005).

Let us accept some level of change in the national political system due to European integration in the following domains: institutional (national executive coordination of EU policies; parliamentary European affairs committees), policy (narrowing of policy choices; implementation of different policy directions affecting existing relationships with producers and consumers) and politics (Eurosceptic parties; politicization of public opinion on EU enlargement). This broad Europeanization of domestic politics and institutions, varying in scope and intensity according to the member state, represents the environmental stimuli inducing change in party organization, slow and incremental stimuli as opposed to one or more critical events, in other words an 'environmental trend' (Harmel and Janda 1994; see also Harmel 2002). How might this transformed domestic environment directly impact on party goals? Let us consider four areas of critical party activities in which the Europeanized domestic environment might impinge to the extent of prompting an adaptive response. They are (1) electoral performance; (2) recruitment; (3) policy development; and (4) resources. It would be reasonable to expect that significant disruption to the normal pursuit of these activities and objectives would generate concern among the party leadership, and appropriate changes would at least be debated, whether or not they are implemented.

Electoral performance

Has the growth in the powers of the EU since the Single European Act undermined or directly affected the chances of national electoral success of the main parties of government? The answer is clearly negative. First of all, whether parties are pro- or anti-EU, the likelihood of electoral success has not altered in the countries under our study. That is, to be explicit, winning or losing national elections over the past 20 years has not been decisively affected by a party's stance on European integration; rather, domestic issues continue to dominate. Second, even in those parties experiencing division over the EU, this internal dynamic does not necessarily translate into an electoral liability with voters. Thirdly, even though explicitly Eurosceptic parties have arisen over the past 10 to 20 years, they remain marginal in the national party system (Mair 2000). Lastly, elections to the EP have remained second-order (Reif and Schmidt 1980; Reif 1984; Marsh and Franklin 1996), and incumbent parties that have lost EP elections have often gone on to win subsequent national elections. All in all therefore, the pro- and anti-EU positions of parties continue to be marginal for electoral performance (van der Eijk and Franklin 2004), and left–right competition still provides the overwhelming basis for voter choice in national elections.

Recruitment

Parties recruit personnel into positions in government. We have seen that for members of parliament in general, and government ministers in particular, there has been no serious change in the selection procedures of parliamentary candidates due to the EU, nor have government positions of any significance dealing with the EU been created. Apart from MEPs, who are not considered part of the party elite, there are very few European-level positions that parties can fill: a European Commissioner (two for the largest member states until 2004, after which one for all states became the rule). Clearly, compared to the number of elected positions parties control within their nation, the EU does not provide them with a significant number of additional political career positions.

Policy development/programme change

The increase in the policy competence of the EU, and the increase in instances in which EU directives and regulations are transposed into national law, may mean that parties have had to adapt to the shift in locus of decision-making, either by creating explicit strategies and/or promises to influence 'Brussels' or by incorporating the EU into a range of domestic policy positions. Nevertheless, evidence suggests that, in terms of programme change reflected in party manifestos, the growth of the EU as an authoritative actor remains marginal. Pennings, in a study of Europeanization and programme change from 1960 to 2003, goes as far as to state that, despite the fact that 'more than 60% of all decision-making and rule-making is (in)directly affected by the EU . . . less than 10% of the explicit co-mentions per policy domain concern Europe . . . suggest[ing] that Europe is deliberately being underemphasized' (2006: 268). Party leaderships, apart from those in explicitly Eurosceptic parties, continue to maintain a domestic focus for their electoral promises, and do not imperil their authority in core policy domains by linking the EU to them. The relatively minor importance of EP national delegations in most large parties means that delegations are unable to lobby for more visibility of EU issues, and the centrality of intergovernmental decision-making in the EU privileges elite control of the agenda. The continuing perception by most party members that EU matters are foreign policy also serves to neutralize any growth of their profile in intra-party policy debates.

Resources

Has the development of the EU had an effect upon the resource base of national political parties? This could be looked at in two ways, one positive and one negative. On the one hand, the EU may have developed in such a way as to become a political/resource opportunity structure, and parties may have adapted an aspect of their organization to be able to secure more money or other type of resource from the Commission or EP. This has not happened, and the recent EU party statute explicitly forbids a transfer of money from Europarties to national party treasuries. In the case of very small parties, the EP delegation may be used in such a fashion as to contribute support to national party conferences on Europe. But for most major national parties, state financing, 'cartel party' status (Katz and Mair 1995) and collateral organization support mean that the EU is irrelevant to their resource replenishment. On the other hand, the EU does not have the power or authority to intrude upon national legislation governing the registration or financing of national parties, so parties have not had to develop strategies to fend off or deter the EU from their fund-raising activities.

   Let us return to the question of how the EU impacts on the attainment of party goals. We have seen that the EU is not a direct factor in office-seeking and vote maximization, or in elite recruitment, or in policy-shaping (here it is probably more accurate to say party leaderships resist making the linkage between the EU and their authority/autonomy in policy development), or finally in disrupting the resource base upon which parties depend. The necessary conditions to trigger party organizational change are therefore absent. What has now become apparent is that, despite the recognized changes the EU has engendered in member state's institutional and policy agendas, national party leaderships continue to practice party politics as if the EU were only a foreign policy matter, detached from core policy debates and other domestic activities. The consequences or implications of this 'depoliticization' (Mair 2000), or issue avoidance (Johansson and Raunio 2001), are dealt with in the final section of this chapter.

Before turning to this matter, it is still necessary to explain what function EU specialists actually play in national party organizations, since after all we have noted the creation of positions during the period of our study. The question is the following: if national parties constrain EU issues within the European arena and continue to debate policy issues in the national arena as if the two were not somehow linked, what actual use to party leaderships are EU specialists?

The interaction of EU specialists and party elites

In much the same way as Pennings pointed to the incongruence between the significance of the EU in policy-making on the one hand and yet scarce mentions of the EU in party manifestos on the other, so too do we find that parties have not greatly increased the posts within their organizations dedicated to EU affairs, despite elite recognition of the expansion of the EU into domestic policy fields. To a substantial degree, this is certainly owing to the endemic shortage of financial resources that tends to constrain parties ability to staff their central offices. Nevertheless, as this study has demonstrated, there has indeed been the creation of a limited number of positions, mostly in the areas of liaison between EU level party actors and the party central office and spokespersons (parliamentary and extra-parliamentary).

This suggests, then, that party leaderships acknowledge the need to monitor EU affairs, but for what purpose? Party actors interact with the EU in two fundamental yet different senses. In the first, the EU represents a governance regime in which party personnel are the ultimate arbitrators. As Hix and Lord state, the EU 'is run by party politicians' (1997: 1). In terms of decision-making, the Council of Ministers has been the most important body in the regular EU decision-making process, with the EP having enhanced its position over the past 15 years. It is government ministers who participate in Council of Ministers meetings, with European Council summits reserved for the political leaders. In these two cases, we are speaking of party elites in general, as they staff government ministries (although Hayes-Renshaw and Wallace (2006) point to the trend for ministers, especially senior ones, not to turn up for meetings). Unencumbered by precise party manifesto details and robust *ex ante* reporting, these party actors are involved with policy details, not high political stakes (which are often passed onto heads of state and/or government in European Council summits). Consequently, most of the decisions that take up the time of national government ministers, or more accurately permanent representatives, as well as of MEPs are non-controversial in terms of domestic politics. EU specialists to whom government ministers have access within the national executive are primarily technical experts, able to advise on the input to intergovernmental negotiations as well as the output of EU decisions and how these may be transposed into national legislation. As referred to above, the party in the national executive does not depend upon the party in parliament or central office to supply it with the necessary policy-technical advice. Party EU specialists, then, are not very important to party elites in government.

The other sense in which party actors engage with the EU is by treating it as a political issue, with the capacity to disrupt domestic patterns of party competition. In this case, the government and opposition status is less important, as the domestic salience of an EU policy or action can reverberate in a particular party for reasons specific to its own internal politics. The likelihood that or frequency with which an EU issue (say a proposed directive from the Commission debated in the EP) will *align* with a national party's internal dynamics, enough to arouse concern or internal party divisions, is quite low. We would expect that for such a situation to occur there must be a prior internal party sensitivity or uneasy balance or equilibrium that would be upset by the proposed EU action. This situation could be a truce within a divided party (e.g. the Swedish Social Democrats); a struggle over ideological identity (e.g. the French Socialist Party); or party identification with a national interest, such as the impact of enlargement (e.g. Austrian parties).

In fact, alignments of the supranational and national arenas are the exception. An example of this phenomenon occurred in early 2006 in France. The proposed liberalization of the services directive registered a significant negative response by the Socialist Party. There are many reasons to explain the internal mobilization against the directive, but the actual response of the party leadership was to instruct its EP delegation to vote against the final compromise agreed between the two main EP groups, the Party of European Socialists and the European People's Party–European Democrats. The French Socialist votes were clearly not going to be enough to derail the compromise motion, but the validation for this position was reflected more importantly in internal party politics. In such scenarios, it is enough for a party leadership to be made aware of the political risks associated with EU legislation, and so a few well placed EU specialists, whether they are in the party's central office or in an EP delegation, suffice to warn of an imminent alignment of EU issues and internal party needs. In other words, apart from the actual technical role carried out by an individual in a particular position, the more significant role of EU specialists for a party leadership is to act as an 'early warning system' to prevent a party from being caught off guard by issues emanating from Brussels. Once an EU issue has entered the domestic arena, the usefulness of EU specialists, including MEPs, is almost nil, as the matter has now become interwoven into regular party management responsibilities, whether in government or in opposition.

Conclusion

Our study has had internal party organizational change as its focus. This has meant, necessarily, that our coverage of relevant actors included MPs, MEPs and unelected staff, and that we paid attention to the operation of parliamentary as well as extra-parliamentary party organizations, and to the role of party elites/party leadership. Guiding our understanding of Europeanization and party change has been the concept of organizational adaptation to significant environmental change, thus making our study fit with the literature on party organizational change. This chapter has summarized our findings and attempted some explanations for our two main highlights: first, that party elites are further empowered, among other factors, by the development of the EU over the past 20 years; second, that there has not been a significant proliferation of party EU specialists, and further that those positions that have been created have not in and of themselves accrued noteworthy additional intra-party power. Our empirical research also contributes to the notion of depoliticization, i.e. that party elites separate the EU policy-making realm from domestic party politics. In our case, we can add that party organizations themselves continue to operate as if the EU and its policy competences were confined to the EU arena, and consequently that national politics remained almost exclusively national (with the occasional intrusion of the EU or an EU policy onto the daily agenda). The continuing perception that the EU is a foreign policy matter further reinforces the lack of attention to it by rank-and-file party members and contributes to the party elites' autonomy. As Mair has stated, this explains why party systems seem to appear unaffected by more general examples of Europeanization: 'the parties make it so' (2000: 47).

This phenomenon also calls into question, at the very least, the relationship of the party organization – parliamentary as well as extra-parliamentary – to its leadership, especially when the party is in government. The concern here is that lack of awareness by the party in general of the dynamics (broadly speaking) of European governance and the impact of the EU on national policy-making renders party policy and programme development and hence party government naïve at best, dishonest at worst. It also means that what might be termed a 'permissive consensus' by party actors, for party elites in government to take decisions as they see fit, is in reality an ignorance of the implications of those decisions, indeed of the very activities that their government ministers engage in when participating in EU decision-making bodies. The effect of European integration on this dimension of party–government relations would suggest a rethinking of the party government model (Katz 2001).

For parties to change, we expect that one or a combination of three triggering factors or conditions must have occurred. One, that adaptation occurs as a result of environmental changes that have a legal basis in affecting party activity. Second, that environmental changes have created a political opportunity, providing parties with incentives to change. Third, that the national political system has changed in such a manner as to jeopardize the attainment of core party goals. We have seen that the first condition does not apply to parties: the EU has not directly intruded into the classic activities of parties in competitive party systems by means of altering or challenging the legal bases of national parties. As far as the second point is concerned, not only has the EU *not* become an attractive political opportunity structure for parties to exploit (apart from parties specifically created to connect with Eurosceptic public opinion), it is viewed by party elites as a volatile and potentially disruptive factor that requires containment. Lastly, the core pursuits and activities of parties have not been directly impeded by the EU. Thus we have the paradoxical situation in which party elites in government are involved in making authoritative decisions at the European level but striving all the same to prevent a 'spillover' of the impact and significance of this decision-making into their own national parties.

This highlights another disjuncture between internal party activities and governance: the effort going into manifesto and programme development and the near uselessness of these documents as realistic indicators of actual future government action (particularly where EU competences are involved). Though the effort of their development may have other uses, for example symbolic of a participatory culture, the divorce between a Europeanized policy dimension and the near total focus on the domestic environment of these documents does point to an unspoken fictional element in party organizational dynamics.

As noted above, we find no overriding incentive for party elites to change this state of affairs. The number and role of party EU specialists meets the present needs of party elites. Any increase in the number of personnel with an EU brief – with a corresponding measure of power and autonomy – would add further complexity for party leaderships. Furthermore, a noticeable increase of such prominent individuals may have the opposite effect of actually highlighting the EU as a political issue. So, we can state that national party organizations have adapted or changed in response to the influence of the EU, but in a limited and – from the perspective of party elites – appropriate manner.

Can this party elite strategy continue? Van der Eijk and Franklin argue that, for party leaders, 'European issues have as a matter of fact proved easier to manage than other new issues in most European countries'. Managing the EU as an issue has meant preventing its politicization, because 'all party leaders understand from long experience the danger to them of an issue that is not already integrated into the left/right spectrum of concerns' (2004: 48). Party leaders, as 'gatekeepers' between the national and the supranational arenas, tend to avoid situations that they cannot control. What is apparent from our study is that the 'permissive consensus' enjoyed by party elites when in government to drive forward the European integration process also exists within many of their party organizations. Here we find another growing paradox. It has been suggested that the defeat of the EU constitution in the French and Dutch referendums in 2005 may introduce public opinion into the integration equation, thus complicating or even slowing the process itself. Sbragia puts this scenario succinctly:

> Since the major political parties in Europe (whether in government or in opposition) have supported treaty ratification since 1958 and supported the ratification of the Constitution, the view that European integration will stall privileges public opinion *vis-à-vis* the opinions of governmental and party elites. In brief, the key support for integration – elite consensus – would become less powerful as an effective driving force.
>
> (2006: 238)

As the 'permissive consensus' ebbs in terms of public opinion, it remains, paradoxically, within the major parties, as no party in our study has introduced robust measures of accountability for its elites. In the French and Dutch referendums, all of the major parties supported a Yes vote, but post-referendum analysis shows that their voters rejected party cues (inter alia, Aarts and van der Kolk 2006; Brouard and Tiberj 2006). Increased politicization of the EU as an issue linked to the left–right spectrum has already become apparent in France, especially within the Socialist Party (Ivaldi 2006). While this party may be exceptional in this case, it is nevertheless instructive that a rising polititicization of the EU in domestic politics may eventually force party elites to devise a post-containment strategy for the 'EU as an issue'. In so doing, it could affect EU governance by engendering 'a greater incidence of deadlock, derogation, and opting-out in intergovernmental bargaining' (Hooghe and Marks 2006: 249) as national electoral factors come to shape party elite strategies.

Notes

1 I would like to thank Nicholas Aylott, Elisabeth Carter and Thomas Poguntke for their helpful suggestions to an earlier draft of this chapter.
2 COSAC (the Conference of European Affairs Committees, usually referred to by its French acronym) brings together representatives from the European Parliament and national parliaments.

References

Aarts, Kees and Henk van der Kolk (2006) 'Understanding the Dutch "No": The Euro, the East, and the Elite', *PS: Political Science and Politics*, 39(2): 243–6.

Bartolini, Stefano (2005) *Restructuring Europe: Centre Formation, System Building, and Political Structuring between the Nation State and the European Union*, Oxford: Oxford University Press.

Brouard, Sylvain and Vincent Tiberj (2006) 'The French Referendum: The Not So Simple Act of Saying Nay', *PS: Political Science and Politics*, 39(2): 261–8.

Cole, Alastair and Helen Drake (2000) 'The Europeanization of the French Polity? Continuity, Change and Adaptation', *Journal of European Public Policy*, 7(1): 26–43.

Dyson, Kenneth and Kevin Featherstone (1999) *The Road to Maastricht: Negotiating Economic and Monetary Union*, Oxford: Oxford University Press.

van der Eijk, Cees and Mark N. Franklin (2004) 'Potential for Contestation on European Matters at National Elections in Europe', in Gary Marks and Marco R. Steenbergen (eds), *European Integration and Political Conflict*, Cambridge: Cambridge University Press, pp. 32–50.

Hanley, David (2006) 'Keeping It in the Family? National Parties and the Transnational Experience', *European View*, 3: 35–43.

Harmel, Robert (2002) 'Party Organizational Change: Competing Explanations?', in Kurt Richard Luther and Ferdinand Müller-Rommel (eds), *Political Parties in the New Europe: Political and Analytical Challenges*, Oxford: Oxford University Press, pp. 119–42.

Harmel, Robert and Ken Janda (1994) 'An Integrated Theory of Party Goals and Party Change', *Journal of Theoretical Politics*, 6(3): 259–87.

Hayes-Renshaw, Fiona and Helen Wallace (2006) *The Council of Ministers*, second edition, Basingstoke: Palgrave.

Hix, Simon and Christopher Lord (1997) *Political Parties in the European Union*, Basingstoke: Palgrave.

Hooghe, Liesbet and Gary Marks (2001) *Multi-Level Governance and European Integration*, Lanham, MD: Rowman & Littlefield.

Hooghe, Liesbet and Gary Marks (2006) 'Europe's Blues: Theoretical Soul-Searching after the Rejection of the European Constitution', *PS: Political Science and Politics*, 39(2): 247–50.

Ivaldi, Gilles (2006) 'Beyond France's 2005 Referendum on the European Constitutional Treaty', *West European Politics*, 29(1): 47–69.

Johansson, Karl Magnus (2002) 'Party Elites in Multilevel Europe: The Christian Democrats and the Single European Act', *Party Politics*, 8(4): 423–40.

Johansson, Karl Magnus and Tapio Raunio (2001) 'Partisan Responses to Europe: Comparing Finnish and Swedish Political Parties', *European Journal of Political Research*, 39(2): 225–49.

Kassim, Hussein (2000) 'Conclusion: The National Co-ordination of EU Policy: Confronting the Challenge', in Hussein Kassim, B. Guy Peters and Vincent Wright (eds), *The National Coordination of EU Policy: The Domestic Level*, Oxford: Oxford University Press, pp. 235–64.

Kassim, Hussein (2005) 'The Europeanization of Member State Institutions', in Simon Bulmer and Christian Lequesne (eds), *The Member' States of the European Union*, Oxford: Oxford University Press, pp. 285–316.

Katz, Richard (2001) 'Models of Democracy: Elite Attitudes and the Democratic Deficit in the European Union', *European Union Politics*, 2(1): 53–80.

Katz, Richard and Peter Mair (1995) 'Changing Models of Party Organization and Party Democracy: The Emergence of the Cartel Party', *Party Politics*, 1(1): 5–28.

Ladrech, Robert (2002) 'Europeanization and Political Parties: Towards a Framework for Analysis', *Party Politics*, 8(4): 389–403.

Ladrech, Robert (2005) 'The Europeanization of Interest Groups and Political Parties', in Simon Bulmer and Christian Lequesne (eds), *The Member States of the European Union*, Oxford: Oxford University Press, pp. 317–37.

Mair, Peter (2000) 'The Limited Impact of Europe on National Party Systems', *West European Politics*, 23(4): 27–51.

Mair, Peter (2006) 'Political Parties and Party Systems', in Paolo Graziano and Maarten P. Vink (eds), *Europeanization: New Research Agendas*, Basingstoke: Palgrave.

Marsh, Michael and Mark N. Franklin (1996) 'The Foundations: Unanswered Questions from the Study of European Elections, 1979–1994', in Cees van der Eijk and Mark N. Franklin (eds), *Choosing Europe? The European Electorate and National Politics in the Face of the Union*, Ann Arbor, MI: University of Michigan Press, pp. 11–32.

Moravcsik, Andrew (1994) *Why the European Community Strengthens the State: Domestic Politics and International Cooperation*, Harvard University Center for European Studies, Working Paper Series, 52: 1–82.

Müller, Wolfgang and Kaare Strøm (eds) (1999) *Policy, Office or Votes? How Political Parties in Western Europe Make Hard Decisions*, Cambridge: Cambridge University Press.

Panebianco, Angelo (1988) *Political Parties: Organization and Power*, Cambridge: Cambridge University Press.

Pennings, Paul (2006) 'An Empirical Analysis of the Europeanization of National Party Manifestos, 1960–2003', *European Union Politics*, 7(2): 257–70.

Radaelli, Claudio (1997) 'How does Europeanization Produce Domestic Policy Change?', *Comparative Political Studies*, 30(5): 553–75.

Raunio, Tapio (2002) 'Why European Integration Increases Leadership Autonomy within Political Parties', *Party Politics*, 8(4): 405–22.

Reif, Karlheinz (1984) *European Elections 1979/81 and 1984: Conclusions and Perspectives from Empirical Research*, Berlin: Quorum.

Reif, Karlheinz and Hermann Schmitt (1980) 'Nine Second Order National Elections: A Conceptual Framework for the Analysis of European Election Results', *European Journal of Political Research*, 8(1): 3–44.

Sbragia, Alberta (2006) 'Introduction – The EU and its "Constitution": Public Opinion, Political Elites, and their International Context', *PS: Political Science and Politics*, 39(2): 237–42.

Smith, Mitchell (2000) 'The Commission Made Me Do It: The European Commission as a Strategic Asset in Domestic Politics', in Neill Nugent (ed.), *At the Heart of the Union: Studies of the European Commission*, Basingstoke: Macmillan, pp. 167–86.

Whitaker, Richard (2005) 'National Parties in the European Parliament: An Influence in the Committee System?', *European Union Politics*, 6(1): 5–28.

Index

For Product Safety Concerns and Information please contact our EU
representative GPSR@taylorandfrancis.com
Taylor & Francis Verlag GmbH, Kaufingerstraße 24, 80331 München, Germany

www.ingramcontent.com/pod-product-compliance
Lightning Source LLC
Chambersburg PA
CBHW050421280326
41932CB00013BA/1951

*   9 7 8 0 4 1 5 4 7 9 7 8 3   *